THE TIMES 1000 1978-1979

LEADING COMPANIES IN BRITAIN AND OVERSEAS

Contents

Edited by Margaret Allen

Advertisements: A. Tollworthy, Financial Advertisement Director, Times Newspapers Limited

Cover design by Ivan and Robin Dodd

Published 1978 by Times Books,
18 Ogle St., London, W.1.

ISBN 0 7230 0223 1

IMI makes it

IMI, one of the UK's top 100 industrial companies, is now completely independent, with 76,000 shareholders. So here we are at last in the Times 1000, in our own right.

IMI's companies make products for building in metal and plastics, they make heat exchangers like car radiators and beer coolers, they make all kinds of pneumatic components, they make zip fasteners, they make simple bits and complicated pieces for general engineering, from coins to valves to cartridges (and something for practically every British car and television set and washing machine).

And in addition they're big in metals, from copper refining and copper strip and rod and tube, to titanium for aircraft and chemical plant.

IMI has grown by going into markets, businesses and technologies that it knows about. IMI continues to invest in new plant and to explore new market opportunities.

How does one parent company control a turnover of £467 million? Simply by letting its 100 plus operating subsidiaries get on with what they know best, within corporate guide lines. It is an enlightened principle of management by which IMI has certainly produced results over the last 12 years, and will go on doing so. Look at the figures.

1966 turnover £69 million (IMI's first year as a public company).

1977 turnover £467 million. IMI, with a world-wide work force of over 33,000, operates in 6 main areas:

Building Products, Heat Exchange, Fluid Power, General Engineering, Zip Fasteners, Refined and Wrought Metals.

IMI Limited Birmingham England B6 7BA

4

THE TIMES 1000

1978-79

The indispensable annual review
of leading world industrial and financial companies

TIMES BOOKS

The Times 1000

Europe's top twenty industrial groups

Rank	Rank last year	Company	Headquarters	Main activity	Sales £000s
1	2	British Petroleum	UK	Oil industry	14,712,200
2	1	Royal Dutch Petroleum	Netherlands	Oil industry	13,640,000
3	3	"Shell" Transport and Trading	UK	Oil industry	11,393,651
4	4	Philips' Lamps Holding	Netherlands	Electrical products	7,172,500
5	6	ENI	Italy	Holding company (petroleum, chemicals, engineering, textiles, etc.)	7,027,000
6	5	Veba AG	Germany	Holding company	6,821,700
7	7	Daimler-Benz AG	Germany	Motor vehicles & engine manufacturers	6,441,800
8	14	Siemens AG	Germany	Electrical & general engineering, electronics	6,275,900
9	8	BAT Industries	UK	Tobacco, retailing, cosmetics	6,070,000
10	10	Volkswagenwerk	Germany	Motor vehicle manufacturers	6,015,400
11	9	Cie Française des Petroles	France	Holding company (oil & petroleum)	5,957,600
12	*	Hoechst AG	Germany	Chemicals, dyes, plastics	5,802,700
13	12	BASF AG	Germany	Chemicals, dyes, plastics	5,773,600
14	11	Renault (Régie Nationale des Usines)	France	Automobile production	5,488,300
15	13	Bayer AG	Germany	Chemical products	5,327,900
16	17	Nestlé Alimentana SA	Switzerland	Holding company (chocolates, milk & food products)	5,239,900
17	16	Unilever NV	Netherlands	Food products, detergents, animal foodstuffs, toilet preparations	5,206,700
18	15	Thyssen AG	Germany	Iron & steel	4,910,000
19	18	Peugeot-Citroën	France	Automobiles, engines	4,669,500
20	19	Imperial Chemical Industries	UK	Chemicals	4,663,000

* Not listed last year.

This new edition of **The Times 1000** includes for the first time details of the major British trade unions and employers' associations. The top 25 of each are shown on pages 16 and 18. For trade unions the criterion of size has been the number of members, and the table also shows members' contributions, net income and the total funds of each union. The Transport and General Workers' Union is by far the largest union on all counts, with almost two million members, over £16m each year in contributions, a net income of £3m plus and total funds in excess of £32m. Only one other union, the Amalgamated Union of Engineering Workers, has more than one million members.

In contrast, the National Farmers' Union, the biggest employers' association, with 134,724 members, takes in almost £4m in subscriptions, has a net income of little over £500,000 and total funds amounting to about £6m. Indeed, the net income of the smallest union in the list, the Institution of Professional Civil Servants, is almost equal to that of the NFU. The criterion of size for employers' organisations is subscription income and the table covers only those associations which have been registered with the Certification Office and for whom a return has been filed.

The European Giants
There has been a change among the top twenty companies in Europe over the past year (see above). British Petroleum has overtaken Royal Dutch Petroleum and is now Europe's biggest industrial group. As usual, the oil industry and chemicals predominate. Britain still has four companies in the twenty biggest groups in Europe, Germany eight, France three, the Netherlands three and Switzerland and Italy one each. The biggest move forward has been made by Hoechst AG, the German-based chemical, dyes and plastics company, which has moved from twenty-third place in Europe to eleventh in just one year. Automobile makers Daimler-Benz, Volkswagenwerk, Renault and Peugeot-Citroën all make the top twenty, but Britain's BL lags far behind.

The Main Table (page 30)
The two major UK oil companies, BP and "Shell" Transport and Trading, continue to dominate this table, retaining their position as 1 and 2 respectively. The only change in the top ten positions concerns the jump from last year's twelfth to eighth position by the Ford Motor Company. Even so, BL remains the UK's largest motor vehicle manufacturer in terms of sales and remains in seventh position.

There are 77 changes in the constituents of the 1000 table. As usual, the majority of these changes arise in the lower areas of the table, but amongst the additions this year are Littlewoods at number 63. This major private company has been excluded in the past, due to problems in ascertaining a turnover figure which could be compared with other companies. Another addition is Imperial Metal Industries at 94. This company has previously been omitted because of our rule excluding from this table subsidiaries of other UK companies, IMI being a subsidiary of Imperial Chemical Industries. ICI's decision to divest them themselves of their controlling interest means that for the first time IMI is eligible for inclusion in its own right.

Companies lose their place in the 1000 table for a variety of reasons, but the major ones are that their turnover is no longer sufficiently large (this year's lowest is almost £22,000,000, compared with just under £19,000,000 in the 1977–78 edition), or because the company has been taken over. This latter category includes Clarke Chapman (160 last year), Reyrolle Parsons (203 last year), Manbré & Garton (229 last year) and Beaverbrook Newspapers (318 last year).

The top ten UK profit makers

Rank	Company	Profit‡ £000	Rank in Table 1
1	British Petroleum	2,393,600	1
2	"Shell" Transport & Trading	1,712,400	2
3	The Post Office	1,110,700	*
4	Electricity Council & Boards	747,400	*
5	Imperial Chemical Industries	612,000	4
6	British Gas Corporation	473,400	*
7	BAT Industries	472,000	3
8	Unilever	348,800	5
9	Rio Tinto-Zinc	322,800	11
10	General Electric	292,000	10

*A nationalised industry.
‡Before interest and tax.

British Petroleum once again achieved the largest absolute rise in profits. This year an increase of £434,200,000 (22.2 per cent) compares with last year's £333,200,000 (20.5 per cent). In contrast, ICI, BL (formerly British Leyland), Unilever and Courtaulds, from being among those companies registering big profit increases, now figure among the ten companies with the largest falls in profits. Last year thirty-five companies appeared in the table of Money Losers; this year the number has fallen to twenty-five companies, but Texaco's loss of £41,935,000 is larger than Chrysler United Kingdom's loss of £31,902,000, which was the biggest last year.

A Changes in profit

10 Biggest rises

Rank in Table 1	Company	£000	per cent change
1	British Petroleum Co.	434,200	+22·2
8	Ford Motor Co.	122,900	+87·7
10	General Electric Co.	72,900	+33·3
2	"Shell" Transport & Trading	61,200	+ 3·7
102	Rank Organisation	50,080	+50·9
19	Reed International	49,000	+75·2
3	BAT Industries	43,000	+10·0
48	Distillers Co.	38,937	+36·8
58	Beecham Group	38,300	+38·3
24	Inchcape & Co.	38,229	+68·4

10 Biggest falls

Rank in Table 1	Company	£000	per cent change
20	Texaco	44,844	−1,541·6
4	Imperial Chemical Industries	43,000	− 6·6
7	BL	39,888	− 35·5
16	Courtaulds	30,300	− 25·9
15	Guest, Keen & Nettlefolds	19,660	− 14·2
22	Dunlop Holdings	16,800	− 16·7
5	Unilever Ltd.	16,600	− 4·5
109	Vickers	12,116	− 25·2
125	Total Oil Great Britain	11,361	− 90·1
53	J. Lyons & Co.	10,520	− 26·3

B Money losers

Rank in Table 1	Company	Loss £000
237	Chevron Oil (UK)	2
833	Addressograph-Multigraph	64
636	Barker & Dobson	117
545	British Enkalon	164
359	Fyffes Group	183
831	Caltex (UK)	228
576	SKF (UK)	277
552	Scott Lithgow	346
982	Murco Petroleum	500
915	Peek Holdings	606 p.a.
849	Reardon Smith Line	857
945	Armstrong Cork Co.	1,015
268	Borregaard Industries	1,103
236	Continental (London)	1,293
976	Titaghur Jute Factory Co.	1,294
731	Inver House Distillers	1,888
497	Govan Shipbuilders	2,906 p.a.
154	Amoco (UK)	2,980
829	Short Brothers	3,977
746	Sena Sugar Estates	5,509
98	Chrysler United Kingdom	8,231
940	Clark Equipment	11,598
580	Roche Products	14,674
646	Harland & Wolff	15,677
20	Texaco	41,935

Corpo **rate** **a** **Im** ge

Will yours stand it?

Companies come under more careful scrutiny today than
perhaps ever before.

It may be from investors and the financial community, at home and
abroad; from employees or potential employees at all levels or from
the people who form or influence public policy—pressure groups,
politicians, civil servants, trade unions, local government.

Some of these groups will have a crucial influence on your future
growth and prosperity.

It makes sound business sense, then, to communicate your aims
and achievements to them clearly and unequivocally. Which means
setting objectives, devising and executing a communications plan,
and researching the results.

Charles Barker City can help better than most. Because CBC is
the most experienced advertising agency specialising in
corporate, financial and public affairs communications in Britain.

For information on CBC's unique range of communications
services, please telephone CBC's Chief Executive,
Reg Valin, on 01-236 3011.

Charles Barker City

30 Farringdon Street, London EC4A 4EA

Newcomers and departures in the Top 1000

Ins

Rank in 1978/79 1000	Name	Rank in 1978/79 1000	Name	Rank in 1978/79 1000	Name
63	Littlewoods Organisation	764	Akzo Chemie UK (Holdings)	946	Warren Plantation Holdings
94	IMI	786	W. J. Oldacre (Holdings)	947	Avana Group
115	Northern Engineering Industries	798	Montedison (UK)	951	Cosalt
144	Food Manufacturers (GB Co.)	830	Forth Wines	953	Biro Bic
230	Mardon Packaging International	838	Prosper de Mulder	958	Sheffield Twist Drill & Steel
312	J. H. Rayner & Co.	847	E. M. Denny (Holdings)	959	William Moss Group
320	Océ-Van der Grinten Finance	861	Strong & Fisher (Holdings)	964	Evode Holdings
336	Twil	867	Alfa Romeo (Great Britain)	966	Elliott Grp of Peterborough
388	Ceres (UK)	877	United Sterling Corpn.	974	Electrocomponents
399	Smurfit	879	Argos Distributors	975	Grundig International
424	International Synthetic Rubber	886	Brunning Group	977	Edbro (Holdings)
458	Corrie Maccoll and Son	887	Scotia Investments	978	Londis (Holdings)
464	M. Golodetz	890	William Leech (Builders)	981	H. E. Samson
539	Dentsply	894	Motorola	983	Colt International & Assoc. Cos
597	Elbar Industrial	899	Wrigley Co.	984	C. G. Hacking & Sons
616	E. G. Cornelius & Co.	900	Longton Transport (Hldgs)	986	D. B. Marshall (Newbridge)
659	Polygram Leisure	912	Gambia Produce Marketing Co.	987	Mills & Allen International
695	J. Murphy & Sons	913	Camford Engineering	989	Home Charm
704	Mothercat	919	Bell & Howell	990	Johnson Wax
711	Star Aluminium Co.	921	Highams	991	Champion Sparking Plug Co.
723	Anglo European Foods Group	924	Fein & Co.	993	Carr's Milling Industries
727	Pure Lard	925	Hogg Robinson Group	997	Dart Industries
729	John M. Henderson & Co. (Hgs)	929	Burco Dean	998	Norton Villiers Triumph
748	H. P. Bulmer Holdings	934	Sotheby Parke Bernet Group	999	Pitman
751	Colombo Commercial (Produce)	939	Sanyo Marubeni (UK)	1000	S. W. Wood Group
759	National Panasonic (UK)	943	Stothert & Pitt		

Outs

Rank in 1977/78 1000	Name	Rank in 1977/78 1000	Name	Rank in 1977/78 1000	Name
149	Leslie & Godwin (Holdings)	691	107 Baker St. Investments	915	Herbert Morris
160	Clarke Chapman	733	Clyde Petroleum	923	Bartella
162	Mars	780	H. P. Bulmer	926	Habitat Design Holdings
203	Reyrolle Parsons	792	Rosgill Holdings	930	Attock Petroleum
229	Manbré & Garton	794	Maple & Co. (Holdings)	933	Louis C. Edwards & Son (Manchester)
302	Vosper	802	Hemdale Film Group		
307	Bond Worth Holdings	809	Dowsett Engineering Construction	935	Bett Brothers
318	Beaverbrook Newspapers	831	Anglo-European Foods	936	Erith & Co.
322	Kinloch (Provision Merchants)	838	G. E. Wallis & Sons	941	John Bright Group
325	Procon (Great Britain)	848	FPA Construction Group	943	Whatlings
333	Ozalid Group Holdings	850	A. Gallenkamp & Co.	945	J. B. Holdings
343	F. J. Wallis	852	Prothofin	955	John Thomas (Sugar Merchants)
364	Tinsley Wire (Sheffield)	854	Kimpher	959	Scotcros
410	Dunford & Elliott	864	AVP Industries	960	H. H. Robertson (UK)
413	Head, Wrightson & Co.	876	IDC Group	972	Sansinena Co.
415	Fairey Co.	884	Carron Company (Holdings)	983	Ideal-Standard
445	Teacher (Distillers)	891	Argyle Securities	984	Blyth, Greene, Jourdain & Co.
456	Gateway Securities	896	Alliance Alders	987	A. G. Barr & Co.
460	London & Overseas Freighters	897	Transparent Paper	988	J. Compton, Sons & Webb (Holdings)
558	AD International	898	K. O. Boardman International	989	Bradbury Wilkinson
572	Harrisons Malaysian Estates	899	WGI	990	Davenports Brewery (Holdings)
593	Yarrow & Co.	900	Audiotronic Holdings	992	M. & W. Mack
607	J. Walter Thompson Group	905	Indesit	994	United Spring & Steel Group
625	Storey Brothers and Co.	908	Arthur Bartfeld Group	997	Aquascutum & Assoc. Cos
646	Essoldo Group Holdings	911	British Rollmakers Corpn.	999	Glenlivet Distillers
657	F. L. Smidth & Co.	912	Fiat Allis UK		
679	Isherwoods (Holdings)				

The top ten UK exporters

Rank	Company	Exports £000s	Rank in Table 1
1	Imperial Chemical Industries	936,000	4
2	Ford Motor	893,500	8
3	BL	854,000	7
4	General Electric	524,000	10
5	Unilever	428,600	5
6	Courtaulds	387,900	16
7	Massey-Ferguson	369,000	83
8	Hawker Siddeley	295,000	41
9	George Wimpey	292,000	69
10	Rolls-Royce	285,000	60

The above figures do not include C. T. Bowring (Number 31 in Table 1), whose total export figure of £546,623,000 included £538,000,000 premium income earned overseas.

Return on Capital Employed

Service companies, as usual, lead in terms of return on capital employed, with CBS United Kingdom still having the highest return of 243.9 per cent. The highest ranked company appearing in the lowest return table is number 125, Total Oil Great Britain, with a return of 1.1 per cent. The very large companies tend to be around the average.

C Return on capital employed*

10 Highest

Rank in Table 1	Company	per cent
857	CBS United Kingdom	243.9
588	Lummus Co.	192.8
626	Peugeot Automobiles UK	146.7
759	National Panasonic (UK)	146.4
810	Fluor (England)	135.3
697	Moutafian Commodities	134.9
704	Mothercat	100.8
775	Luncheon Vouchers	90.3
987	Mills & Allen International	87.4
619	Saatchi & Saatchi Compton	83.1

10 Lowest

Rank in Table 1	Company	per cent
608	Westminster Dredging Group	0.2
329	General Foods	0.3
370	Burrough Machines	0.5
594	Wilkins & Mitchell	0.5
385	Alcoa of Great Britain	0.6
912	Gambia Produce Marketing Co.	0.7
272	Burton Group	0.8
425	Firestone Tyre & Rubber Co.	0.9
832	Guardian & Manchester Evening News	0.9
125	Total Oil Great Britain	1.1

*At beginning of year.

Equity Market Capitalisation

There are only two changes in the ten highest equity market capitalisations: Marks & Spencer and Unilever change place at 6 and 7, and Great Universal Stores replaces Guest, Keen and Nettlefolds at 10. BP and 'Shell' Transport and Trading continue to head this table. At the other end, Titaghur Jute Factory has the smallest market value – £100,000 (last year £200,000).

D Equity market capitalisation

10 Highest

Rank in Table 1	Company	14 July 1978 £ million
1	British Petroleum Co.	3,362.7
2	"Shell" Transport & Trading	3,116.4
4	Imperial Chemical Industries	2,114.5
10	General Electric Co.	1,476.0
3	BAT Industries	1,128.9
26	Marks & Spencer	1,006.0
5	Unilever Ltd.	974.8
58	Beecham Group	964.1
44	Boots Co.	730.1
38	Great Universal Stores	696.4

10 Lowest

Rank in Table 1	Company	14 July 1978 £ million
976	Titaghur Jute Factory Co.	0.1
915	Peek Holdings	0.3
746	Sena Sugar Estates	0.7
933	P. Panto & Co.	1.0
650	Mears Bros. Holdings	1.0
719	Joseph Stocks & Sons (Holdings)	1.3
609	Staflex International	1.3
936	Glass, Glover Group	1.3
708	J. E. England & Sons (Wellington)	1.3
979	Randalls Group	1.7
914	Morgan Edwards	1.7
593	Charles Hurst	1.7

Acquisitions and Mergers (page 73)

The largest takeover last year was Coral Leisure Group's acquisition of Pontin's, valued at £44,246,000, followed by the £39,697,000 scheme of arrangement by which Générale Occidentale acquired Cavenham. Coral Leisure Group appear a second time in the twenty largest bids with the acquisition of Centre Hotels (Cranston), valued at £14,164,000. Only thirteen of the top fifty did not feature a cash element (last year eighteen).

Largest Shareholdings (page 74)

This year thirty-seven companies appear, and only Lonrho, Great Universal Stores, P & O Steam Navigation and Lucas Industries, who were all eligible, did not supply information. Prudential Assurance remain the major shareholders and in only four of the thirty-seven companies (BL, Burmah Oil Co., C. T. Bowring & Co. and Allied Breweries) do they not hold at least 1 per cent of the equity capital. The existence of nominee holdings prevents a more detailed appraisal of individual holdings.

Nationalised Industries, State Holding Companies (page 77)

The much-publicised improvement in their results continues, although the only major change in order is the National Enterprise Board's replacement of the British Steel Corporation at 3.

Only British Steel and London Transport returned pre-interest losses and the turnovers of the top six are all higher than the company placed tenth in the top 1000 table. The largest nationalised industry (Electricity Council & Boards) would be fourth in the main table. Apart from the loss makers, only National Freight Corporation and British National Oil Corporation failed to cover their interest charges from current profits.

The Financial Section

Among finance houses Forward Trust has slipped from third to fifth place, whilst Lloyds and Scottish has moved up from sixth to third, but Lombard North Central is still comfortably leading the table in terms of outstanding balances and capital employed. United Dominions Trust remains the most profitable, although Lombard North Central has considerably closed the gap.

Now that N. M. Rothschild & Sons (in ninth place) is included among the accepting houses, this table now includes all members of the Accepting Houses Committee. Kleinwort, Benson, Lonsdale continue to head the table, this time from Hill Samuel Group.

Among unit trusts, Union Capital has dropped from fifth to seventh place, but otherwise the top ten remain the same as last year. Investment Trust Units is still the largest, but although the trust value increases, the number of unit holders has fallen. Save and Prosper manage five of the twenty largest, and M & G Group four, including numbers 2 and 3.

The European Table (page 99)

ENI, the Italian holding company, with interests in petroleum, chemicals, engineering and textiles, has replaced Veba AG in third place, but the two Dutch concerns, Royal Dutch Petroleum and Philips' Lamps Holdings continue to be 1 and 3 respectively. The top fifty now consists of twenty-one German companies, twelve French companies, seven Dutch, four Italian, three Swiss, one Austrian, one Belgian and one Swedish.

The most important point to be made about this table concerns the future. The adoption by EEC member states of the 4th Directive, which may be followed by a further directive on Consolidated Accounts, may eventually lead to the possibility of making true comparisons between companies from differing countries and perhaps a truly European **Times 1000**.

Margaret Allen

Don't just buy a car...

Have one made

The Aston Martin V8 is the result of rare skills and 55 years of unique experience. From the men who design and specify to standards most would find it impossible to attain, to the team who hand-build each car under the guidance of an individual craftsman engineer, everyone at Aston Martin is dedicated to one end. That is the production of a motor car which is as near perfect as possible.

The fact that the V8 is in demand in every country in the world and that it surpasses the requirements of pollution control and safety standards wherever it goes demonstrate the magnificent success of these men and the cars that they build. The Aston Martin V8 . . . to drive it is to love it.

Aston Martin Lagonda (1975) Limited, Tickford Street, Newport Pagnell, Buckinghamshire MK16 9AN.
Telephone: Newport Pagnell (0908) 610620. Telegrams: Astomartia, Newport Pagnell. Telex: 82341

Compilation

Extel Statistical Services are once again responsible for almost all the tabulations in **The Times 1000**. The figures are compiled on the basis used for Extel Statistical Cards. For any queries regarding figures in the tables, readers should either telephone 01-253 3400 or write to Extel at 37-45 Paul Street, London EC2A 4PB.

We are indebted to the Nomura Research Institute of Technology and Economics, whose research facilities were drawn on in the compilation of the Japanese table.

Extel and *The Times* would like to record their appreciation for the assistance given to them by the staff of the Certification Office for Trade Unions and Employers' Associations in the compilation of the tables covering trade unions and employers' associations.

The list of foreign bank branches in the UK was drawn up in the offices of *The Times*.

The guide can now be used to make valid comparisons of the size of companies in various parts of the world, at least in terms of total sales. Only the South African tables are exceptional, in that capital employed, and not total turnover, is the criterion of size. Any attempt to carry comparisons of size beyond sales, however, can be of doubtful validity. Definitions of capital employed and profit, for example, vary from one country to another – in some countries, for instance, published profits may be just enough to cover dividends to shareholders.

Certain companies include in their reported turnover figures relating to the turnover of associated companies. To aid comparison with companies that do not adopt such a policy, these details have been excluded in arriving at the turnover reported in the tables.

There is the further problem, when making comparisons, of differing year ends. Most companies now draw up their balance sheets on 31 December, but by no means all of them do. In the Top 1000 table and the other tables relating to British groups, almost every company whose year ended on 31 December 1977 or 31 March 1978 is included. *No full accounts published after 30 June 1978 have been included.* As a further aid to readers, the Top 1000 table shows the accounting period to which each company's figures refer.

The table of top UK advertisers was prepared for us by the research department of J. Walter Thompson, the advertising agency. This analysis of advertising expenditure is based on data supplied by Media Expenditure Analysis Limited, a company which monitors all display advertisements in national and provincial newspapers and the larger-circulation general, women's and special interest magazines. For television, details are taken from all contractors' daily transmission logs. In every case information about special positions is coded.

The space or time for each advertisement is then costed at published card rates, allowing for published premium position rates. No allowance has been made for GHI or other special schemes or for column or series discounts, etc. The figures do not claim to be exact estimates of companies' total advertising expenditure. Only television and the press are covered.

Exchange rates used for conversion purposes in all the tables involving foreign companies were supplied to Extel by the Press Association as at 31 December 1977 for Europe and at 30 June 1978 for the other overseas tables. As the pound has continued to float, the depreciation in sterling over the year would once again have led to a misrepresentation of the growth rate of foreign companies in comparison with those in the UK. To avoid this, Extel have converted 1976 figures at the same rate for sterling as that for 1977. This means that the 1976 figures are not the same as those in the previous edition of **The Times 1000**; calculated by this means, however, the sales and profit figures reflect real growth or decline, adjusted only by the companies' home-based inflation.

Extel has used declared turnover in grading the companies. This is usually net for French companies and gross for most others. Wherever available, consolidated accounts and, as a consequence, consolidated turnover, have been used. Readers should note, however, that profit figures for European and British companies are not strictly comparable, since in a number of cases for which the consolidated turnover may be available, consolidated profits are not, and only the parent company's own profits are included.

We have kept notes down to a minimum and have included only essential definitions. Details of chairmen and managing directors are based on available information as we went to press. Every effort has been made to ensure complete accuracy, and we are grateful to the many companies in all fields who have helped us to produce information which is as up-to-date as possible.

Butler Till Ltd.

Money Brokers

Local Authority, Commercial,
Hire Purchase Deposits,
Sterling Certificates of Deposits
All Negotiable Bills
and Inter-Bank brokers

Dealing Telephone No: 01-623 1161.
Speak to Don Turner
or Gerry Wilton

**Head Office
Adelaide House,
London Bridge,
London EC4R 9HN
01-623 7782**

**Edinburgh House,
3/11 North St. Andrew Street,
Edinburgh
EH2 1HJ
Edinburgh 031-556 9241**

The top 25 trade unions

Rank	Name—General Secretary	Number of members	Members' contributions £	Net income £	Funds £
1	Transport and General Workers' Union *M. Evans*	1,929,834	16,783,945	3,338,974	32,458,570
2	*Amalgamated Union of Engineering Workers *T. Duffy*	1,421,132	15,448,000	2,937,000	18,307,000
3	National Union of General & Municipal Workers *D. Basnett*	945,324	10,421,850	986,349	17,149,972
4	National Union of Public Employees *A. W. Fisher*	693,097	6,416,119	2,535,370	7,737,572
5	National and Local Government Officers' Association *G. Drain*	683,011	8,418,000	2,868,000	8,755,000
6	Union of Shop Distributive and Allied Workers *Rt. Hon. Lord Allen of Fallowfield*	441,539	3,966,469	877,953	4,440,745
7	Association of Scientific, Technical & Managerial Staffs *C. Jenkins*	441,000	5,680,100	1,029,729	2,471,696
8	Electrical, Electronic, Telecommunication and Plumbing Union *F. J. Chapple*	432,628	3,708,971	234,543	5,993,124
9	National Union of Mineworkers *L. Daly*	370,541	3,263,356	152,550	1,849,698
10	Union of Construction, Allied Trades and Technicians *G. F. Smith*	297,264	3,189,978	233,117	2,196,766
11	National Union of Teachers *F. Jarvis*	296,092	2,479,465	706,353	6,078,360
12	Civil and Public Services Association *K. R. Thomas*	230,905	2,772,844	917,199	2,976,146
13	Confederation of Health Service Employees *E. A. G. Spanswick*	211,636	1,980,286	528,810	1,726,780
14	Society of Graphical and Allied Trades *W. H. Keys*	198,182	2,546,481	287,680	2,853,137
15	Union of Post Office Workers *T. Jackson*	197,247	3,844,738	745,511	3,654,648
16	National Union of Railwaymen *S. Weighell*	177,548	2,905,924	1,105,747	13,260,549
17	Association of Professional, Executive, Clerical & Computer Staff *R. A. Grantham*	146,385	1,763,592	306,826	2,601,040
18	Amalgamated Society of Boilermakers, Shipwrights, Blacksmiths & Structural Workers *J. Chalmers*	129,956	1,477,451	185,047	3,164,565
19	Post Office Engineering Union *B. Stanley*	124,535	1,936,218	501,609	2,646,640
20	National Union of Tailors and Garment Workers *J. Macgougan*	117,840	840,308	126,579	3,251,952
21	Iron & Steel Trades Federation *W. Sirs*	117,401	1,541,862	376,670	9,750,962
22	National Union of Bank Employees *L. A. Mills*	116,739	965,405	77,479	335,302
23	National Graphical Association *J. Wade*	109,438	1,983,321	460,111	9,974,759
24	Society of Civil and Public Servants *B. A. Gillman*	105,320	2,380,699	851,141	2,307,447
25	Institution of Professional Civil Servants *W. McCall*	99,009	1,940,621	503,912	1,484,508

NOTE: * Comprising four constituent branches: Constructional (34,056 members); Engineering(1,168,990); Foundry (56,479); Technical Administrative and Supervisory (161,607).

Talk to the Prudential about pension fund investment

John Clark is the man to talk about professional fund management.

❝ At the end of June, 1978 Prudential Pensions, through its Group Investment Linked Pension policies, was managing assets exceeding £300 million on behalf of over 140 pension funds.

Trustees of exempt approved pension funds can choose how their contributions are split between our equity, fixed interest or property funds or leave that decision to us.

We're a wholly-owned subsidiary of the Prudential and we have the benefits of their experience and expertise developed in managing assets exceeding £5,000 million, including a property portfolio valued at over £1,000 million.

Ring 01-405 9222 ext. 6048 for all the details.

A fully descriptive booklet and our latest annual report are also available. **❞**

Prudential Pensions Ltd.
142, Holborn Bars, London EC1N 2NH

Keith Spickett is the man to talk about insured pension plans.

❝ The Prudential has been a market leader in insured pensions since 1933. We manage schemes involving over half a million lives and some 95,000 pensioners.

We have a variety of plans to offer – cash accumulation contracts for groups of 25 people or more, cash retirement schemes for any number of employees, executive pension plans which are tailor made for directors and key staff.

We can meet your investment needs and offer a most comprehensive range of services for insured plans – advisory, administrative and documentary.

Ring 01-405 9222 ext. 2206 and we'll be happy to discuss your needs, arrange meetings with you or your professional advisers, and give you any further information. **❞**

The Prudential Assurance Company Ltd.
142, Holborn Bars, London EC1N 2NH

The top 25 employers' associations

Rank	Name—*General Secretary*	Subscription income	Number of members	Net income £	Funds £
1	National Farmers' Union *H. M. Haynes*	3,907,222	134,724	**514,975**	6,046,541
2	*Engineering Employers' Federation *H. K. Mitchell*	3,485,000	5,187	**360,000**	5,172,000
3	National Federation of Building Trades Employers *H. L. Foster*	2,487,833	11,399	**183,927**	1,761,861
4	British Shipping Federation/General Council of British Shipping *M. W. Gamble*	1,586,000	245	**45,000**	798,000
5	Chemical Industries Association *A. J. Chant*	996,469	290	**17,480**	50,890
6	British Paper & Board Industry Federation *H. Proctor*	596,000	109	**Deficit 5,000**	127,000
7	Incorporated National Association of British & Irish Millers *E. T. J. Hurle*	590,623	43	**28,632**	264,049
8	Newspaper Society *C. G. Page*	538,372	285	**35,512**	140,346
9	Freight Transport Association *G. Turvey*	461,361	14,726	**221,413**	740,349
10	British Printing Industries Federation *E. Dixon*	441,587	3,728	**7,402**	350,594
11	Road Haulage Association *G. H. Newman*	433,000	15,714	**6,000**	463,000
12	Electrical Contractors' Association *P. A. Dey*	420,564	2,151	**3,221**	304,238
13	Newspaper Publishers' Association *J. E. Le Page*	407,043	10	**12,172**	5,130
14	National Federation of Retail Newsagents *K. E. J. Peters*	387,000	29,851	**Deficit 23,000**	647,000
15	Federation of Master Builders *W. Williams*	340,545	19,874	**3,857**	218,565
16	Cement Makers' Federation *Admiral C. K. Wheen*	298,792	6	**330**	67,677
17	Heating & Ventilating Contractors' Association *E. F. Staznes*	264,445	997	**5,720**	117,092
18	British Rubber Manufacturers' Association *R. Byford*	256,000	117	**Deficit 1,000**	62,000
19	Dairy Trade Federation *W. R. Freeman*	253,000	4,400	**Deficit 11,000**	10,000
20	National Farmers' Union of Scotland *D. S. Johnston*	250,000	19,644	**46,000**	109,000
21	British Textile Employers' Association (Cotton, Man-Made and Allied Fibres) *J. Platt*	203,501	254	**741**	47,530
22	Northern Brick Federation *J. Hall*	181,078	26	**857**	11,825
23	National Association of Master Bakers, Confectioners and Caterers *M. F. Zimmerman*	171,372	4,335	**24,190**	113,524
24	National Pharmaceutical Association *J. Wright*	150,756	7,184	**1,299**	156,046
25	Coal Merchants' Federation of Great Britain *R. Matthews*	142,901	7,000	**21,807**	195,160

NOTE: * Comprising 18 separate engineering employers' associations.

Ten-year record table

Rank by turnover	Company	Item		Accounting period ended
1	BRITISH PETROLEUM CO.	Net Capital Employed Ratio of Turnover to *Net Capital Employed Net Profit before Interest and Tax % to *Net Capital Employed	£000 £000	Dec. 31
2	"SHELL" TRANSPORT & TRADING[1]	Net Capital Employed Ratio of Turnover to *Net Capital Employed Net Profit before Interest and Tax % to *Net Capital Employed	£000 £000	Dec. 31
3	B.A.T. INDUSTRIES[3]	Net Capital Employed Ratio of Turnover to *Net Capital Employed Net Profit before Interest and Tax % to *Net Capital Employed	£000 £000	Sept. 30
4	IMPERIAL CHEMICAL INDUSTRIES	Net Capital Employed Ratio of Turnover to *Net Capital Employed Net Profit before Interest and Tax % to *Net Capital Employed	£000 £000	Dec. 31
5	UNILEVER LTD.	Net Capital Employed Ratio of Turnover to *Net Capital Employed Net Profit before Interest and Tax % to *Net Capital Employed	£000 £000	Dec. 31
6	IMPERIAL GROUP	Net Capital Employed Ratio of Turnover to *Net Capital Employed Net Profit before Interest and Tax % to *Net Capital Employed	£000 £000	Oct. 31
7	BL	Net Capital Employed Ratio of Turnover to *Net Capital Employed Net Profit before Interest and Tax % to *Net Capital Employed	£000 £000	Sept. 30 1969–1975 Dec. 31 1976–1977
8	FORD MOTOR CO.	Net Capital Employed Ratio of Turnover to *Net Capital Employed Net Profit before Interest and Tax % to *Net Capital Employed	£000 £000	Dec. 31
9	ESSO PETROLEUM CO.	Net Capital Employed Ratio of Turnover to *Net Capital Employed Net Profit before Interest and Tax % to *Net Capital Employed	£000 £000	Dec. 31
10	GENERAL ELECTRIC CO.	Net Capital Employed Ratio of Turnover to *Net Capital Employed Net Profit before Interest and Tax % to *Net Capital Employed	£000 £000	Mar. 31
11	RIO TINTO-ZINC CORPORATION	Net Capital Employed Ratio of Turnover to *Net Capital Employed Net Profit before Interest and Tax % to *Net Capital Employed	£000 £000	Dec. 31
12	BOWATER CORPORATION	Net Capital Employed Ratio of Turnover to *Net Capital Employed Net Profit before Interest and Tax % to *Net Capital Employed	£000 £000	Dec. 31
13	CAVENHAM	Net Capital Employed Ratio of Turnover to *Net Capital Employed Net Profit before Interest and Tax % to *Net Capital Employed	£000 £000	Mar. 31

NOTES: *Net capital employed at beginning of year.
[1] Based on 40% of Royal Dutch/Shell Group.
[2] On capital employed at end of year.
[3] Figures for years 1967-1975 relate to British-American Tobacco Co.
N/A Not available

1968	1969	1970	1971	1972	1973	1974	1975	1976	1977
1,587,700	1,827,900	1,971,600	2,117,500	2,293,600	2,941,400	3,635,500	4,296,100	5,124,500	5,517,300
1·4	1·4	1·4	1·6	1·6	2·0	3·2	2·6	3·0	2·9
371,200	384,300	466,500	738,500	776,400	1,213,300	2,405,500	1,626,400	1,959,600	2,393,800
24·8	24·2	25·5	37·5	36·7	52·9	81·8	44·7	45·6	46·7
1,825,567	1,961,690	2,005,791	2,173,208	2,363,900	2,612,588	3,111,600	3,745,200	4,461,200	5,002,400
1·3	1·3	1·3	1·5	1·5	1·8	2·6	2·3	2·7	2·6
315,667	355,435	397,348	491,430	500,354	856,802	1,720,000	1,431,600	1,651,200	1,712,400
19·3	18·4	20·3	24·5	23·0	36·2	65·8	46·0	44·1	38·4
607,090	667,720	779,030	833,740	913,320	1,265,100	1,442,610	1,742,260	2,373,000	2,493,000
2·6	2·4	2·5	2·3	2·4	3·1	2·8	3·0	3·0	2·6
130,300	141,560	167,590	169,610	178,360	249,660	305,760	327,190	429,000	472,000
26·3	23·3	25·1	21·2	21·4	27·3	24·2	22·7	23·2	19·9
1,505,400	1,581,300	1,713,000	1,851,800	1,936,800	2,216,300	2,493,200	2,841,000	3,629,000	3,805,000
0·9	0·9	0·9	0·9	0·9	1·1	1·3	1·3	1·5	1·3
193,100	212,700	196,400	191,800	217,500	417,000	581,700	427,000	655,000	612,000
13·9	14·1	12·4	11·2	11·7	21·5	26·2	17·1	23·1	16·9
542,500	548,000	570,800	580,900	644,900	728,100	838,000	979,000	1,268,100	1,421,200
1·9	2·1	2·4	2·6	2·6	3·0	3·4	3·4	3·9	3·1
75,000	68,000	74,100	89,200	108,200	149,400	175,800	227,800	365,400	348,800
13·9	12·6	13·5	15·6	17·9	23·2	24·1	27·2	33·3	27·5
546,100	528,208	568,480	604,753	782,723	797,162	780,162	924,915	791,279	1,116,047
2·3	2·1	2·4	2·2	2·3	2·0	2·4	3·0	3·1	3·3
58,128	62,057	72,353	80,203	88,685	127,689	114,352	151,463	168,098	171,135
13·0	11·2	13·7	14·1	14·7	16·3	14·3	19·4	18·2	17·6
347,644	408,371	436,550	429,364	467,878	511,464	510,485	552,015	814,322	994,971
N/A	2·8	2·5	2·7	3·0	3·3	3·1	3·7	4·2	3·2
50,275	55,594	25,616	55,629	51,458	76,446	42,190	Loss 23,631	112,407 p.a.	72,519
N/A	16·0	6·3	12·7	12·0	16·3	8·2	—	20·4 p.a.	8·9
216,200	239,600	264,100	293,700	277,600	356,600	463,200	453,200	474,900	741,900
1·6	2·3	2·5	2·2	2·7	3·2	2·7	2·5	3·6	4·7
7,888	43,100	26,800	Loss 19,200	56,500	76,500	25,100	40,800	140,200	263,100
3·2	18·0	11·2	—	19·2	27·6	7·0	8·8	30·9	55·4
327,450	346,773	404,443	445,431	478,995	530,309	621,273	930,031	1,160,778	1,416,533
1·7	1·7	1·8	1·7	1·6	1·7	2·7	2·6	2·1	1·9
18,911	14,809	11,846	32,287	61,614	65,384	152,100	133,890	117,171	139,317
6·1	4·5	3·4	7·9	13·6	13·7	28·7	21·6	12·6	12·0
309,676	620,333	583,599	582,201	563,681	624,131	618,150	786,400	896,000	1,036,600
1·6	1·6	1·4	1·6	1·7	1·8	1·8	2·1	2·3	2·3
22,374	45,179	81,819	84,023	92,961	133,777	165,884	177,200	219,100	292,000
19·2	14·6	13·2	14·4	16·0	23·7	26·6	26·0	28·5	32·6
457,685	528,411	714,800	863,500	1,027,700	1,247,200	1,255,900	1,556,100	1,926,000	1,924,600
0·9	0·7	0·8	0·6	0·7	0·9	0·9	0·9	1·1	0·9
62,831	80,400	98,500	81,400	119,200	264,600	317,200	191,600	328,700	322,800
18·6	17·6	18·6	11·4	13·8	25·7	25·4	15·3	21·1	16·8
270,355	296,732	293,583	267,452	391,309	490,365	530,839	609,800	728,500	760,800
0·9	1·0	1·0	0·9	1·5 [2]	2·6	2·4	2·1	2·5	2·4
23,033	27,359	25,026	16,970	37,241	67,629	89,309	84,900	113,000	120,100
9·3	10·1	8·5	5·8	9·5 [2]	17·3	18·2	15·0	18·5	16·5
4,272	4,293	5,564	9,982	135,905	167,699	291,021	316,312	341,239	378,530
7·5	6·4	2·3	3·5 [2]	0·9 [2]	3·5	4·4	4·8	5·2	5·0
Loss 223	302	953	2,465	6,860	25,544	39,329	46,654	53,313	58,723
—	7·1	22·2	24·7 [2]	5·0 [2]	18·8	23·5	16·0	16·9	17·2

Rank by turnover	Company	Item		Accounting period ended
14	GRAND METROPOLITAN	Net Capital Employed Ratio of Turnover to *Net Capital Employed Net Profit before Interest and Tax % to *Net Capital Employed	£000 £000	Sept. 30
15	GUEST, KEEN & NETTLEFOLDS	Net Capital Employed Ratio of Turnover to *Net Capital Employed Net Profit before Interest and Tax % to *Net Capital Employed	£000 £000	Dec. 31
16	COURTAULDS	Net Capital Employed Ratio of Turnover to *Net Capital Employed Net Profit before Interest and Tax % to *Net Capital Employed	£000 £000	Mar. 31 1969–1978
17	GEORGE WESTON HOLDINGS	Net Capital Employed Ratio of Turnover to *Net Capital Employed Net Profit before Interest and Tax % to *Net Capital Employed	£000 £000	Mar. 31
18	ROTHMANS INTERNATIONAL	Net Capital Employed Ratio of Turnover to *Net Capital Employed Net Profit before Interest and Tax % to *Net Capital Employed	£000 £000	June 30 1968–1973 Mar. 31 1974–1977
19	REED INTERNATIONAL	Net Capital Employed Ratio of Turnover to *Net Capital Employed Net Profit before Interest and Tax % to *Net Capital Employed	£000 £000	Mar. 31
20	TEXACO	Net Capital Employed Ratio of Turnover to *Net Capital Employed Net Profit before Interest and Tax % to *Net Capital Employed	£000 £000	Dec. 31
21	GALLAHER	Net Capital Employed Ratio of Turnover to *Net Capital Employed Net Profit before Interest and Tax % to *Net Capital Employed	£000 £000	Dec. 31
22	DUNLOP HOLDINGS	Net Capital Employed Ratio of Turnover to *Net Capital Employed Net Profit before Interest and Tax % to *Net Capital Employed	£000 £000	Dec. 31
23	S. & W. BERISFORD	Net Capital Employed Ratio of Turnover to *Net Capital Employed Net Profit before Interest and Tax % to *Net Capital Employed	£000 £000	Sept. 30
24	INCHCAPE & CO.	Net Capital Employed Ratio of Turnover to *Net Capital Employed Net Profit before Interest and Tax % to *Net Capital Employed	£000 £000	Mar. 31
25	TATE & LYLE	Net Capital Employed Ratio of Turnover to *Net Capital Employed Net Profit before Interest and Tax % to *Net Capital Employed	£000 £000	Sept. 30
26	MARKS & SPENCER	Net Capital Employed Ratio of Turnover to *Net Capital Employed Net Profit before Interest and Tax % to *Net Capital Employed	£000 £000	Mar. 31 1969–1978

NOTES: *Net capital employed at beginning of year.
      2 On capital employed at end of year.
      N/A Not available.

1968	1969	1970	1971	1972	1973	1974	1975	1976	1977
44,502	76,285	137,598	211,477	554,289	666,505	737,054	880,562	888,747	922,539
1·5	1·0	1·7²	1·5²	1·1²	1·6	1·5	1·6	1·7	1·8
4,568	6,089	20,380	28,066	76,843	86,588	82,670	98,375	113,106	133,527
20·8	13·7	14·8²	13·2²	13·9²	15·6	12·4	13·3	12·8	15·0
317,080	320,940	322,900	395,610	443,720	522,050	626,070	818,520	1,020,430	1,068,000
1·6	1·6	1·5	1·7	1·6	1·8	2·2	1·9	1·8	1·6
37,108	42,822	49,140	56,420	57,530	88,390	128,920	105,000	138,460	118,800
13·8	13·5	15·3	17·5	14·5	19·9	24·7	16·8	16·9	11·6
456,983	510,475	556,122	563,985	640,655	758,027	841,100	909,200	942,300	943,200
1·5	1·4	1·3	1·2	1·4	1·5	1·5	1·4	1·7	1·7
61,457	67,046	59,816	61,809	85,603	140,107	148,100	75,200	116,800	86,500
15·9	14·7	11·7	11·1	15·2	21·9	19·5	8·9	12·8	9·2
N/A	N/A	N/A	N/A	N/A	229,670	278,245	306,777	373,697	433,741
					4·1	3·8	3·9	4·3	4·0
					41,314	47,164	57,808	76,550	91,266
					23·2	20·5	20·8	25·0	24·4
47,208	53,251	61,260	63,162	65,684	226,992	265,721	297,548	330,660	405,715
2·4	2·8	2·7	2·6	2·6	4·1²	4·4	3·8	4·1	4·5
8,180	9,569	9,519	11,902	12,317	50,883	53,183 p.a.	44,870	62,593	93,157
17·1	20·3	17·9	19·4	19·5	22·4²	23·4 p.a.	16·8	21·0	28·2
221,184	235,688	238,741	344,700	337,400	409,300	478,600	519,000	623,100	790,800
1·2	1·3	1·3	1·9	1·9	1·8	1·8	2·0	2·0	2·4
20,875	23,866	28,330	34,300	43,400	56,100	84,200	107,300	65,200	114,200
9·8	10·8	12·0	10·0²	12·6	16·6	20·6	22·4	12·6	18·3
N/A	130,841	147,618	178,490	200,477	234,892	313,368	300,055	466,884	N/A
	N/A	1·9	2·0	1·6	2·4	3·9	3·1	4·8	
	Loss 2,854	4,566	2,327	8,791	Loss 4,003	Loss 4,277	2,909	Loss 41,935	
	—	3·5	1·6	4·9	—	—	0·9	—	
123,402	125,141	121,641	127,041	140,798	169,962	184,733	207,225	230,043	319,577
3·5	3·7	3·5	3·7	4·1	3·9	4·3	5·0	5·5	6·1
18,437	19,564	20,487	23,627	29,471	38,003	39,657	44,586	47,123	40,087
15·9	15·9	16·4	19·4	23·2	27·0	23·3	24·1	22·7	17·4
270,451	307,284	325,844	453,960	445,395	517,700	595,943	628,500	774,100	789,000
1·9	1·8	1·8	1·8	1·4	1·6	1·7	1·7	2·1	1·8
35,271	36,116	38,369	50,932	53,386	54,633	66,135	75,000	100,900	84,100
14·5	13·4	12·5	15·6	11·8	12·0	12·8	12·6	16·1	10·9
10,674	12,342	14,250	20,502	27,243	32,239	28,211	37,145	78,851	122,499
11·3	10·1	10·5	10·6	6·6	12·6²	16·5	21·2	20·7	16·0
1,073	2,537	2,747	3,081	3,431	7,694	12,380	12,308	14,994	27,361
12·4	23·8	22·3	21·6	16·7	23·9²	38·4	43·6	40·4	34·7
43,474	53,608	60,982	75,777	85,342	118,201	191,361	238,472	323,530	433,360
1·9	2·6	2·4	2·7	2·9	4·0	4·5	3·8	3·8	3·9
3,892	6,540	7,516	10,074	13,647	20,506	39,074	41,739	55,887	94,116
10·9	15·0	14·0	16·5	18·0	24·1	33·1	21·8	23·4	29·1
146,432	166,385	172,980	174,564	185,066	181,210	197,210	264,693	283,809	407,881
1·7	1·6	1·6	2·0	2·4	2·5	3·8	6·4	5·0	4·4
14,407	11,954	15,157	16,348	21,125	22,709	46,760	55,536	58,212	57,070
10·6	8·2	9·1	9·5	12·1	12·3	25·8	28·2	22·0	20·1
157,305	169,502	174,061	183,193	210,217	235,817	407,034	446,724	479,839	562,026
2·1	2·2	2·3	2·5	2·9	2·7	3·1	2·2	2·5	2·6
40,225	46,419	53,293	56,944	73,214	80,003	85,078	88,937	114,491	129,539
27·5	29·5	31·4	32·7	40·0	38·1	36·1	21·9	25·6	27·0

Rank by turnover	Company	Item		Accounting period ended
27	LONRHO	Net Capital Employed Ratio of Turnover to *Net Capital Employed Net Profit before Interest and Tax % to *Net Capital Employed	£000 £000	Sept. 30
28	CZARNIKOW GROUP[4]	Net Capital Employed Ratio of Turnover to *Net Capital Employed Net Profit before Interest and Tax % to *Net Capital Employed	£000 £000	Sept. 30
29	RANKS HOVIS MCDOUGALL	Net Capital Employed Ratio of Turnover to *Net Capital Employed Net Profit before Interest and Tax % to *Net Capital Employed	£000 £000	Aug. 31
30	ALLIED BREWERIES	Net Capital Employed Ratio of Turnover to *Net Capital Employed Net Profit before Interest and Tax % to *Net Capital Employed	£000 £000	Sept. 30
31	C. T. BOWRING & CO.	Net Capital Employed Ratio of Turnover to *Net Capital Employed Net Profit before Interest and Tax % to *Net Capital Employed	£000 £000	Dec. 31
32	AMALGAMATED METAL CORPN.	Net Capital Employed Ratio of Turnover to *Net Capital Employed Net Profit before Interest and Tax % to *Net Capital Employed	£000 £000	Dec. 31
33	THORN ELECTRICAL INDUSTRIES	Net Capital Employed Ratio of Turnover to *Net Capital Employed Net Profit before Interest and Tax % to *Net Capital Employed	£000 £000	Mar. 31
34	BICC	Net Capital Employed Ratio of Turnover to *Net Capital Employed Net Profit before Interest and Tax % to *Net Capital Employed	£000 £000	Dec. 31
35	BURMAH OIL CO.	Net Capital Employed Ratio of Turnover to *Net Capital Employed Net Profit before Interest and Tax % to *Net Capital Employed	£000 £000	Dec. 31
36	SEARS HOLDINGS	Net Capital Employed Ratio of Turnover to *Net Capital Employed Net Profit before Interest and Tax % to *Net Capital Employed	£000 £000	Jan. 31 1969–1978
37	P. & O. STEAM NAVIGATION CO.	Net Capital Employed Ratio of Turnover to *Net Capital Employed Net Profit before Interest and Tax % to *Net Capital Employed	£000 £000	Sept. 30 1968–1974 Dec. 31 1975–1977
38	GREAT UNIVERSAL STORES	Net Capital Employed Ratio of Turnover to *Net Capital Employed Net Profit before Interest and Tax % to *Net Capital Employed	£000 £000	Mar. 31
39	CONSOLIDATED GOLD FIELDS	Net Capital Employed Ratio of Turnover to *Net Capital Employed Net Profit before Interest and Tax % to *Net Capital Employed	£000 £000	June 30

NOTES: * Net capital employed at beginning of year.
[2] On capital employed at end of year.
[4] Figures for years 1969-1974 relate to C. Czarnikow.
N/A Not available.

1968	1969	1970	1971	1972	1973	1974	1975	1976	1977
58,611	124,759	139,879	143,520	156,120	183,690	211,520	355,530	519,120	626,580
3·8	1·2²	1·5	1·4	1·5	1·6	1·8	1·5²	2·8	2·3
8,007	16,549	17,680	18,870	22,520	33,860	51,950	74,870	107,900	101,310
30·2	13·3²	14·2	13·5	15·7	21·7	28·3	21·1²	30·3	19·5
N/A	6,911	8,041	9,425	10,772	11,444	17,087	13,809	17,578	20,898
	37·9	51·8	53·8	64·2	50·5	64·9	86·2²	60·4²	63·5
	888	886	942	1,425	1,062	3,449	6,713	3,648	5,514
	12·9	9·9	11·7	15·1	9·8	30·1	48·6²	20·8²	31·4
137,943	164,025	171,508	177,799	183,413	213,132	243,232	266,245	289,827	332,117
2·4	2·6	2·3	2·4	2·5	2·8	3·3	3·3	3·5	3·8
20,707	20,418	20,947	22,951	28,943	33,931	33,171	42 432	51,508	51,127
16·6	14·8	12·8	13·4	16·3	18·5	15·6	17·4	19·3	17·6
292,954	319,332	327,984	352,235	405,943	513,184	528,199	569,900	610,600	734,200
1·2	1·2	1·2	1·3	1·4	1·3	1·2	1·4	1·6	1·8
34,492	37,460	41,897	50,157	63,574	74,388	69,917	75,199	77,800	95,800
13·9	12·8	13·1	15·3	18·0	18·3	13·6	14·2	13·7	15·7
27,222	54,896	64,026	89,452	104,077	123,143	114,810	151,299	175,311	213,909
12·2	5·1²	6·2	6·0	4·9	4·9	4·0	5·9	6·2	6·2
4,568	13,331	17,577	21,993	26,609	36,392	36,309	34,105	44,081	47,438
27·7	24·3²	32·0	34·3	29·7	35·0	29·5	29·7	29·1	27·1
20,192	25,317	20,650	20,223	23,787	28,660	31,451	48,930	61,064	56,772
10·6	13·3	11·9	11·8	9·6	13·9	23·8	15·3²	21·5	17·3
2,744	3,167	2,248	137	1,327	4,999	13,079	9,628	12,464	9,662
14·7	15·7	8·9	0·7	6·6	21·0	45·6	30·6²	25·5	15·8
95,079	145,820	169,397	203,138	234,877	253,628	318,730	388,904	411,279	469,810
2·4	1·8²	2·0	2·0	2·0	2·2	2·5	2·3	2·2	2·5
16,843	33,363	34,811	41,415	53,265	73,853	80,831	76,869	83,296	112,952
23·2	22·9²	23·9	24·4	26·2	31·4	31·9	24·1	21·4	27·5
187,894	212,801	225,595	224,402	249,293	313,206	356,687	347,894	371,748	383,369
1·9	2·2	2·2	2·0	2·1	2·5	2·5	2·1	2·6	2·7
23,611	26,162	31,677	35,584	38,918	52,411	53,211	44,489	53,073	58,561
13·9	13·9	14·9	15·8	17·3	21·0	17·0	12·5	15·3	15·8
302,895	766,182	713,621	784,303	905,637	981,738	964,100	1,001,916	653,000	638,807
0·9	0·8	0·4	0·5	0·6	0·7	1·0	1·1	1·0	1·5
42,139	45,396	49,914	50,156	54,097	75,469	55,350	29,793	17,472	24,445
17·6	15·0	6·5	7·0	6·9	8·3	5·6	3·1	1·7	3·7
220,360	218,205	207,636	219,766	332,899	352,925	397,190	426,236	457,842	598,818
1·3	1·3	1·4	1·6	2·2	1·6	1·7	1·8	1·9	2·1
17,412	28,291	33,339	38,271	53,160	55,057	43,555	56,111	55,550	74,612
13·6	12·8	15·3	18·4	24·2	16·5	12·3	14·1	13·0	16·3
255,862	273,250	305,066	330,567	336,356	556,473	750,267	819,469	828,817	816,680
0·7	0·7	0·7	0·8	0·7	0·7	0·8	0·8	0·9	1·2
11,072	15,056	16,070	9,978	19,554	42,682	70,290	38,583 p.a.	59,358	64,983
4·6	5·9	5·9	3·3	5·9	12·7	12·6	5·1 p.a.	7·2	7·8
196,910	218,257	235,761	254,410	277,694	341,101	382,060	426,343	472,721	543,822
2·0	1·9	1·9	1·9	2·0	2·2	1·9	1·9	2·0	2·1
45,861	49,451	52,667	54,729	62,660	80,208	85,964	92,541	101,835	116,223
25·4	25·2	24·1	23·2	24·6	28·9	25·2	24·2	23·9	24·6
151,802	185,575	205,059	197,965	203,343	260,738	324,431	380,018	445,084	442,400
1·2	1·2	1·1	1·1	1·1	1·2²	1·8	1·7	1·8	2·1
19,367	27,781	33,254	28,025	29,330	41,945	77,218	82,626	64,291	73,800
17·8	18·3	17·9	13·7	14·8	16·1²	29·6	25·5	16·9	16·6

Rank by turnover	Company	Item		Accounting period ended
40	TOZER, KEMSLEY & MILLBOURN	Net Capital Employed Ratio of Turnover to *Net Capital Employed Net Profit before Interest and Tax % to *Net Capital Employed	£000 £000	Dec. 31
41	HAWKER SIDDELEY GROUP	Net Capital Employed Ratio of Turnover to *Net Capital Employed Net Profit before Tax and Interest % to *Net Capital Employed	£000 £000	Dec. 31
42	BASS CHARRINGTON	Net Capital Employed Ratio of Turnover to *Net Capital Employed Net Profit before Interest and Tax % to *Net Capital Employed	£000 £000	Sept. 30
43	LUCAS INDUSTRIES	Net Capital Employed Ratio of Turnover to *Net Capital Employed Net Profit before Interest and Tax % to *Net Capital Employed	£000 £000	July 31
44	BOOTS CO.	Net Capital Employed Ratio of Turnover to *Net Capital Employed Net Profit before Interest and Tax % to *Net Capital Employed	£000 £000	Mar. 31 1969–1978
45	CADBURY SCHWEPPES	Net Capital Employed Ratio of Turnover to *Net Capital Employed Net Profit before Interest and Tax % to *Net Capital Employed	£000 £000	Dec. 31
46	UNIGATE	Net Capital Employed Ratio of Turnover to *Net Capital Employed Net Profit before Interest and Tax % to *Net Capital Employed	£000 £000	Mar. 31
47	EMI	Net Capital Employed Ratio of Turnover to *Net Capital Employed Net Profit before Interest and Tax % to *Net Capital Employed	£000 £000	June 30
48	DISTILLERS CO.	Net Capital Employed Ratio of Turnover to *Net Capital Employed Net Profit before Interest and Tax % to *Net Capital Employed	£000 £000	Mar. 31
49	THOMAS TILLING	Net Capital Employed Ratio of Turnover to *Net Capital Employed Net Profit before Interest and Tax % to *Net Capital Employed	£000 £000	Dec. 31
50	METAL BOX	Net Capital Employed Ratio of Turnover to *Net Capital Employed Net Profit before Interest and Tax % to *Net Capital Employed	£000 £000	Mar. 31 1969–1978

NOTES: * Net capital employed at beginning of year.
² On capital employed at end of year.
N/A Not available.

1968	1969	1970	1971	1972	1973	1974	1975	1976	1977
9,903	14,600	20,103	33,862	43,761	82,641	111,984	70,830	85,886	84,990
N/A	N/A	N/A	13·6	11·3	11·5	8·5	5·8	12·8	10·7
1,626	2,630	3,649	5,325	7,326	11,601	17,281	13,994	19,156	17,413
18·7	26·6	25·0	26·5	21·6	26·5	20·9	12·5	27·0	20·3
209,900	238,548	243,299	223,470	254,383	276,455	331,602	408,515	408,924	443,956
1·6	1·9	1·9	1·9	2·1	2·3	2·3	2·5	2·4	1·9
22,643	20,410	21,137	28,172	37,824	51,886	59,855	74,083	99,727	107,209
9·2	9·7	8·9	11·6	16·9	21·1	21·7	22·3	24·4	22·3
325,657	332,377	337,008	353,130	382,700	518,600	545,200	571,700	625,400	662,200
N/A	1·0	1·0	1·1	1·2	1·3	1·1	1·2	1·4	1·4
30,263	32,549	38,728	46,051	56,500	66,200	61,700	69,500	77,900	100,100
N/A	10·0	11·7	13·7	16·0	17·3	11·9	12·7	13·6	16·0
106,634	116,017	134,022	179,323	217,984	242,028	266,000	293,085	384,808	473,179
2·6	2·4	2·4	2·4	1·9	1·8	1·9	2·1	2·1	2·3
16,733	20,186	16,093	22,067	27,762	32,566	25,758	42,856	65,967	90,790
19·9	18·9	13·9	16·5	15·5	14·9	10·6	16·1	22·5	23·6
108,535	110,397	123,205	129,368	154,414	184,653	232,535	280,000	337,900	414,400
2·3	2·1	2·3	2·5	2·8	2·7	2·7	2·6	2·6	2·6
20,084	21,114	25,905	35,256	57,716	64,792	66,820	82,202	101,100	109,300
22·1	19·5	23·5	28·6	44·6	42·0	36·2	35·4	36·1	32·3
59,301	118,716	181,438	177,376	199,708	262,812	292,100	357,800	398,800	420,300
2·6	1·5	1·4	1·6	2·0	2·2	2·1	2·2	2·2	2·2
11,491	21,646	21,456	24,884	31,715	38,426	36,841	49,100	57,800	62,300
19·4[2]	21·1	11·4	13·7	17·9	19·2	14·0	16·8	16·2	15·6
70,737	91,466	94,217	99,440	103,564	130,010	141,044	162,592	164,599	200,124
4·3	4·3	3·4	3·6	4·0	3·9	3·6	4·2	4·7	5·2
10,961	10,736	11,043	12,009	14,718	16,031	19,996	25,779	28,598	30,727
16·1	15·2	12·1	12·7	14·8	15·5	15·4	18·3	17·6	18·7
86,504	107,226	120,115	145,810	141,568	158,017	172,420	176,990	217,206	285,207
2·1	2·0	2·0	1·9	1·7	2·0[2]	2·5	2·9	3·8	3·9
12,849	20,369	25,179	14,924	23,684	34,826	43,419	46,277	67,206	77,611
22·4	23·5	23·5	12·4	16·2	22·0[2]	27·5	26·8	38·0	35·7
311,128	331,597	358,814	370,118	423,632	444,889	488,639	579,416	633,934	731,548
1·2	1·2	1·1	1·2	1·2	1·1	1·2	1·3	1·2	1·3
43,617	53,013	46,091	60,512	70,281	79,285	94,658	84,869	105,864	144,801
14·6	17·0	16·9	16·9	16·9	19·0	18·7	21·1	17·4	18·3	22·8
77,683	99,519	109,026	120,086	145,668	191,374	224,489	235,400	266,700	340,700
2·3	2·4	2·5	2·9	3·3	3·5	2·9	2·8	2·9	3·0
11,746	12,939	15,975	22,179	29,413	40,433	40,586	44,700	52,400	65,500
16·5	16·7	16·1	20·3	24·5	27·8	21·2	19·9	22·3	24·6
108,613	125,708	141,693	155,153	183,906	196,122	250,311	282,104	340,925	386,171
1·7	1·8	1·8	1·7	1·8	1·9	2·3	2·1	2·5	2·4
15,798	16,476	18,407	17,546	18,674	29,968	36,798	42,235	66,547	65,681
16·8	17·2	17·1	15·1	14·7	19·2	23·2	16·9	23·6	19·3

The 50 leading UK advertisers[†]

Rank	Company	1977			1976			Rank last year
		Total £000's	TV £000's	Press £000's	Total £000's	TV £000's	Press £000's	
1	Unilever	29,259	23,678	5,581	25,700	22,941	2,759	1
2	Imperial Group	21,021	8,056	12,065	18,436	2,503	10,864	2
3	Cadbury Schweppes	16,697	15,531	1,166	12,230	11,070	1,160	5
4	Mars	14,159	13,987	172	12,061	11,450	611	4
5	H.M. Government	13,310	5,117	8,193	12,300	5,449	6,851	3
6	Beecham Group	12,801	10,397	2,404	9,020	7,095	1,925	6
7	Co-operative Wholesale Society	10,629	3,883	6,746	8,337	2,377	5,960	8
8	Reed International	9,878	6,000	3,878	7,014	4,864	2,150	12
9	Rowntree Mackintosh	9,520	8,800	720	5,993	5,119	874	16
10	Proctor & Gamble	8,485	8,235	250	7,293	7,152	144	11
11	Gallaher	8,108	2,230	5,878	8,942	1,984	6,958	7
12	British Leyland	7,934	3,819	4,115	7,407	3,149	4,258	10
13	Allied Breweries	7,876	5,861	2,015	7,888	6,028	1,860	9
14	Electricity Council	7,596	4,549	3,047	6,180	3,243	2,937	15
15	Boots	7,586	2,265	5,321	5,624	1,917	3,707	19
16	Reckitt & Colman	7,359	5,711	1,648	6,733	5,625	1,108	13
17	Nestlé	7,320	5,056	2,264	4,316	3,088	1,228	25
18	Gas Council	7,126	3,987	3,139	4,893	2,290	2,603	22
19	Tesco	6,556	3,140	3,416	—			
20	Rothmans International	6,380	—	6,380	6,621	—	6,621	14
21	BAT Industries	6,279	4,969	1,310	3,778	3,286	492	31
22	Arthur Guinness	5,964	5,508	456	5,262	4,406	856	20
23	Ranks Hovis McDougall	5,839	4,730	1,109	5,975	5,381	594	17
24	Brooke Bond Liebig	5,668	4,698	976	3,800	3,739	61	29
25	United Biscuits	5,598	4,394	1,204	4,565	4,420	141	23
26	Bass Charrington	5,485	3,905	1,580	6,635	2,745	890	34
27	Unigate	5,439	4,855	584	2,812	2,692	120	43
28	General Electric	5,412	4,459	953	—	—	—	
29	Imperial Chemical Industries	5,402	3,419	1,983	5,951	4,405	1,546	18
30	Heinz	5,186	4,311	875	5,210	3,948	1,262	21
31	Grand Metropolitan	4,885	3,411	1,474	4,278	2,998	1,280	26
32	Allied Retailers	4,661	3,567	1,094	4,256	3,193	1,064	27
33	Thorn Electrical	4,544	1,242	3,302	3,491	814	2,678	35
34	Midland Bank	4,525	1,996	2,529	2,743	566	2,177	44
35	F. W. Woolworth	4,508	1,971	2,537	3,233	1,869	1,366	38
36	Post Office	4,313	2,891	1,432	3,301	1,918	1,383	36
37	Barclays Bank	4,151	143	4,008	—	—	—	
38	Spillers	4,140	3,413	727	2,637	2,311	325	46
39	Gillette	4,091	3,743	348	2,823	2,569	254	42
40	Scottish & Newcastle Breweries	3,955	3,627	328	3,284	3,125	159	37
41	Debenhams	3,878	638	3,240	4,414	240	4,174	24
42	J. Lyons	3,852	2,964	888	3,678	3,072	606	33
43	Sears Holdings	3,835	365	3,470	—			
44	British Rail	3,757	1,160	2,597	—	—	—	
45	Colgate Holdings (UK)	3,674	3,597	77	2,458	2,261	197	49
46	Fiat	3,611	814	2,797	—	—	—	
47	Kellogg Co. of Great Britain	3,431	3,044	387	4,094	3,326	763	28
48	Whitbread & Co.	3,336	2,224	1,112	3,784	2,266	1,519	30
49	Wittington Investments	3,249	1,462	1,787	2,991	2,141	850	39
50	National Westminster Bank	3,244	767	2,447	—	—	—	

† See page 14 for further information.
(a) The method includes only display advertisements; classified, financial, trade and technical are broadly omitted; (b) not *all* the press is covered, nor are local advertisers;
(c) The method of costing, on gross card rates, will usually over-estimate the actual charge to the advertiser; (d) production costs are not included; (e) the definition Holding Company is normally taken to be that used in *Who Owns Whom*, but there are such exceptions as H.M. Government which as a non-commercial company does not feature there.
Sources: *MEAL A1 Reports* and *Who Owns Whom* 1977/78.

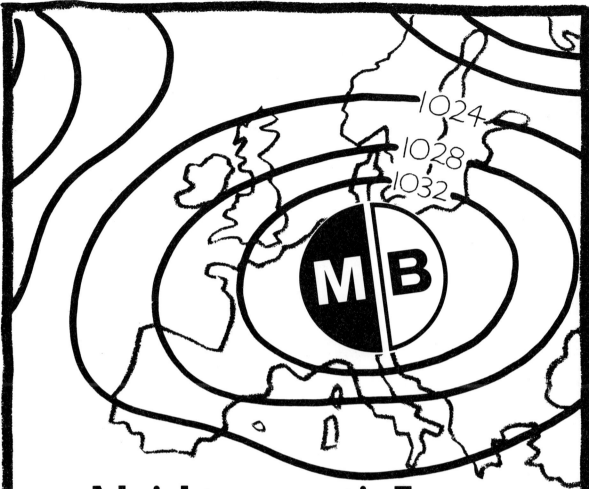

A bright prospect in Europe; it's Metal Box's business.

For years, Metal Box has been selling containers into Europe.

But today, we're increasingly involved in on-the-spot manufacturing, consultancy and marketing.

We are now manufacturing in Germany and Portugal (tinplate containers), France (collapsible plastics tubes), Italy and Greece (food, drink and aerosol cans), with additional sales operations in Scandinavia and Holland.

Our central heating subsidiary Stelrad, has operations in Belgium, Holland, France, Germany and Austria, as well as in the UK.

We're winning new customers by offering a mixture of advanced technology, expertise and a better service.

And the outlook is fine.

One of the factories of Metal Box's Italian subsidiary Superbox SpA in Sant' Ilario.

Metal Box
A good business to be in

Queens House, Forbury Road, Reading RG1 3JH. Telephone: 0734 581177. Telex: 847437.

1 The 1000 largest UK industrial companies

Rank by turn-over	COMPANY	Main activity	Chairman and Managing Directors (in italics) §‖	Accounting period ended
1 (1)	British Petroleum Co.	Oil Industry	Sir David Steel (J.M.D.) *(see page 70)*	31–12–77
2 (2)	"Shell" Transport & Trading[19]	Oil Industry	C. C. P. Pocock (J.M.D.), *P. B. Baxendell*	31–12–77
3 (3)	BAT Industries	Tobacco, Retailing, Paper & Cosmetics	P. Macadam	30– 9–77
4 (4)	Imperial Chemical Industries	Chemicals, Fibres, Paints, etc.	M. A. E. Hodgson	31–12–77
5 (5)	Unilever Ltd.	Food Products, Detergents, etc.	Sir David Orr	31–12–77
6 (6)	Imperial Group	Tobacco, Food, Drink and Packaging	Sir John Pile	31–10–77
7 (7)	British Leyland	Motor Vehicle Manufacturers	M. O. Edwardes	31–12–77
8 (12)	Ford Motor Co.	Motor Vehicle Manufacturers	*Sir Terence Beckett (M.D.)*	31–12–77
9 (8)	Esso Petroleum Co.	Oil Industry	A. W. Pearce	31–12–77
10 (9)	General Electric Co.	Electrical Engineers	Lord Nelson of Stafford, *Sir Arnold Weinstock*	31– 3–77
11 (10)	Rio Tinto-Zinc Corporation	Mining & Industrial—Metals & Fuel	Sir Mark Turner	31–12–77
12 (13)	Bowater Corporation	Paper Manufacturers, Intl. Trading	Lord Erroll of Hale, *C. F. Popham*	31–12–77
13 (11)	Cavenham	Food, Drink, Tobacco etc., Products	Sir James Goldsmith, *J. Greenhalgh*	2– 4–77
14 (16)	Grand Metropolitan	Hotel Props, Milk Prds. Brewers, etc.	Maxwell Joseph, *S. G. Grinstead, E. H. Sharp*	30– 9–77
15 (15)	Guest, Keen & Nettlefolds	Steel & Eng. Products, Fastenings, etc.	Sir Barrie Heath, *T. Holdsworth*	31–12–77
16 (14)	Courtaulds	Man-Made Fibres, Textiles, Chemicals	Sir Arthur Knight	31– 3–78
17 (18)	George Weston Holdings	Food Manufacturers & Distributors	W. G. Weston	2– 4–77
18 (20)	Rothmans International	Tobacco Manufacturers	Sir David Nicolson	31– 3–77
19 (24)	Reed International	Paper, Packaging, Printing & Publishing	A. A. Jarratt	31– 3–77
20 (28)	Texaco	Oil Industry	T. E. Cottrell	31–12–76
21 (22)	Gallaher	Tobacco, Cigarette, Cigar & Snuff Man.	A. W. H. Stewart-Moore	31–12–77
22 (19)	Dunlop Holdings	Rubber Goods & Sports Requisites, etc.	*Sir Campbell Fraser (M.D.)*	31–12–77
23 (41)	S. & W. Berisford	Sugar Importers & Mchts., etc.	*E. S. Margulies (M.D.)*	30– 9–77
24 (32)	Inchcape & Co.	International Merchants	Earl of Inchcape *(see page 70)*	31– 3–77
25 (17)	Tate & Lyle	Sugar Refiners, etc.	Earl Jellicoe, *S. Tate*	30– 9–77
26 (23)	Marks & Spencer	General Store Proprietors	Sir Marcus Sieff (J.M.D.) *(see page 70)*	31– 3–78
27 (26)	Lonrho	Mining, Agric., Textiles, Constr., etc.	Lord Duncan Sandys, *R. W. Rowland*	30– 9–77
28 (21)	Czarnikow Group	Commodity Brokers, etc.	R. E. Liddiard	30– 9–77
29 (31)	Ranks Hovis McDougall	Food Manufacturers and Distributors	J. Rank, *P. W. J. Reynolds*	3– 9–77
30 (35)	Allied Breweries	Brewers, Vintners, Hoteliers, etc.	K. S. Showering	24– 9–77
31 (30)	C. T. Bowring & Co.	Insurance Brokers, Finance, Eng., etc.	P. Bowring, *G. A. Cooke*	31–12–77
32 (25)	Amalgamated Metal Corpn.	Metal & Ores	Sir John Saunders	31–12–77
33 (36)	Thorn Electrical Industries	Electrical & Electronic Engineers	Sir Richard G. Cave, *G. J. Strowger*	31– 3–77
34 (34)	BICC	Cable Makers, Elec. Engineers & Contrs.	C. H. Broughton Pipkin	31–12–77
35 (27)	Burmah Oil Co.	Oil Industry	Sir Alastair Down, *S. J. Wilson*	31–12–77
36 (39)	Sears Holdings	Footwear, Stores, Engineering, etc.	L. Sainer	31– 1–78
37 (44)	P. & O. Steam Navigation Co.	Shipowners	Earl of Inchcape, *A. B. Marshall*	31–12–77
38 (37)	Great Universal Stores	Stores & Mail Order	Sir Isaac Wolfson (J.M.D.), *Sir Leonard Wolfson*	31– 3–77
39 (50)	Consolidated Gold Fields	Mining Finance, Industry, Commerce	Lord Erroll of Hale	30– 6–77
40 (33)	Tozer, Kemsley & Millbourn	Internl. Finance & Investment	K. A. C. Thorogood	31–12–77
41 (29)	Hawker Siddeley Group	Mech. & Electrical Eng. & Metals	*Sir Arnold Hall (M.D.)*	31–12–77
42 (38)	Bass Charrington	Brewers	D. Palmar *(Chief Executive)*	30– 9–77
43 (46)	Lucas Industries	Vehicle & Aircraft Accessory Manfrs.	B. F. W. Scott, *R. G. C. Messervy*	31– 7–77
44 (45)	Boots Co.	Manfg., Wholesale & Retail Chemists	G. I. Hobday, *D. E. M. Appleby*	31– 3–78
45 (40)	Cadbury Schweppes	Confectionery, Soft Drinks, Food etc.	Sir Adrian Cadbury, *B. E. S. Collins*	31–12–77
46 (42)	Unigate	Dairymen & Food Manufacturers, etc.	J. Clement	26– 3–77
47 (51)	EMI	Music, Electronics, Leisure, T.V., etc.	Sir John Read *(see page 70)*	30– 6–77
48 (49)	Distillers Co.	Whisky Distillers	J. R. Cater	31– 3–77
49 (52)	Thomas Tilling	Industrial Holding Co.	Sir Robert Taylor, *P. M. Meaney*	31–12–77
50 (48)	Metal Box	Packaging Containers & Closures	Sir Alexander Page, *D. I. Allport*	31– 3–78

NOTES: *Total tangible assets less current liabilities (other than bank loans and overdrafts and future tax).   †As percentage of capital employed at beginning of the year.   ‡As at 14 July 1978.   §Appendix on page 70 gives list of Managing Directors which cannot be fitted into the main text.   ‖M.D. = Managing Director; J.M.D. = Joint Managing Director; A.C. = Acting Chairman.   ¶As percentage of capital employed at the end of the year.   N/A Not available.   [1]UK only.   [7]Including added value and sales taxes in overseas territories, but excluding UK VAT.   [10]Including excise duties but excluding VAT.   [11]Including excise duties and VAT.   [17]Including duties and sales taxes.   [18]Including £538,000,000 premium income earned overseas.   [19]Based on 40% of Royal Dutch/"Shell" Group.   [20]Including sales taxes, excise duties and similar levies.   [30]Including estimated results of IMI Ltd. (formerly Imperial Metal Industries Ltd) for 10 months to date of disposal.   [40]Including results (t/over £82,758,000) of former UK Aerospace subs for 4 months to date of nationalisation.

TURNOVER		*CAPITAL EMPLOYED			NET PROFIT BEFORE INTEREST AND TAX						**No. of employees	‡Equity market cap. £M.
Total £000	Export £000	£000	Rank Latest year	Previous year	Latest year £000	Rank	Previous year £000	% to turnover Latest year	†% to capital employed Latest year	Previous year		
14,712,200[17]	1,188,000	5,517,300	1	1	2,393,800	1	1,959,600	16·3	46·7	45·6	81,000	3,362·7
11,393,651[20]	—	5,002,400	2	2	1,712,400	2	1,651,200	15·0	38·4	44·1	—	3,116·4
6,070,000[7]	154,000	2,493,000	4	4	472,000	4	429,000	7·8	19·9	23·2	152,000	1,128·9
4,663,000[30]	936,000[30]	3,805,000	3	3	612,000[30]	3	655,000	13·1	16·9	23·1	154,000	2,144·5
3,957,900	428,600	1,421,200	6	6	348,800	5	365,400	8·8	27·5	37·3	91,923[1]	974·8
3,196,200	51,900	1,116,047	8	9	171,135	10	168,098	5·4	17·6	18·2	95,600	565·0
2,602,003	854,000	994,971	11	14	72,519	41	112,407p.a.	2·8	8·9	20·4p.a.	194,610	53·2
2,253,100	893,500	741,900	18	29	263,100	8	140,200	11·7	55·4	30·9	71,000	USA
2,235,933[11]	86,300	1,416,533	7	7	139,317	13	117,171	6·2	12·0	12·6	8,666[1]	USA
2,054,600	524,000	1,036,600	10	11	292,000	7	219,100	14·2	32·6	28·5	192,000	1,476·0
1,823,300	89,700	1,924,600	5	5	322,800	6	328,700	17·7	16·8	21·1	11,573[1]	548·0
1,723,300	21,900	760,800	17	16	120,100	17	113,000	7·0	16·5	18·5	37,000	272·0
1,716,477	8,804	378,530	53	47	58,723	53	53,313	3·4	17·2	16·9	59,100	FR
1,640,741	54,759	922,539	13	12	133,527	15	113,106	8·1	15·0	12·8	99,199[1]	464·2
1,639,200	174,700	1,068,000	9	8	118,800	18	138,460	7·2	11·6	16·9	107,468	393·4
1,575,700	387,900	943,200	12	10	86,500	36	116,800	5·5	9·2	12·8	107,536[1]	327·9
1,498,404	29,355	433,741	41	43	91,266	32	76,550	6·1	24·4	25·0	71,850[1]	UQ
1,491,967	67,274	405,715	48	50	93,157	31	62,593	6·2	28·2	21·0	7,010[1]	76·7
1,488,400	70,600	790,800	15	20	114,200	20	65,200	7·7	18·3	12·6	86,300	150·9
1,455,000[10]	115,000	466,884	35	54	Loss 41,935	1000	2,909	—	—	0·9	4,290[1]	USA
1,407,556	24,437	319,577	64	71	40,087	80	47,123	2·8	17·4	22·7	28,845	USA
1,361,000	141,000	789,000	16	15	84,100	37	100,900	6·2	10·9	16·1	102,000	108·8
1,261,567	16,052	122,499	150	186	27,361	116	14,994	2·2	34·7	40·4	3,100	115·7
1,259,763	75,000	433,360	42	51	94,116	30	55,887	7·5	29·1	23·4	6,576[1]	319·5
1,257,181	87,000	407,881	47	57	57,070	56	58,212	4·5	20·1	22·0	20,015	92·7
1,254,055	53,212	562,026	27	28	129,539	16	114,491	10·3	27·0	25·6	45,257[1]	1,006·0
1,171,340	30,160	626,580	24	25	101,310	26	107,900	8·6	19·5	30·3	120,000	111·4
1,117,000	8,432	20,898	525	612	5,514	392	3,648	0·5	31·4	¶20·8	564[1]	UQ
1,107,000	8,986	332,117	63	56	51,127	66	51,508	4·6	17·6	19·3	57,248	147·2
1,105,900	38,800	734,200	19	21	95,800	28	77,800	8·7	15·7	13·7	59,234	467·5
1,088,091	546,623[18]	213,909	88	93	47,438	71	44,081	4·4	27·1	29·1	9,500	111·5
1,058,000	14,000	56,772	266	222	9,662	274	12,464	0·9	15·8	25·5	1,297[1]	20·4
1,038,753	105,800	469,810	34	35	112,952	21	83,296	10·9	27·5	21·4	83,632	480·2
998,000	213,000	383,369	52	42	58,561	54	53,073	5·9	15·8	15·3	53,100	177·4
986,833[17]	75,165	638,807	23	17	24,445	129	17,472	2·5	3·7	1·7	31,900	90·7
981,068	47,000	598,818	25	31	74,612	39	55,550	7·6	16·3	13·0	56,000[1]	314·0
980,442	—	816,680	14	13	64,983	47	59,358	6·6	7·8	7·2	15,936[1]	120·1
975,158	22,544	543,822	29	30	116,223	19	101,835	11·9	24·6	23·9	37,005[1]	696·4
954,100	29,700	442,400	40	32	73,800	40	64,291	7·7	16·6	16·9	97,000	264·4
916,000	69,000	84,990	198	171	17,413	169	19,156	1·9	20·3	27·0	4,678	27·4
911,955[40]	295,000[40]	443,956	39	27	107,209[40]	24	99,727	11·8	22·3	24·4	50,900	411·7
904,500	10,500	662,200	21	18	100,100	27	77,900	11·2	16·0	13·6	60,038[1]	430·6
886,070	139,930	473,179	33	41	90,790	33	65,967	10·2	23·6	22·5	68,778[1]	272·5
883,800	44,400	414,400	45	49	109,300	23	101,100	12·4	32·3	36·1	67,044[1]	730·1
883,600	49,100	420,300	43	37	62,300	48	57,800	7·1	15·6	16·2	45,424	198·1
862,854	7,203	200,124	97	96	30,727	102	28,598	3·6	18·7	17·6	38,000[1]	121·3
851,121	128,564	285,207	68	76	77,611	38	67,206	9·1	35·7	38·0	51,300	149·6
847,172	244,900	731,548	20	19	144,801	12	105,864	17·1	22·8	18·3	19,156[1]	671·9
811,200	33,300	340,700	58	64	65,500	46	52,400	8·1	24·6	22·3	39,100	253·0
807,459	59,300	386,171	51	48	65,681	45	66,547	8·1	19·3	23·6	33,916[1]	190·7

The following letters in the Market Capitalisation column denote unquoted companies and country of control: FR = France.   UQ = Unquoted.
USA = United States of America.

Rank by turn-over	COMPANY	Main activity	Chairman and Managing Directors (in italics) §‖	Accounting period ended
51 (54)	J. Sainsbury	Retail Distribution of Food	J. D. Sainsbury	4– 3–78
52 (47)	Tube Investments	General Engineers	B. S. Kellett (J.M.D.), *R. M. Bagnall,* *T. E. Barnsley*	31– 3–77
53 (55)	J. Lyons & Co.	Food Products, Catering, Property	N. L. Salmon, *L. Badham*	31– 3–78
54 (64)	Brooke Bond Liebig	Tea, Coffee, Meat & Other Food Prods.	Sir Humphrey Prideaux	30– 6–77
55 (43)	Rank Xerox	Xerographic Equipment, etc.	J. M. Thomas, *W. F. Glavin*	31–10–76
56 (56)	Dalgety	International Merchants	D. L. Donne, *J. A. Turner*	30– 6–77
57 (53)	F. W. Woolworth & Co.	General Retail Merchants	S. J. Owen (J.M.D.), *G. Rodgers*	31– 1–78
58 (67)	Beecham Group	Pharmaceuticals, Toiletries, Drinks, etc.	G. J. Wilkins	31– 3–77
59 (80)	Gill & Duffus Group	Commodity Brokers, Mchts. & Processrs.	F. M. Gill, *T. P. H. Aitken, C. G. Palmer*	31–12–77
60 (60)	Rolls-Royce	Aero Engines	Sir Kenneth Keith	31–12–77
61 (61)	Tesco Stores (Holdings)	Multiple Retailing	L. Porter, *I. C. Maclaurin*	26– 2–77
62 (63)	BOC International	Manfrs. of Gases & Associated Eqpmt.	Sir Leslie Smith	30– 9–77
63 (N/A)	Littlewoods Organisation	Mail Order Trading & Retail Stores	P. Moores, *P. D. Carter*	31–12–77
64 (72)	Western United Inv. Co.¹²	Foodstuffs & By-products	*None*	31–12–75
65 (57)	Babcock & Wilcox	Engineers & Contractors	J. L. King, *T. Carlile*	31–12–77
66 (68)	Mobil Oil Co.	Oil Industry	G. W. Pusack, *Sir Nevil J. W. Macready*	31–12–77
67 (75)	Tarmac	Roadstone & Civil Eng.	R. G. Martin	31–12–77
68 (62)	Coats Patons	Thread, Yarns, Fashion & Clothing	W. R. Henry	31–12–77
69 (65)	George Wimpey & Co.	Bldg., Civil, Mech. & Elec. Eng. Contrs.	R. B. Smith, *D. G. Fitzgerald, D. Wight*	31–12–77
70 (69)	Philips Electronic & Assoc.	Electric & Electronic Products	G. Jeelof (M.D.)	31–12–76
71 (74)	Vauxhall Motors	Motor Vehicle Manufacturers	W. R. Price (M.D.)	31–12–77
72 (71)	United Biscuits (Holdings)	Manfrs. of Biscuits, Cakes, Crisps, etc.	Sir Hector Laing	31–12–77
73 (58)	Spillers	Millers, Bakers, Food Manufacturers	W. M. Vernon	29– 1–77
74 (59)	Lonconex	Metal and Ore Merchants		30– 9–76
75 (83)	Trafalgar House	Contracting, Civil Eng., Shipping, etc.	N. Broackes, *E. W. Parker*	30– 9–77
76 (70)	Harrisons & Crosfield	Eastern Mchts. Exporters & Importers	T. Prentice	31–12–77
77 (76)	IBM United Kingdom Holdings	Information Handling Eqpt. Mfrs.	Earl of Cromer, *E. R. Nixon*	31–12–77
78 (84)	Whitbread & Co.	Brewers	C. H. Tidbury	25– 2–78
79 (77)	Plessey Co.	Electric & Electronic Products	Sir John Clark	31– 3–77
80 (78)	Reckitt & Colman	Food & H/hold Products, Pharms., etc.	J. A. S. Cleminson	31–12–77
81 (73)	Ready Mixed Concrete	Building Materials Suppliers, etc.	J. Camden (M.D.)	31–12–77
82 (82)	Trust Houses Forte	Hotels, Catering and Leisure Group	Lord Thorneycroft	31–10–77
83 (81)	Massey-Ferguson Holdings	Manfrs. of Agricultural Machinery	H. A. R. Powell (M.D.)	31–10–77
84 (101)	Booker McConnell	International Food, Eng. & Tdg. Co.	Sir George Bishop	31–12–77
85 (85)	British Electric Traction	Industrial Holding Co.	Sir John Spencer Wills, *H. S. L. Dundas*	31– 3–77
86 (91)	Arthur Guinness Son & Co.	Brewers	Earl of Iveagh, *R. A. McNeile, A. J. Purssell*	24– 9–77
87 (87)	House of Fraser	Departmental Stores	Sir Hugh Fraser, *W. G. Crossan*	28– 1–78
88 (93)	Glaxo Holdings	Pharmaceutical Preparations, etc.	A. E. Bide	30– 6–77
89 (79)	British Aircraft Corpn. (Hldgs)	Aircraft Manufacturers		1– 1–77
90 (112)	Hanson Trust	Agriproducts, Industrial Services	Sir James Hanson	30– 9–77
91 (66)	Ultramar Co.	Petroleum Exploration & Development	C. L. Nelson (M.D.)	31–12–77
92 (95)	Rowntree Mackintosh	Confectionery & Grocery Products	Sir Donald Barron	31–12–77
93 (88)	Delta Metal Co.	Metals, Alloys, Engineers, etc.	Viscount Caldecote, *T. R. M. Kinsey,* *G. H. Wilson*	31–12–77
94 (—)	IMI	Metals, Fabricated Products, etc.	Sir Michael J. S. Clapham, *E. Swainson*	31–12–77
95 (86)	Standard Telephones & Cables	Telecommunications & Electronics	Lord Caccia, *K. G. Corfield*	31–12–77
96 (126)	Wood Hall Trust	Civil & Gen. Eng., Pastoral Tdg., etc.	M. Richards, *A. I. Annand*	30– 6–77
97 (96)	Ocean Transport & Trading	Shipping, Distribution, etc.	Sir Lindsay Alexander	31–12–77
98 (107)	Chrysler United Kingdom	Motor Vehicle Manufacturers	G. A. Hunt, *G. A. Lacy*	31–12–77
99 (114)	Conoco	Petroleum Products	R. J. Maisonpierre, *R. A. Fowler*	31–12–76
100 (99)	Fitch Lovell	Food Mfrs., Wholesalers & Retailers	M. G. T. Webster	30– 4–77

NOTES: *Total tangible assets less current liabilities (other than bank loans and overdrafts and future tax). †As percentage of capital employed at beginning of the year. ‡As at 14 July 1978. §Appendix on page 70 gives list of Managing Directors which cannot be fitted into the main text. ‖M.D. = Managing Director. ¶As percentage of capital employed at the end of the year. N/A Not available. ¹UK only. ¹¹Including excise duties and VAT. ¹²Turnover, exports and employees relate to gorup. Other figures relate to parent co. only. ¹³Not calculated. ²⁴Contract value of work executed. ²⁵Contract work overseas. M.D. = Managing Director; J.M.D. = Joint Managing Director; A.C. = Acting Chairman.

TURNOVER		*CAPITAL EMPLOYED			NET PROFIT BEFORE INTEREST AND TAX						**No. of employees	‡Equity market cap. £M.
Total £000	Export £000	£000	Rank Latest year	Rank Previous year	Latest year £000	Rank	Previous year £000	% to turnover Latest year	†% to capital employed Latest year	†% to capital employed Previous year		
797,302	0	209,266	93	87	28,096	111	28,583	3·5	15·0	15·7	32,203	168·4
791,800	148,300	460,100	37	39	68,500	42	63,933	8·7	17·6	18·0	51,490[1]	214·3
790,000	21,420	247,332	76	58	29,501	107	40,021	3·7	10·8	14·0	19,985[1]	36·3
769,154	17,570	337,892	59	72	59,591	51	33,125	7·7	26·0	16·1	9,730[1]	115·7
759,454	90,767	598,548	26	22	215,755	9	192,741	28·4	38·4	41·8	30,313	USA
725,200	19,700	261,400	72	69	30,000	105	26,800	4·1	12·8	13·4	13,822	104·0
724,099	4,129	307,510	65	60	51,973	63	46,823	7·2	18·6	17·4	64,122[1]	245·7
720,800	66,200	367,900	54	62	138,400	14	100.100	19·2	50·1	47·6	31,700	964·1
713,000	14,950	88,949	190	218	22,471	143	15,523	3·2	36·4	51·0	574[1]	55·3
703,900	285,000	404,800	49	40	21,700	145	Loss 9,300	3·1	5·6	—	61,786	UQ
701,291	53	126,379	144	141	30,424	103	25,105	4·3	28·2	26·6	37,480	147·0
670,600	60,900	638,900	22	24	105,200	25	94,270	15·7	19·8	21·6	40,900	243·1
666,948	0	335,175	60	—	53,167	62	41,236	8·0	20·0	18·3	29,453	UQ
662,200	15,060	6,141	888	910	344	944	165	—[13]	4·3	3·7	18,255[1]	UQ
656,669	81,718	210,404	92	73	35.997	86	44,978	5·5	15·9	25·2	36,948	120·9
656,163[11]	83,700	222,948	85	85	31,972	98	26,952	4·9	15·8	15·9	2,342[1]	USA
649,510	4,072	162,263	115	104	29,556	106	26,311	4·6	18·7	19·0	24,019[1]	82·7
639,534	59,960	391,644	50	45	90,448	34	83,628	14·1	24·9	27·7	68,000	199·2
638,000[24]	292,000[25]	356,687	57	55	61,834	50	51,391	9·7	20·9	27·1	26,000[1]	192·0
630,000	144,583	457,329	38	34	15,454	188	1,100	2·5	3·6	0·3	45,698[1]	H
627,546	195,400	148,726	125	115	5,273	404	7,349	0·8	3·8	6·3	30,180	USA
623,300	21,200	212,998	90	106	44,052	74	38,099	7·1	28·3	28·1	38,000	209·6
621,000	13,900	170,617	108	94	23,598	136	21,510	3·8	14·1	14·4	29,097[1]	45·6
620,366	50,000	3,857	937	920	695	885	351	0·1	21·2	17·7	—	USA
587,262	1,918	361,119	55	61	58,237	55	41,540	9·9	20·9	16·1	17,972[1]	199·3
579,000	26,000	96,466	178	169	24,814	128	24,332	4·3	28·7	35·7	5,141[1]	121·8
578,842	263,730	292,999	66	67	110,268	22	86,962	19·0	45·5	41·6	13,814	USA
573,369	11,613	508,651	32	33	55,782	58	54,835	9·7	11·4	12·3	39,670	213·8
568,800	93,999	334,788	61	52	50,514	68	44,474	8·9	15·7	16·4	63,890	216·3
557,000	35,500	225,320	83	83	62,220	49	60,710	11·2	29·8	35·7	34,000	294·2
547,103	575	144,709	126	112	32,970	93	28,898	6·0	22·7	21·6	8,949[1]	88·2
531,000	2,200	413,700	46	46	56,100	57	41,700	10·6	15·7	13·9	67,046	221·1
527,679	369,000	195,936	100	110	53,514	61	54,090	10·1	35·1	43·6	21,486	CAN
523,000	58,700	104,489	167	160	27,358	117	17,563	5·2	30·1	¶19·3	17,204	77·0
512,862	34,500	418,259	44	44	66,547	44	52,989	13·0	18·2	15·3	55,000	154·3
498,849	48,300	243,281	79	82	47,892	70	46,327	9·6	22·7	25·5	18,627	135·8
492,950	16,429	269,750	70	70	40,373	77	32,591	8·2	17·3	15·3	29,020[1]	170·1
488,028	111,700	358,818	56	53	95,113	29	80,506	19·5	31·0	36·8	30,540	477·4
483,410	270,141	122,517	149	131	43,533	76	31,812	9·0	41·3	37·0	34,528	UQ
477,400	8,400	135,700	136	118	31,000	101	24,622	6·5	23·4	32·0	12,000	87·4
472,652	—	213,413	89	74	35,846	88	25,499	7·6	16·0	14·4	176[1]	111·5
469,212	49,872	211,127	91	109	47,246	72	37,074	10·1	31·0	28·6	30,900	223·2
469,130	71,000	245,530	78	68	36,910	85	35,150	7·4	15·3	18·5	32,000	98·5
467,016	84,700	245,590	77	—	41,096	76	36,278	8·8	17·9	20·1	26,664[1]	127·1
460,083	103,685	248,008	75	78	45,604	73	39,682	9·9	21·2	20·1	36,970[1]	USA
460,028	23,479	85,729	197	203	10,935	254	10,754	2·4	15·1	18·1	2,200[1]	23·1
459,034	2,400	464,282	36	38	51,694	64	52,586	11·3	13·3	16·8	15,979	118·7
457,983	175,607	125,630	145	128	Loss 8,231	996	Loss 31,902	—	—	—	22,800	USA
453,017	116,901	221,267	87	105	15,392	190	12,810	3·4	10·0	9·2	2,400	USA
446,919	10,588	57,310	264	241	11,258	243	8,577	2·5	19·8	15·8	17,120[1]	38·9

The following letters in the Market Capitalisation column denote unquoted companies and country of control: CAN = Canada.   H = Holland.   UQ = Unquoted   USA = United States of America.

Rank by turn-over	COMPANY	Main activity	Chairman and Managing Directors (in italics) §‖	Accounting period ended
101 (97)	Debenhams	Department Stores, Supermarkets, etc.	Sir Anthony Burney	28– 1–78
102 (89)	Rank Organisation	Films, Entertainment, Xerox	H. Smith, *R. W. Evans*	31–10–77
103 (100)	Richard Costain	Bldg. & Civil Engineering Contrs.	J. P. Sowden	31–12–77
104 (115)	Associated Dairies	Dairymen, Supermarkets, etc.	A. N. Stockdale, *E. G. Bousfield*	30– 4–77
105 (103)	Wheatsheaf Distbn. & Trdng³³	Wholesale & Retail Distribution	V. G. Williams	25– 2–78
106 (127)	ICL	Data Processing Systems	T. C. Hudson, *C. M. Wilson*	30– 9–77
107 (102)	John Lewis Partnership	Department Stores & Food Retailing	P. T. Lewis	28– 1–78
108 (106)	Turner & Newall	Asbestos, Plastics, Insulation, etc.	P. W. C. Griffith, *C. W. Newton, J. K. Shepherd*	31–12–77
109 (90)	Vickers	Engineering, Office Eqpt., etc.	Lord Robens of Woldingham, *Sir Peter Matthews*	31–12–77
110 (122)	Thomas Borthwick & Sons	International Meat Traders	W. A. Bullen, *D. F. Burditt*	30– 9–77
111 (94)	John Laing & Son	Building & Civil Eng. Contractors	Sir Maurice Laing	31–12–77
112 (111)	W. H. Smith & Son (Holdings)	Newspaper Distributors, Booksellers	P. W. Bennett, *S. Hornby*	28– 1–78
113 (118)	Pilkington Bros.	Glass Manufacturing & Processing	Sir Alastair Pilkington	31– 3–77
114 (113)	Ladbroke Group	Bookmaking, Hotel, Leisure, Property	C. Stein (M.D.)	3– 1–78
115 (—)	Northern Engineering Indsts.	Electrical & Mechanical Eqpt. Mfrs.	Sir James Woodeson, *D. McDonald*	31–12–77
116 (105)	Dickinson Robinson Group	Paper, Packaging Materials, Printers	J. S. Camm (M.D.)	31–12–77
117 (109)	FMC	Meat & By-products	D. H. Darbishire, *G. H. B. Cattell*	30– 4–77
118 (169)	Anglo Chemical & Ore Co.	Metal Dealers	*None*	31–12–76
119 (98)	Blue Circle Industries	Cement and Allied Products	Sir Rowland Wright, *J. D. Milne*	31–12–77
120 (117)	Johnson, Matthey & Co.	Gold, Silver & Platinum Refiners, etc.	Lord Robens of Woldingham, *H. R. Hewitt*	31– 3–77
121 (130)	Stenhouse Holdings	Insurance Bkg, Gen. Engineers, etc.	J. G. Stenhouse	30– 9–77
122 (92)	Taylor Woodrow	Builders & Civil Eng. Contractors	R. G. Puttick, *Sir Frank Taylor*	31–12–77
123 (110)	Tootal	Thread & Textile Manufacturers	Sir George Kenyon, *R. F. Audsley*	31– 1–78
124 (134)	Guinness Peat Group	Manufacturers, Gen. Mchts. & Brokers	Lord Kissin	30– 4–77
125 (133)	Total Oil Great Britain	Marketing of Petroleum Products	T. E. Hutton	31–12–76
126 (116)	Scottish & Newcastle Brews.	Brewers	P. E. G. Balfour	1– 5–77
127 (170)	NAFTA (GB)	Traders in Petroleum Products	*Details refused*	31–12–76
128 (139)	Powell Duffryn	Shipg., Eng., Fuel Dis., Timber, Indl. Serv.	C. S. Aston, *W. J. Franklin*	31– 3–78
129 (104)	Tampimex Oil	Oil Traders	J. B. Eldridge, *M. G. Schubert*	31–12–76
130 (119)	Michelin Tyre Co.	Tyre Manufacturers	M. J. De Logeres, *G. Gazareth*	31–12–77
131 (108)	Bunge & Co.	Grain, Cotton & Commodity Merchants	W. Hugaerts, *R. G. Pendered*	31–12–76
132 (123)	Wellcome Foundation	Pharmaceuticals, Chemicals, etc.	A. J. Shepperd	27– 8–77
133 (148)	Inco Europe	Nickel Refiners	A. T. Shadforth, *R. B. Nicholson*	31–12–76
134 (128)	Albright & Wilson	Manfrs. of Chemical & Allied Prods.	G. H. Meason, *D. W. Livingstone*	26–12–77
135 (129)	Thomson Organisation	Printers & Publishers, Travel, etc.	Lord Thomson of Fleet, *G. C. Brunton*	31–12–77
136 (121)	UDS Group	Retail Stores and Mail Order	B. Lyons (M.D.)	28– 1–78
137 (124)	S. Pearson & Son	Newspapers, Publishing, Indl., etc.	Lord Gibson	31–12–77
138 (131)	Louis Dreyfus & Co.	Merchants and Shippers	J. Louis-Dreyfus	31–12–77
139 (156)	Hoechst UK	Chemicals, Pharms, Dyestuffs, Paints	N. M. Mischler, *D. von Winterfeldt*	31–12–77
140 (132)	Carrington Viyella	Textile Manufacturers	L. Regan	31–12–77
141 (137)	Lex Service Group	Car Dealers, Hoteliers, etc.	T. E. Chinn (M.D.)	1– 1–78
142 (159)	Davy International	Industrial Plant Manufacturers	Sir John Buckley, *R. J. Withers*	31– 3–77
143 (171)	Linfood Holdings	Wholesale, Retail, Cash & Carry Distn.	Lord Kissin, *D. G. T. Linnell*	30– 4–77
144 (N/A)	Food Manufacturers (GB Co.)¹⁶	Food Manufacturers	R. C. Edwards	31–12–76
145 (180)	Petrofina (UK)	Petroleum Products	Baron E. De Selys Longchamps, *H. D. Newlyn*	31–12–76
146 (135)	Associated Engineering	Precision Component Manfrs. & Distbs.	J. N. Ferguson, *J. G. Collyear*	30– 9–77
147 (143)	Glynwed	Eng. & Building Products, Steel	L. Fletcher	31–12–77
148 (138)	Blackwood Hodge	Earth Moving Eqpmt., Sales & Service	W. A. Shapland (M.D.)	31–12–77
149 (144)	Gulf Oil (Great Britain)	Distbn. of Petroleum Products	W. H. Hamilton	31–12–76
150 (141)	Fisons	Chemical Fertilisers, etc.	Sir George Burton	31–12–77

NOTES: *Total tangible assets less current liabilities (other than bank loans and overdrafts and future tax). †As percentage of capital employed at beginning of the year. ‡As at 14 July 1978. §Appendix on page 70 gives list of Managing Directors which cannot be fitted into the main text. ‖M.D. = Managing Director; J.M.D. = Joint Managing Director; A.C. = Acting Chairman. ¶As percentage of capital employed at the end of the year. N/A Not available. ¹UK only. ⁴Gross sale value of all equipment exported (only rental or net selling price included in turnover). ¹⁰Including excise duties but excluding VAT. ¹¹Including excise duties and VAT. ¹³Not calculated ¹⁶Co. published accounts on current cost accounting basis (E.D.18). ²⁶Combined profit of Clarke Chapman Ltd. and its subs and Reyrolle Parsons Ltd. and its subs prior to merger. ³³Now a sub. co. of Linfood Holdings Ltd. ⁴³Including results of shipbuilding subs for 6 months to date of nationalisation.

| TURNOVER | | *CAPITAL EMPLOYED | | | NET PROFIT BEFORE INTEREST AND TAX | | | | | | **No. of employees | ‡Equity market cap £M. |
Total £000	Export £000	£000	Rank Latest year	Rank Previous year	Latest year £000	Rank	Previous year £000	% to turnover Latest year	†% to capital employed Latest year	†% to capital employed Previous year		
442,983	5,000	224,874	84	75	24,434	130	26,771	5·5	11·2	13·5	27,401[1]	120·3
442,666	42,289	559,466	28	23	148,504	11	98,424	33·5	26·5	19·6	36,856	426·3
432,000	1,000	102,511	169	175	38,066	82	25,398	8·8	45·7	36·1	5,282[1]	102·9
429,000	108	52,884	281	337	23,950	133	14,981	5·6	67·5	66·0	13,974[1]	187·8
426,009	0	30,380	412	446	3,345	556	6,179	0·8	14·6	35·0	6,532	—[32]
418,650	83,000[4]	261,044	73	80	40,125	78	30,856	9·6	18·8	17·7	32,156	108·2
414,574	6,747	152,676	121	116	32,362	95	27,124	7·8	23·6	22·8	25,800	UQ
413,792	93,700	332,727	62	63	54,682	60	41,896	13·2	20·4	20·3	40,062	195·6
409,388[42]	40,500[42]	291,364	67	59	35,876[42]	87	47,992	8·8	12·6	18·8	27,095	74·4
405,414	6,475	70,702	223	196	10,545	257	11,738	2·6	14·2	21·7	1,862[1]	20·3
404,000	537	120,483	151	143	23,919	134	18,682	5·9	22·3	19·9	19,200[1]	96·1
393,786	1,528	86,607	195	202	21,274	148	17,201	5·4	29·4	27·5	20,292	124·5
390,066	47,244	523,650	30	36	89,369	35	55,798	22·9	21·8	18·1	30,400	335·9
387,693	7	102,746	168	187	25,276	125	16,699	6·5	32·1	28·8	13,157	90·4
387,000	95,000	153,387	120	—	28,753	110	25,977[26]	7·4	¶18·7	—[13]	33,678	75·6
382,978	35,706	162,279	114	103	26,636	120	24,570	7·0	16·6	17·7	25,886	98·8
376,622	8,093	44,083	318	307	5,413	397	2,800	1·4	13·5	8·2	8,200[1]	6·8
375,535	827	23,501	479	583	3,964	494	3,481	1·1	25·9	27·4	—	USA
370,800	47,400	513,600	31	26	67,200	43	60,800	18·1	13·6	14·6	11,854[1]	194·5
370,388	109,591	154,867	119	121	25,643	124	18,424	6·9	20·0	16·3	5,635[1]	73·8
363,000	2,473	22,523	490	500	11,520	239	9,394	3·2	59·0	55·6	7,401	38·7
362,000	39,353	200,638	96	86	26,105	123	25,143	7·2	13·5	16·3	10,373[1]	83·9
361,191	55,241	179,466	103	97	28,048	112	24,307	7·8	16·8	16·6	20,397[1]	83·3
359,917	14,486	92,766	184	250	16,316	179	10,792	4·5	29·5	20·3	1,944[1]	79·7
353,725[11]	21,800	138,056	133	136	1,234	829	12,604	0·4	1·1	11·6	1,239	FR
345,897	6,576	268,831	71	65	39,060	81	35,186	11·3	14·7	14·6	26,160[1]	181·7
345,643	0	106,291	163	135	4,543	456	3,538	1·3	3·9	11·2	—	USSR
343,630	34,105	110,117	160	180	15,702	184	13,876	4·6	17·1	17·1	12,045	55·4
343,532	18,340	5,996	891	904	2,050	720	2,118	0·6	44·4	46·8	—	USA
342,184	82,609	238,613	80	81	34,351	90	39,506	10·0	16·3	21·6	18,658[1]	FR
342,000	8,489	44,346	314	327	8,782	291	6,194	2·6	26·6	16·6	858[1]	NA
341,762	73,351	260,686	74	77	55,536	59	49,885	16·2	25·6	28·0	6,996[1]	UQ
340,723	219,403	176,090	105	134	17,349	170	15,613	5·1	14·5	17·8	7,898[1]	CAN
338,007	91,900	201,916	95	89	40,102	79	37,140	11·9	22·1	23·3	10,364	220·3
332,680	13,927	111,696	159	150	24,076	132	18,741	7·2	24·9	22·0	20,086[1]	352·3
331,269	39,900	221,927	86	79	26,125	122	23,826	7·9	12·2	12·3	27,026	137·3
328,491	69,824	271,926	69	66	51,501	65	45,404	15·7	20·4	21·4	28,946[1]	149·2
319,594	2,367	86,791	194	223	2,846	609	4,323	0·9	3·8	7·2	275[1]	FR
311,578	15,574	119,225	156	149	17,276	171	15,096	5·5	14·6	15·5	6,503[1]	G
304,322	38,901	172,810	107	102	22,557	142	18,762	7·4	13·9	14·0	28,841[1]	68·7
299,584	1,127	95,051	180	184	18,816	163	14,402	6·3	23·6	20·5	8,145[1]	42·7
297,435	111,000	88,400	192	265	19,934	156	11,463	6·7	40·3	29·7	9,498	93·5
293,898	263	23,530	478	629	6,333	361	3,359	2·2	¶26·9	32·4	8,531[1]	29·2
290,075	28,513	84,523	201	—	8,646	298	8,943p.a.	3·0	16·4	¶16·9p.a.	9,249[1]	USA
286,576	29,814	105,141	164	216	7,036	339	10,364	2·5	11·0	18·6	1,921	B
286,517	46,000	159,109	117	127	37,209	83	26,242	13·0	29·8	25·0	28,953	99·2
285,440	10,000	104,724	166	151	16,559	175	18,088	5·8	17·2	23·9	17,218	66·7
282,274	10,400	131,322	141	119	26,267	121	22,340	9·3	20·1	22·9	5,800	36·1
280,772[10]	63,081	139,930	132	123	11,849	236	12,610	4·2	9·3	9·5	1,191[1]	USA
275,659	48,253	195,991	99	95	25,213	127	23,287	9·1	14·8	15·9	12,466	135·4

The following letters in the Market Capitalisation column denote unquoted companies and country of control: B = Belgium. CAN = Canada. FR = France. G = Germany. NA = Netherlands Antilles. UQ = Unquoted. USA = United States of America. USSR = Union of Soviet Socialist Republics.

Rank by turn-over	COMPANY	Main activity	Chairman and Managing Directors (in italics) §‖	Accounting period ended
151 (157)	British Sugar Corpn.	Sugar Products	Sir Gerald Thorley (*see page 70*)	25– 9–77
152 (147)	Alcan Aluminium (UK)	Aluminium & Associated Products	D. A. Pinn (M.D.)	31–12–77
153 (140)	Mitchell Cotts Group	Eng., Transport, Commodity Trdg., etc.	P. P. Dunkley, *K. N. Jenkins, J. R. C. Wren*	30– 6–77
154 (200)	Amoco (UK)	Marketing of Petroleum Products	J. A. Parker	31–12–77
155 (150)	Chloride Group	Battery, etc., Manufacturers	Sir Francis Hawkings	31– 3–77
156 (146)	British Home Stores	Retail Stores	Sir Jack Callard, *C. W. Paterson*	1– 4–78
157 (166)	Ciba-Geigy (UK)	Manufacture & Sale of Chemicals	A. A. S. Rae, *R. H. Wilson, H. R. Wust*	26–12–76
158 (125)	Guthrie Corporation	Plantations, Carpets & Floorcovering	Sir Eric Griffith-Jones, *I. L. Coates*	31–12–77
159 (163)	BPB Industries	Gypsum, Bldg. Materials, Paper & Eng.	N. M. Barrow	31– 3–77
160 (152)	BTR	General Rubber Manufacturers	Sir David Nicolson, *O. Green*	31–12–77
161 (174)	Redland	Construction Materials	C. R. Corness	26– 3–77
162 (177)	Heron Corpn.	Property Inv. & Trdg., Garage Opertrs.	H. Ronson	31– 3–77
163 (158)	Northern Foods	Dairymen, Food Manufacturers, Brewers	N. Horsley	30– 9–77
164 (145)	Gestetner Holdings	Duplicating Machines, etc., Manfrs.	D. Gestetner, *J. Gestetner*	5–11–77
165 (178)	Croda International	Chemical Processors	Sir Frederick Wood (*see page 70*)	1– 1–78
166 (175)	Kodak	Photographic Goods Manufacturers	F. J. Moorfoot (M.D.)	30–10–77
167 (181)	Smiths Industries	Vehicle, Aviation & Marine Eqpmt., etc.	E. R. Sisson, *W. A. Mallinson*	30– 7–77
168 (275)	Gerald Metals	Metal Merchants	G. L. Lennard, *R. Kestenbaum*	30– 4–77
169 (199)	Montague L. Meyer	Timber Merchants	*J. M. Meyer*	31– 3–77
170 (151)	Consolidated Petroleum	Oil Industry	N/A	31–12–76
171 (204)	Hepworth Ceramic Holdings	Manfrs. of Vitrified Clay Pipes, etc.	P. Goodall	31–12–77
172 (154)	Thos. W. Ward	Heavy Engineering, etc.	J. P. Frost (M.D.)	30– 9–77
173 (209)	Overseas Containers	Container Operators	R. O. C. Swayne	27–11–76
174 (161)	Marley	Manfrs. of Building Trade Products	O. A. Aisher	31–10–77
175 (179)	Br. & Commonwealth Shipping	Ship and Aircraft Operators, etc.	Sir W. Nicholas Cayzer	31–12–76
176 (153)	Steetley Company	Minerals, Chems., High Temp. Ceramics	H. Smith	31–12–77
177 (120)	Tradax, England	Grain & Commodity Merchants	R. S. Hurren	31– 5–77
178 (206)	Coral Leisure Group	Turf Accountants, etc.	N. Coral, *J. M. Hoare*	29– 4–77
179 (173)	AAH	Fuel Distbn., Builders Supplies, etc.	W. M. Pybus	31– 3–77
180 (195)	John Brown & Co.	Engineering, Machine Tools, etc.	J. Mayhew-Sanders	31– 3–77
181 (190)	Nurdin & Peacock	Cash & Carry Wholesalers	J. A. Peacock, *G. A. King, T. V. Grimwood*	31–12–77
182 (239)	APV Holdings	Process Engineers & Plant Manfrs.	H. P. N. Benson, *D. K. Fraser, K. A. G. Miller*	31–12–77
183 (172)	H. J. Heinz Company	Food Manufacturers	H. J. Heinz II, *C. F. Lowe*	23– 4–77
184 (193)	Granada Group	Entertainments	Lord Bernstein	1–10–77
185 (299)	Cocoa Merchants	General Produce Merchants	M. Weldon (M.D.)	30– 9–77
186 (155)	London and Northern Group	Contracting, Quarrying, Bldg. Prods., etc.	J. H. M. Mackenzie, *J. Barker*	31–12–76
187 (186)	British Aluminium Co.	Aluminium, Aluminium Alloys, Chemicals	B. S. Kellett, *R. E. Utiger*	31–12–77
188 (207)	BSG International	Vehicle Distbn. Servicing, Leasing, etc.	H. G. Cressman, *T. C. Cannon*	31–12–77
189 (167)	Bunzl Pulp & Paper	Paper & Paper Products	G. G. Bunzl, *E. G. Beaumont, F. R. Davenport*	31–12–77
190 (217)	English China Clays	China Clay Manufacturers	Lord Aberconway	30– 9–77
191 (182)	Monsanto	Chemical & Plastic Products	E. Sharp	31–12–77
192 (164)	Danish Bacon Co.	Sale & Distbn. of Groceries & Provs.	E. Trautmann (M.D.)	31–12–77
193 (184)	Johnson & Firth Brown	Specialist Engineers	J. M. Clay	30– 6–77
194 (136)	Lead Industries Group	Metal Refining & Smelting, Paints, etc.	I. G. Butler (J.M.D.), *R. G. Harper*	31–12–77
195 (165)	Simon Engineering	Engineers & Plant Contractors	H. C. Harrison	31–12–77
196 (213)	William Press & Son	Civil & Mech. Engineering Contrs.	W. A. Hawken, *R. A. Daniels*	31–12–77
197 (188)	Duport	Steel Foundry, Eng., Domestic Eqpmt.	E. C. Sayers, *J. H. Russell*	31– 1–78
198 (194)	Birmid Qualcast	Mfrs. of Foundry Products, etc.	J. F. Insch, *B. K. Fitton*	29–10–77
199 (189)	Berec Group	Battery Manfrs. and Engineers	L. W. Orchard	25– 2–78
200 (187)	Associated Biscuit Manfrs.	Biscuit Manufacturers, etc.	G. W. N. Palmer	31–12–77

NOTES: *Total tangible assets less current liabilities (other than bank loans and overdrafts and future tax). †As percentage of capital employed at beginning of the year. ‡As at 14 July 1978. §Appendix on page 70 gives list of Managing Directors which cannot be fitted into the main text. ‖M.D. = Managing Director; J.M.D. = Joint Managing Director; A.C. = Acting Chairman. ¶As percentage of capital employed at the end of the year. N/A Not available. ¹UK only. ¹⁰Including excise duties but excluding VAT.

| TURNOVER | | *CAPITAL EMPLOYED | | | NET PROFIT BEFORE INTEREST AND TAX | | | | | | **No. of employees | ‡Equity market cap. £M. |
Total £000	Export £000	£000	Rank Latest year	Rank Previous year	Latest year £000	Rank	Previous year £000	% to turnover Latest year	†% to capital employed Latest year	Previous year		
268,267	1,708	133,529	139	162	24,246	131	18,392	9·0	27·1	19·8	5,686	66·0
266,889	64,900	180,906	102	92	32,323	96	18,828	12·1	17·9	13·9	8,923[1]	65·5
263,706	5,635	76,265	214	207	15,566	186	12,830	5·9	22·2	21·6	10,500	21·3
262,653[10]	38,590	107,659	162	194	Loss 2,980	993	Loss 1,322	—	—	—	1,345	USA
260,451	23,663	166,710	110	132	31,794	99	23,259	12·2	26·1	23·4	20,536	145·3
259,788	0	96,950	177	153	27,407	115	26,201	10·5	28·8	26·6	25,014	191·4
253,750	93,038	198,817	98	90	16,949	174	5,347	6·7	9·4	¶3·0	10,911[1]	SWZ
252,816	13,571	175,200	106	88	25,217	126	20,174	10·0	13·5	12·5	30,000	100·5
243,237	10,085	144,187	127	126	32,968	94	26,284	13·6	27·0	28·7	11,400	98·1
240,763	21,500	119,436	155	147	33,192	92	29,147	13·8	33·0	40·0	17,500	165·5
233,970	6,910	151,830	122	124	37,010	84	29,930	15·8	29·4	26·7	7,285[1]	133·0
232,418	—	148,899	124	117	15,807	182	12,759	6·8	11·7	10·3	4,771	UQ
232,315	1,253	70,036	224	247	19,830	158	16,780	8·5	35·6	37·7	12,816[1]	104·8
228,023	45,493	162,463	113	100	33,790	91	28,723	14·8	20·6	23·8	4,151[1]	107·1
226,572	37,600	94,183	182	178	15,332	193	16,731	6·8	18·8	23·2	6,536[1]	55·5
224,712	83,463	123,120	147	138	35,504	89	28,574	15·8	31·6	30·1	11,364[1]	USA
224,050	39,000	120,338	152	146	23,087	140	18,228	10·3	22·8	19·9	20,400	80·2
223,260	2	6,717	870	934	2,586	640	1,109	1·2	76·1	52·3	—	USA
222,000	3,366	104,775	165	192	19,585	160	11,952	8·8	26·0	18·1	7,965	44·2
221,820	0	50,316	286	231	21,606	146	20,681	9·7	36·8	27·3	—	UQ
220,767	29,510	130,109	143	158	29,138	108	20,485	13·2	31·5	25·9	11,000[1]	109·5
220,713	11,154	97,967	173	154	11,282	242	12,576	5·1	11·9	14·0	9,094[1]	35·3
220,676	—	150,321	123	133	50,405	69	21,197p.a.	22·8	42·1	18·3p.a.	2,870[1]	UQ
218,667	15,722	132,620	140	145	18,374	165	20,380	8·4	17·9	24·4	7,692[1]	76·6
218,100	5,454	232,058	81	84	28,983	109	20,706	13·3	14·1	10·4	8,200[1]	90·7
217,909	21,693	142,397	129	122	27,534	114	23,683	12·6	21·6	21·0	6,228	80·2
217,527	2,537	7,617	851	607	2,248	685	1,960	1·0	16·0	20·1	379	PAN
216,788	0	46,796	300	632	20,431	154	10,698	9·4	¶43·7	96·0	8,918[1]	80·1
216,701	11,983	23,331	480	498	6,775	349	5,724	3·1	34·7	27·5	4,700[1]	14·4
214,741	75,332	71,320	222	199	13,476	214	4,836	6·3	18·3	7·9	14,400[1]	63·0
214,085	0	16,481	609	637	4,858	431	4,441	2·3	37·3	46·2	1,915	21·6
213,400	34,400	92,131	186	172	18,922	162	14,046	8·9	22·1	27·2	7,643[1]	62·3
213,129	5,603	94,541	181	173	18,090	166	17,111	8·5	21·2	21·3	10,212	USA
212,411	4,415	158,324	118	98	31,293	100	24,141	14·7	19·0	18·7	10,724	122·4
210,988	0	5,863	896	966	1,679	772	1,086	0·8	81·3	35·7	—	LU
208,388	4,493	58,703	257	232	14,685	199	15,170	7·0	21·6	21·3	10,458[1]	16·5
208,150	51,577	125,289	146	148	32,059	97	21,923	15·4	32·0	24·1	9,174[1]	69·0
205,700	6,982	47,546	297	296	11,227	245	8,649	5·5	26·0	20·3	5,508[1]	27·4
203,883	15,095	92,258	185	164	15,142	194	16,603	7·4	17·1	24·2	7,566	27·5
203,742	87,353	185,773	101	108	30,222	104	25,882	14·8	19·5	18·2	10,977[1]	117·6
202,727	70,114	227,160	82	107	11,113	249	16,848	5·5	6·8	17·0	5,300[1]	USA
202,650	0	19,465	558	542	2,324	673	2,502	1·1	13·1	18·5	3,012[1]	2·0
200,308	30,901	118,856	157	156	16,323	177	11,401	8·1	17·5	13·6	12,020[1]	63·5
198,531	29,400	143,057	128	137	23,124	139	22,559	11·6	20·0	25·0	5,637[1]	59·9
197,363	68,008	64,248	235	253	15,437	189	13,467	7·8	28·6	36·8	8,087	46·4
196,000	6,400	37,978	350	376	10,225	264	9,579	5·2	33·9	43·7	13,700[1]	28·7
195,587	22,377	89,858	189	189	9,916	271	13,156	5·1	12·7	22·0	11,647[1]	29·0
194,871	18,792	83,138	204	198	11,737	237	12,552p.a.	6·0	15·9	20·7p.a.	16,361[1]	40·2
194,033	53,522	141,407	130	125	27,125	118	31,350	14·0	21·6	34·9	16,736	106·3
193,171	14,880	64,787	234	220	12,932	222	12,005	6·7	21·0	20·4	19,630	38·5

The following letters in the Market Capitalisation column denote unquoted companies and country of control: LU = Luxembourg. PAN = Panama. SWZ = Switzerland. UQ = Unquoted. USA = United States of America.

Rank by turn-over	COMPANY	Main activity	Chairman and Managing Directors (in italics) §‖	Accounting period ended
201 (211)	Kenning Motor Group	Motor Distributors	G. Kenning (J.M.D.), *D. B. Kenning*	30– 9–77
202 (208)	Transport Development Group	Road Transport, Warehousing, etc.	J. B. Duncan (M.D.)	31–12–77
203 (222)	UBM Group	Builders Merchants, etc.	M. G. Phillips (J.M.D.), *J. M. F. Dibben*	28– 2–78
204 (183)	Hoover	Household Appliance Manufacturers	P. C. Boon, *G. L. Lloyd*	31–12–77
205 (197)	Mallinson-Denny	Timber Merchants & Manufacturers	Sir Frederick Catherwood, *R. T. S. Macpherson*	31–12–77
206 (210)	Goodyear Tyre & Rubber (GB)	Tyres and Rubber Products	W. Hansen (M.D.)	31–12–77
207 (220)	Nestle Company	Food Manufacturers & Distributors	W. A. Manahan, *R. A. Wilson*	31–12–76
208 (196)	Furness, Withy & Co.	Shipowners, etc.	Sir James Steel, *B. P. Shaw*	31–12–77
209 (221)	Safeway Food Stores	Food Retailing	T. E. Spratt (M.D.)	1–10–77
210 (218)	C. & J. Clark	Footwear	J. D. Clark (M.D.)	31–12–77
211 (205)	Wilkinson Match	Matches, Personal Products, etc.	D. Randolph, *C. Lewington*	31– 3–77
212 (231)	Caterpillar Tractor Co.	Manfrs. of Earthmoving Equipment	M. W. Dargel	30– 9–76
213 (260)	Racal Electronics	Radio Communication, Electronic Eqpt.	E. T. Harrison (M.D.)	31– 3–78
214 (192)	Decca	Records, TV, Radio, Radar, Electronics	Sir Edward Lewis	31– 3–77
215 (219)	600 Group	Machine Tool Mfrs., Engineers, etc.,	Sir Jack Wellings (M.D.)	31– 3–77
216 (262)	Henry W. Peabody Grain	Grain Shippers	J. B. Faller	30 –9–77
217 (168)	Stone-Platt Industries	Textile Machy, Marine Eng., Pumps, etc.	Sir Francis Hawkings, *E. G. Smalley*	31–12–77
218 (198)	Foseco Minsep	Special Products for Industry	E. Weiss, *D. V. Atterton*	31–12–77
219 (214)	Matthew Hall & Co.	Industrial Engineers, etc.	Sir Rupert Spier, *A. H. J. Hoskins*	31–12–77
220 (256)	De La Rue Co.	Security Printers, Plastics, Graphics	Sir Arthur Norman	31– 3–77
221 (212)	Cawoods Holdings	Fuel Distribution, etc.	E. Binks (M.D.)	31– 3–77
222 (301)	General Motors	Vehicle Comps. & Domestic Appl. Mnfrs.	R. A. White	31–12–77
223 (142)	Bridon	Wire, Wire Rope, Fibre & Plastic Prod.	H. Smith, *D. Smith*	31–12–77
224 (191)	Charringtons Industrial Hldg.[43]	Fuel & Vehicle Distribution, etc.	C. E. Needham	31– 3–77
225 (201)	Fairclough Construction GP	Civil Eng. & Building Contractors	O. Davies	31–12–77
226 (225)	John Menzies (Holdings)	Newsagents, Booksellers, Stationers	J. M. Menzies, *D. G. Macdonald*	28– 1–78
227 (176)	Marchwiel Holdings	Building & Civil Eng. Contractors	A. J. McAlpine	31–10–77
228 (223)	J. Bibby & Sons	Feeds, Seeds, Foods, Farm Prods., Paper	J. B. Bibby, *L. C. Young*	31–12–77
229 (241)	Geest Holdings	Shipping, Importing, etc., of Produce	L. van Geest	1– 1–77
230 (N/A)	Mardon Packaging Intl.	Packaging Manufacturers & Printers	J. F. D. Cornish (M.D.)	30– 9–76
231 (266)	United City Merchants	Intl. Merchants, Leather Mfrs.	E. C. Sosnow	30– 6–77
232 (242)	Ellerman Lines	Shipowners, Brewers, Insurance	D. F. Martin-Jenkins, *P. Laister*	31–12–77
233 (224)	Smith & Nephew Assoc. Cos.	Surgical, Medical & Sanitary Prods.	K. R. Kemp	31–12–77
234 (226)	Currys	TV, Radio, Domestic Appliance Retlr.	D. Curry, *M. Curry, T. R. Curry*	25– 1–78
235 (244)	Procter & Gamble	Detergents and Allied Products	W. R. Gurganus, *A. D. Garrett*	30– 6–77
236 (380)	Continental (London)	Commodity Dealers	D. G. Turner	31–12–76
237 (263)	Chevron Oil (UK)	Petroleum Distributors	J. R. Smits, *P. J. M. Wilson*	31–12–76
238 (237)	Weir Group	Engineers	Viscount Weir, *J. J. B. Young*	30–12–77
239 (253)	Henlys	Motor Car Dealers	G. R. Chandler (M.D.)	30– 9–77
240 (255)	Automotive Products	Vehicle & Aircraft Eqpmt. Manfrs.	J. B. Emmott, *G. D. Pears*	30–12–77
241 (246)	Chubb & Son	Security Systems, etc.	Lord Hayter, *W. E. Randall*	31– 3–77
242 (270)	J. B. Eastwood	Farmers & Builders	Sir John Eastwood	1– 4–77
243 (273)	Phillips-Imperial Petroleum	Oil Refiners	*None*	1– 4–77
244 (233)	News International	Printing, Publishing, Paper, etc.	K. R. Murdoch, *H. C. Hardy*	31–12–77
245 (303)	Cable and Wireless	International Telecommunications	Lord Glenamara	31– 3–77
246 (230)	Norcros	Industrial Investments	J. V. Sheffield, *W. K. Roberts*	31– 3–77
247 (216)	Masius, Wynne-Williams & D'Arcy MacManus	Advertising & Marketing Advisers	A. J. Abrahams	31–12–76
248 (248)	Cape Industries	Bldg., Friction & Insulation Matls., etc.	R. H. Dent, *G. A. Higham*	31–12–77
249 (227)	British Printing Corpn.	Printers, Publishers, Bookbinders, etc.	P. Robinson (M.D.)	31–12–77
250 (252)	Freemans (London SW9)	Mail Order Business	A. Rampton, *R. H. C. Aldred*	28– 1–78

NOTES: *Total tangible assets less current liabilities (other than bank loans and overdrafts and future tax). †As percentage of capital employed at beginning of the year. ‡As at 14 July 1978. §Appendix on page 70 gives list of Managing Directors which cannot be fitted into the main text. ‖M.D. = Managing Director; J.M.D. = Joint Managing Director; A.C. = Acting Chairman. ¶As percentage of capital employed at the end of the year. N/A Not available. [1]UK only. [23]Virtually all revenue earned abroad. [43]Now a sub. co. of Coalite & Chemical Products Ltd. [46]Including £86,428,000 turnover of partnership.

| TURNOVER | | *CAPITAL EMPLOYED | | | NET PROFIT BEFORE INTEREST AND TAX | | | | | | **No. of employees | ‡Equity market cap. £M. |
Total £000	Export £000	£000	Rank Latest year	Rank Previous year	Latest year £000	Rank	Previous year £000	% to turnover Latest year	†% to capital employed Latest year	Previous year		
192,786	2,808	57,599	261	272	8,194	308	5,621	4·3	17·2	14·1	6,930	22·1
192,616	2,484	108,461	161	152	19,920	157	16,388	10·3	20·7	19·6	13,400	91·7
192,614	7,496	50,221	287	275	5,700	381	5,348	3·0	11·3	11·5	8,146	29·8
190,991	38,061	97,945	174	157	12,290	227	17,083	6·4	13·2	20·0	16,664	60·5
190,064	13,182	68,997	227	238	13,097	221	12,923	6·9	21·3	27·1	4,596	23·8
187,571	31,932	98,156	171	174	4,520	460	5,412	2·4	5·4	7·7	11,432[1]	USA
185,741	21,986	130,716	142	139	11,973	235	10,829	6·4	10·7	9·4	7,795[1]	SWZ
184,600	1,480	206,881	94	91	23,572	137	27,468	12·8	13·1	16·5	6,320[1]	61·6
184,580	—	21,499	514	418	6,879	344	4,799	3·7	26·0	19·3	6,622	USA
183,260	10,867	82,140	206	237	14,117	204	12,558	7·7	24·5	25·5	12,099[1]	UQ
182,698	18,285	118,763	158	155	16,465	176	13,583	9·0	17·5	14·0	15,876	47·4
182,286	99,730	58,832	256	294	22,857	141	12,622	12·5	52·7	34·8	4,898[1]	USA
181,681	94,061	133,805	138	239	50,991	67	33,499	28·1	49·9	¶32·8	5,824[1]	282·3
181,400	51,800	102,029	170	181	19,303	161	16,464	10·6	21·1	24·0	12,064	75·0
180,424	42,685	84,925	199	195	13,168	219	10,529	7·3	17·8	15·2	7,600	40·5
179,226p.a.	431p.a.	6,692	872	759	1,704p.a.	767 Loss	749	1·0	25·2p.a.	—	—	SWZ
176,013	69,600	88,704	191	170	17,256	172	18,316	9·8	20·0	25·1	12,611	47·2
174,896	9,613	75,002	216	205	16,319	178	17,633	9·3	23·2	32·0	8,356	77·8
173,625	45,930	16,705	604	648	6,203	364	4,620	3·6	49·8	51·9	6,528[1]	25·6
172,920	66,503	62,054	240	204	27,905	113	13,670	16·1	38·6	23·1	12,293	134·2
171,744	6,946	22,499	491	502	7,142	336	5,173	4·2	36·8	34·9	2,186	33·0
171,542	40,300	59,595	251	350	12,006	233	6,883	7·0	23·6	¶13·5	8,807	USA
171,405	37,810	137,816	134	130	15,725	183	21,709	9·2	12·8	20·2	10,555	54·3
170,188	1,953	33,879	383	348	5,554	388	4,890	3·3	17·7	14·6	4,847	—[43]
170,041	8,979	26,544	444	459	7,155	335	6,279	4·2	32·5	30·9	9,612[1]	27·3
168,682	432	17,509	593	603	5,191	414	3,280	3·1	36·0	22·9	6,605	21·8
168,664	258	57,594	262	266	13,718	211	12,223	8·1	27·9	34·1	11,110	48·8
168,176	1,386	39,152	343	312	7,656	319	5,929	4·6	19·4	17·0	3,935	19·3
167,425	1,352	33,451	388	400	2,174	698	3,570	1·3	7·7	11·3	5,443[1]	UQ
166,023	3,921	74,336	217	—	13,875	207	11,707	8·4	20·6	18·7	11,001	UQ
165,457	13,134	14,200	656	680	4,804	438	3,492	2·9	42·8	36·1	630[1]	14·2
163,971	0	136,393	135	140	11,162	248	14,220	6·8	9·2	15·8	5,861[1]	UQ
163,184	27,021	98,135	172	168	21,321	147	17,986	13·1	24·6	22·9	14,405	104·4
163,137	—	47,190	298	306	9,572	275	9,782	5·9	23·8	27·9	6,633	43·1
163,015	31,200	37,501	354	356	9,156	280	9,047	5·6	27·5	27·8	3,489	USA
161,522	73	15,130	631	768	Loss 1,293	989 Loss	163	—	—	—	—	USA
161,240	—	54,121	277	288	Loss 2	976 Loss	950	—	—	—	—	USA
160,432	57,709	64,205	237	226	12,408	226	11,750	7·7	20·9	22·0	10,000	29·9
160,200	—	34,769	374	365	5,232	410	2,637	3·3	16·6	8·3	3,859[1]	16·7
159,844	33,325	80,232	209	200	15,351	191	10,844	9·6	21·0	20·4	12,512	46·7
158,438	22,700	83,823	202	208	15,975	181	13,609	10·1	23·3	23·0	15,158	59·3
156,765	11,491	58,098	260	267	11,681	238	8,720	7·5	23·8	21·0	5,513[1]	29·4
156,677	38,915	29,281	424	436	3,505	528	1,443	2·2	14·3	7·1	—	UQ
156,643	1,751	75,730	215	249	20,762	151	17,813	13·3	29·7	31·9	9,102	50·2
156,480[23]	—	168,023	109	114	58,932	52	29,009	37·7	42·4	24·2	9,488	UQ
156,480	16,475	76,937	213	214	15,595	185	15,340	10·0	23·6	29·5	12,471	48·9
155,440[46]	—	8,605	808	770	3,816	510	1,838	2·5	62·3	28·9	505[1]	USA
155,366	14,555	83,398	203	191	13,715	212	15,834	8·8	18·2	26·8	8,323[1]	30·5
154,863	16,400	69,900	225	206	9,327	279	8,319	6·0	13·3	13·8	12,255	14·8
154,839	1,873	56,164	268	287	13,735	210	10,742	8·9	30·8	25·6	4,881	73·9

The following letters in the Market Capitalisation column denote unquoted companies and country of control: SWZ = Switzerland.   UQ = Unquoted.
USA = United States of America.

Rank by turn-over	COMPANY	Main activity	Chairman and Managing Directors (in italics) §‖	Accounting period ended
251 (238)	Grattan Warehouses	Mail Order Business	J. M. Pickard, *M. M. Place*	31– 1–78
252 (215)	French Kier Holdings	Bldg. & Civil Engineering Contrs.	J. C. S. Mott	31–12–77
253 (308)	Kwik Save Discount Group	Supermarket Operators	I. F. D. Hill, *I. M. Howe, M. J. R. Weeks*	27– 8–77
254 (265)	Dixons Photographic	Retailers of Photographic Eqpt., etc.	S. Kalms (M.D.)	30– 4–77
255 (278)	McKechnie Bros.	Non-Ferrous Metals & Chemicals, Eng.	C. C. Taylor	31– 7–77
256 (235)	Haden Carrier	Bldg. Services & Metal Finishing Eng.	Sir Alan Pullinger, *D. J. Hyam*	31–12–77
257 (185)	Newarthill	Construction, Property and Investmt.	T. R. Grieve	31–10–77
258 (324)	Caledonian Airways	Air Transportation	A. Thomson	31–10–77
259 (285)	Du Pont (UK)	Chemical Manufacturers	E. F. Ruppe, *W. B. Hirons*	17–12–76
260 (268)	Cope Allman International	Packaging, Leisure, Eng., Fashions	L. J. Manson	2– 7–77
261 (202)	Paterson, Zochonis & Co.	West African Merchants	J. B. Zochonis, *B. Spoudeas*	31– 5–77
262 (254)	Pauls & Whites	Maltsters & Manfrs. of Animal Foods	M. G. Falcon, *J. R. Clayton*	31– 3–78
263 (257)	Empire Dairies	Dairy Produce Distributors	A. L. Friis, *S. T. Murphy*	31– 3–77
264 (236)	Esso Chemical	Production & Sale of Chemicals	M. R. Schimmenti (M.D.)	31–12–77
265 (251)	Charterhouse Group	Indl. Investment & Merchant Banking	G. N. Mobbs, *G. C. Rowett*	30– 9–77
266 (269)	Matthews Holdings[5]	Food Manfrs. & Wholesalers	W. A. Bullen	8– 1–77
267 (240)	BSR	Manfrs. of Record Changers, etc.	J. N. Ferguson (M.D.)	7– 1–78
268 (232)	Borregaard Industries	Pulp, Paper, Textiles, etc.	A. Sanengen	31–12–76
269 (272)	International Timber Corpn.	Timber	R. E. Groves	2– 4–77
270 (271)	Dutton-Forshaw Group	Vehicle Distrs. & Automobile Eng.	R. F. Hockin, *C. R. Gray*	31–12–77
271 (234)	Moore Business Forms	Business, Systems, Eng., Packaging, etc.	J.-P. R. M. Evans, *W. M. Nichols*	31–12–76
272 (247)	Burton Group	Retailers, Men's Outerwear Manfrs.	L. O. Rice, *C. Spencer*	27– 8–77
273 (250)	Westland Aircraft	Helicopter Manufacturers, etc.	Lord Aldington	30 –9–77
274 (249)	Tioxide Group	Titanium Oxide & Titanium Compounds	J. K. Pitts	31–12–77
275 (258)	Derby & Co.	Metal & Mineral Merchants	*E. Fraenkel*	31–12–76
276 (283)	Intl. Harvester Co. of GB	Agricultural & Construction Eqpmt.	G. C. D'Arcy Biss, *L. A. Abbott*	31–10–77
277 (261)	Dowty Group	Engineering	R. F. Hunt	31– 3–77
278 (282)	Wadham Stringer	Motor Vehicle Distributors, etc.	F. C. Stringer, *M. J. Stringer*	31–12–77
279 (259)	Hunting Gibson	Crude Oil, Shipowning, etc.	L. C. Hunting	31–12–77
280 (276)	Compair	Air Compressors, Pneumatic Tools, etc.	Sir William Mather	2–10–77
281 (291)	Palmer and Harvey	Wholesale Tobacconists & Confectnrs.	Sir Donald Gosling, *J. H. Chedzoy*	31– 3–76
282 (305)	European Ferries	Sea Transport, Harbour Services	K. D. Wickenden, *K. Siddle*	31–12–77
283 (295)	Imperial Continental Gas As.	Fuel and Power Industries	F. E. Zollinger, *J. Watt, P. V. C. Colebrook*	31– 3–77
284 (304)	Tenneco International Hlgs.	Agricultural Eqpt. Mfrs., Chemicals, etc.	*R. A. Robinson*	31–12–76
285 (289)	Associated Newspapers Group	Newspaper Proprietors, etc.	Vere Harmsworth, *R. M. P. Shields*	31– 3–77
286 (297)	United Glass	Manfrs. of Glass & Plastic Containers.	D. A. Blair, *V. C. Hender*	3–12–77
287 (281)	Ferranti	Electrical & Electronic Engineers	S. Z. De Ferranti, *J. D. Alun-Jones*	31– 3–77
288 (279)	John Mowlem & Co.	Bldg., Civil Eng., Prop. Devmt. & Invmt.	Sir Edgar Beck	31–12–77
289 (274)	USMC International	Machry. for Leather & Plastics Indry.	R. J. Hodge, *L. E. Dowley*	31–12–77
290 (287)	Acrow	Engineering	W. A. De Vigier, *W. Jack*	31– 3–77
291 (286)	Rolls-Royce Motors Hldgs.	Transport Engineers	I. J. Fraser, *D. A. S. Plastow*	31–12–77
292 (277)	Laird Group	Metal Ind., Transport Eng., etc.	Sir Ian Morrow	31–12–77
293 (311)	Illingworth, Morris & Co.	Manfrs. of Wool & Cotton Textiles	I. C. Hill (*see page 70*)	31– 3–77
294 (340)	Seagram Distillers	Prodn. of Whisky & Gin, Blending, etc.	E. M. Bronfman	31– 7–77
295 (329)	Makro Self Service Whslrs.	Cash & Carry Merchants	*R. P. Hoegen*	2– 1–77
296 (335)	Renault	Motor Vehicle Distributors	C. J. Weets, *P. Acolas*	31–12–76
297 (294)	Renold	Power Transmission Prods, Machinery	L. J. Tolley, *C. A. Percival*	3– 4–77
298 (245)	Hargreaves Group	Fuel, Trnpt., Quarrying, Contrg., etc.	D. A. E. R. Peake, *G. D. Lavers*	31– 3–78
299 (243)	Foster Wheeler	Petroleum & Chemical Engineers	H. Dudek (M.D.)	31–12–76
300 (264)	Barrow Hepburn Group	Merchanting & Consumer Products, etc.	R. Smith	31–12–77

NOTES: *Total tangible assets less current liabilities (other than bank loans and overdrafts and future tax). †As percentage of capital employed at beginning of the year. ‡As at 14 July 1978. §Appendix on page 70 gives list of Managing Directors which cannot be fitted into the main text. ‖M.D. = Managing Director; J.M.D. = Joint Managing Director; A.C. = Acting Chairman. ¶As percentage of capital employed at the end of the year. N/A Not available. ¹UK only. ²Incl. annualised profs of Weston Pharmaceuticals Ltd. and its subs. ⁵Now a sub. co. of Thomas Borthwick & Sons Ltd.

TURNOVER		*CAPITAL EMPLOYED			NET PROFIT BEFORE INTEREST AND TAX						**No. of employees	‡Equity market cap £M.
Total £000	Export £000	£000	Rank Latest year	Rank Previous year	Latest year £000	Rank	Previous year £000	% to turnover Latest year	†% to capital employed Latest year	Previous year		
154,739	4,001	53,467	279	261	12,258	228	12,166	7·9	24·3	25·4	5,130	51·5
154,700	6,300	29,623	421	372	6,961	341	5,320	4·5	22·5	12·5	5,223[1]	16·6
152,387	0	17,802	586	664	8,775	292	5,261	5·8	73·0	69·9	2,446	51·8
152,114	1,770	46,198	302	343	10,979	253	7,429[2]	7·2	31·8	21·5	4,802[1]	51·4
150,611	13,900	81,315	207	225	17,532	168	13,513	11·6	29·3	24·5	4,545[1]	36·5
148,184	701	19,790	551	453	2,294	677	3,668	1·5	10·2	15·9	7,343	7·6
148,000	299	66,979	232	242	12,229	229	5,958	8·3	21·6	12·2	6,073[1]	15·2
146,616p.a.	—	39,806	340	328	7,870p.a.	313	8,473	5·4	18·5p.a.	22·8	4,866[1]	UQ
146,400	43,894	77,541	212	228	7,631	321	2,683	5·2	12·9	4·8	2,768[1]	USA
145,725	21,425	58,880	255	257	11,490	240	7,450	7·9	22·3	16·0	7,220[1]	24·5
145,537	30,993	57,136	265	188	20,045	155	20,931	13·8	25·7	¶26·8	2,564[1]	28·5
144,774	7,810	50,356	285	308	7,172	333	6,785	5·0	17·9	21·1	2,089[1]	28·2
144,507	672	9,597	781	832	977	866	755	0·7	14·0	11·8	214	NZ
143,998	52,012	42,396	328	309	13,261	216	12,945	9·2	33·2	38·3	834[1]	USA
143,983	14,547	91,050	187	166	13,676	213	12,193	9·5	15·7	15·9	9,539	58·7
143,027	1,652	19,713	554	621	4,011	491	3,626p.a.	2·8	29·6	31·7p.a.	4,862[1]	—[5]
141,670	68,080	97,597	175	179	20,737	152	29,824	14·6	25·5	50·2	15,699[1]	85·6
140,872	—	79,903	210	182	Loss 1,103	988	Loss 198	—	—	—	—	NOR
140,156	1,247	73,890	219	219	10,172	267	3,680	7·3	16·2	5·3	4,129[1]	21·1
139,843	913	33,320	390	415	4,957	424	4,067	3·5	18·7	17·0	3,740	12·2
139,403	6,245	82,946	205	176	11,039	252	9,537	7·9	14·3	12·3	9,231	CAN
139,138	1,597	165,405	112	101	1,358	814	1,362	1·0	0·8	0·7	16,418[1]	43·4
138,926	41,080	93,270	183	167	6,490	357	10,994	4·7	7·5	15·2	12,894[1]	19·3
137,946	29,700	122,564	148	144	13,930	206	23,092	10·1	13·1	25·7	5,100	UQ
137,640	—	31,941	403	540	8,217	306	5,007	6·0	46·2	31·7	287[1]	USA
137,568	90,968	60,018	249	271	17,998	167	14,466	13·1	36·5	39·3	6,430[1]	USA
136,308	32,408	84,659	200	212	19,785	159	14,693	14·5	30·1	26·3	13,886	142·9
134,831	1,311	30,377	413	452	4,456	465	3,431	3·3	21·5	17·3	4,337	13·2
131,152	—	30,256	414	486	1,406	804	2,615	1·1	5·8	12·9	662[1]	2·6
129,762	34,064	68,564	230	234	15,346	192	11,918	11·8	27·6	25·2	5,152[1]	47·9
129,244	—	9,967	771	891	3,177	570	1,848	2·5	59·4	36·1	2,554	UQ
127,868	0	140,759	131	129	26,722	119	16,650	20·9	21·6	¶13·5	5,743	135·1
127,079	1,169	179,244	104	99	23,903	135	17,004	18·8	14·5	11·4	3,625	159·6
126,635	60,917	68,034	231	284	11,475	241	6,981	9·1	25·4	17·4	7,003[1]	USA
126,361	2,836	58,240	258	274	12,060	231	8,501	9·5	23·6	20·8	12,826	50·8
125,556	8,110	68,835	228	233	13,102	220	8,256	10·4	22·3	13·7	10,775	GB/USA
125,359	22,070	61,782	242	254	8,391	302	5,836	6·7	15·8	17·8	16,786	UQ
124,417	—	24,735	466	511	6,268	362	4,365	5·0	33·0	32·5	6,220[1]	19·0
122,466	36,790	60,542	245	224	13,793	209	10,743	11·3	23·0	18·0	8,891	USA
122,208	67,711	57,533	263	279	13,411	215	10,696	11·0	29·4	24·4	7,407[1]	49·0
121,940	45,230	51,407	283	280	12,768	223	10,571	10·5	28·0	30·8	9,861	55·0
119,241	10,416	60,164	248	213	10,796	256	10,776	9·1	16·8	18·9	7,880[1]	36·2
118,925	48,597	61,050	243	251	7,694	317	3,548	6·5	14·1	7·3	9,849	12·1
118,028	63,300	161,435	116	120	20,863	150	5,199	17·7	13·5	4·0	2,219[1]	CAN
116,545	—	8,726	805	916	2,488	653	352	2·1	61·1	6·8	1,862	H
116,209	—	20,909	524	689	1,090	848	1,599	0·9	10·1	15·5	780	FR
116,162	25,569	119,832	154	142	17,097	173	14,002	14·7	15·9	13·8	13,825	51·0
114,695	10,007	23,953	474	468	3,882	503	3,823	3·4	18·3	20·7	2,652	15·0
114,341	70,198	8,068	832	758	3,397	553	1,190	3·0	37·7	12·4	3,214[1]	USA
114,325	17,206	23,266	482	428	5,568	387	6,196	4·9	21·9	25·7	1,147[1]	6·6

The following letters in the Market Capitalisation column denote unquoted companies and country of control: CAN = Canada.   FR = France.   GB = Great Britain.
H = Holland.   NOR = Norway.   NZ = New Zealand.   UQ = Unquoted.   USA = United States of America.

Rank by turn-over	COMPANY	Main activity	Chairman and Managing Directors (in italics) §‖	Accounting period ended
301 (330)	Low & Bonar Group	Packaging, Eng., Textiles, Flooring	A. J. M. Miller, *B. G. Gilbert*	30–11–77
302 (296)	Rubery, Owen Holdings	Manufacturers & Merchants	A. D. Owen (M.D.)	01–10–76
303 (298)	Bishop's Stores	Wholesale & Retail Grocers	J. H. Bradfield	25– 2–78
304 (290)	Carpets International	Manfr. & Sale of Floorcoverings	R. Wake	31–12–77
305 (367)	LCP Holdings	Industrial Holding Co.	D. M. Rhead	31– 3–77
306 (310)	Nottingham Manufacturing Co.	Knitwear, Hosiery & Carpet Manfrs.	H. A. S. Djanogly, *J. E. Parsons*	31–12–77
307 (280)	Rudolf Wolff & Co.	Metal & Commodity Brokers	F. F. Wolff, *F. L. Holford*	31–12–75
308 (341)	Williams Hudson Group	Transport, Fuel Distbn., Shipping, etc.	D. J. Rowland (M.D.)	31– 3–77
309 (358)	Datsun UK	Vehicle Importers & Distributors	O. Botnar (M.D.)	31–12–76
310 (342)	Mothercare	Maternity & Children's Wear, etc.	S. K. Zilkha (M.D.)	31– 3–78
311 (315)	Avon Rubber Co.	Tyre Manufacturers, etc.	Lord Farnham, *P. M. Fisher*	1–10–77
312 (N/A)	J. H. Rayner & Co.	Commodity Merchants		31– 1–75
313 (326)	Greenall, Whitley & Co.	Brewers, Bottlers & Distillers	C. J. B. Hatton, *J. D. Pritchard-Barrett*	30– 9–77
314 (293)	S. Hoffnung & Co.	Gen. Merchants, Retail & Manfg.	H. R. Bourne	31– 3–77
315 (292)	Higgs & Hill	Bldg. & Civil Engineering Contrs.	E. W. Phillips, *B. J. Hill*	31–12–77
316 (300)	BBA Group	Manfrs. of Insulating & Friction Mat.	D. M. Pearson, *C. M. Fenton*	31–12–77
317 (339)	William Baird & Co.	Textiles, Industrials, Investments	S. A. Field	31–12–77
318 (284)	Mather & Platt	General Engineering	Sir William Mather, *H. C. Smith*	31–12–75
319 (288)	Staveley Industries	Machine Tools, Foundries, Elect., Chem.	Sir Harry Moore, *A. Frankel*	2–10–76
320 (—)	Oce-Van Der Grinten Finance	Reprographic Eqpt. Manfrs., etc.	J. J. Kaptein	30–11–77
321 (312)	Christian Salvesen	Housebuilding, Cold Storage, Fish, etc.	L. M. Harper Gow, *G. H. Elliot*	30– 9–77
322 (319)	Laporte Industries (Hldgs.)	Chemical Manufacturers	R. M. Ringwald, *G. F. Sommerville*	1– 1–78
323 (327)	Sime Darby London	Commodity Traders, Engineers, etc.	L. R. Patterson, *S. P. Wareing*	30– 6–77
324 (337)	Securicor Group	Industrial Security	P. A. C. Smith	30– 9–77
325 (348)	Davies & Newman Holdings	Shipbrokers & Agent & Airline Oprts.	F. E. F. Newman (M.D.)	31–12–77
326 (316)	Averys	Weighing, Testing & Measuring Equipt.	R. C. Hale (M.D.)	31–12–77
327 (349)	3M United Kingdom	Coated Materials & Related Products	M. J. Monteiro, *D. R. Osmon*	31–10–77
328 (338)	Barratt Developments	Builders, Estate Developers	L. A. Barratt (M.D.)	30– 6–77
329 (374)	General Foods	Manfrs. & Dealers in Food Products	J. C. Tappan, *G. Westrop*	2– 4–77
330 (356)	Trebor Group	Confectionery Manufacturers, etc.	J. G. Marks	31–12–77
331 (360)	May & Baker	Chemicals & Pharmaceuticals	G. G. A. Pirrone, *N. Chancellor*	31–12–76
332 (344)	Dobson Park Industries	Mining & Specialised Engineers	C. F. Ward	1–10–77
333 (320)	Associated Fisheries	Trawling, Eng., Food, Cold Storage, etc.	P. M. Tapscott	30– 9–77
334 (336)	Magnet & Southerns	Timber Imptrs., Joinery etc. Products	S. Oxford (*see page 70*)	31– 3–77
335 (369)	Wolseley-Hughes	Merchanting, Eng., Agric. & Gardng. Eqpt.	J. Lancaster (M.D.)	31– 7–77
336 (—)	Twil	Wire Manufacturers	M. H. J. Veys	31– 7–77
337 (306)	James Budgett & Son	Sugar, Dried Fruits, Canned Goods, etc.	R. A. Budgett	28– 1–77
338 (370)	Electrolux	Domestic Appliances	Lord Luke, *J. B. Redman*	31–12–76
339 (373)	Tricentrol	Oil & Gas Expln., Motor Trade, etc.	J. B. Godber, *J. G. S. Longcroft*	31–12–77
340 (408)	Entores	Metal Merchants	J. N. Palmer	31–12–76
341 (353)	Empire Stores (Bradford)	Mail Order House	J. Gratwick, *R. Scott*	28– 1–78
342 (407)	Swift & Co.	Food Distributors & Manufacturers	R. C. Joscelyne	23–10–76
343 (361)	London Brick Co.	Brick Manufacturers, etc.	Sir Ronald Stewart (J.M.D.), *J. Rowe, M. O. Wright*	31–12–77
344 (345)	Sangers Group	Wholesale Chemists	H. T. Nicholson, *S. G. Folkes*	28– 2–78
345 (331)	Wilmot-Breeden (Holdings)	Mfrs. of Eng. Products	D. L. Breeden (J.M.D.), *M. L. Breeden*	31–12–77
346 (317)	Steel Brothers Holdings	Construction, Foodstuffs, Mfg., etc.	J. H. Gaunt	31–12–77
347 (355)	Appleyard Group of Cos.	Distrs. & Retlrs. of Vehicles, etc.	I. Appleyard, *K. D. Fraser, J. Limb*	31–12–77
348 (385)	Associated Television Corpn.	Television Contrs., Theatres, etc.	Lord Grade	27– 3–77
349 (350)	Morgan Crucible Co.	Materials & Components for Industry	I. Weston Smith, *J. C. R. Gilbert*	1– 1–78
350 (372)	Rockware Group	Glass & Plastic Container Manfrs.	J. H. Craigie	1– 1–78

NOTES: *Total tangible assets less current liabilities (other than bank loans and overdrafts and future tax).   †As percentage of capital employed at beginning of the year.   ‡As at 14 July 1978.   §Appendix on page 70 gives list of Managing Directors which cannot be fitted into the main text.   ‖M.D. = Managing Director; J.M.D. = Joint Managing Director; A.C. = Acting Chairman.   ¶As percentage of capital employed at the end of the year.   N/A Not available.   ¹UK only.   ²²Comparative figures for previous year not available.

TURNOVER		*CAPITAL EMPLOYED			NET PROFIT BEFORE INTEREST AND TAX						**No. of employees	‡Equity market cap. £M.
Total £000	Export £000	£000	Rank Latest year	Rank Previous year	Latest year £000	Rank	Previous year £000	% to turnover Latest year	†% to capital employed Latest year	Previous year		
113,317	11,940	62,685	238	268	7,985	311	7,028	7·0	16·4	19·5	4,112[1]	18·4
112,213	13,940	55,517	269	255	3,730	515	3,312	3·3	7·0	6·3	8,780[1]	UQ
111,504	0	14,634	643	647	1,008	861	2,176	0·9	8·1	21·1	4,000	7·1
110,670	13,900	59,640	250	236	3,930	500	6,260	3·6	6·8	11·8	7,807	13·5
110,466	1,426	36,096	361	429	5,215	412	3,327	4·7	20·7	13·6	3,226	24·5
110,421	13,054	58,226	259	270	14,383	203	12,021	13·0	30·1	28·2	14,227	64·8
108,859	—	13,155	675	630	984	865	2,703	0·9	13·0	35·7	—	CAN
108,381	1,693	41,509	334	211	6,566	355	3,148	6·1	9·8	4·4	2,210[1]	PAN
108,249	1,242	15,286	628	710	5,809	377	4,795	5·4	55·8	71·0	386	CI
108,063	10,960	35,514	370	399	13,965	205	11,954	12·9	49·3	62·0	5,009	111·1
108,020	26,919	33,044	393	382	6,838	347	4,182	6·3	23·2	14·7	7,134[1]	13·6
107,346	—	10,472	754	—	1,415	802	4,622p.a.	1·3	21·8	¶71.2p.a.		LU
107,006	887	88,134	193	190	11,209	246	9,665	10·5	14·5	13·2	9,336	64·0
106,828	3,247	35,768	367	349	5,719	380	4,957	5·4	16·9	21·3	2,517	15·5
106,000	—	14,873	636	597	3,125	579	2,195	2·9	21·3	16·1	2,511[1]	6·0
105,808	12,708	47,980	294	283	8,370	304	8,935	7·9	18·5	25·2	7,015	23·2
105,797	7,221	37,139	356	393	9,365	278	5,800	8·9	32·7	27·9	12,307	27·3
105,747	14,960	51,132	284	259	7,167	334	5,383	6·8	15·2	14·4	12,300	AUS
103,846	15,847	38,193	347	321	7,601	324	4,785	7·3	22·7	16·5	6,505[1]	39·5
103,245p.a.	10,924p.a.	45,910	305	—	5,257p.a.	405	—[22]	5·1	¶11·5p.a.	—	3,610[1]	H
103,230	8,200	85,996	196	177	10,201	265	10,053	9·9	12·5	12·0	6,480[1]	UQ
102,442	36,276	96,308	179	165	12,582	225	17,667	12·3	14·3	23·2	4,655[1]	51·4
102,104	3,136	22,292	496	615	3,841	506	2,690	3·8	28·1	¶19·7	3,370[1]	MAL
100,828	—	22,262	497	532	5,248	408	3,964	5·2	28·6	24·1	24,095[1]	11·6
100,652	27,544	11,806	716	687	1,262	826	2,316	1·3	11·6	25·0	3,020[1]	6·3
100,146	14,061	60,848	244	252	15,550	187	14,820	15·5	28·4	30·7	8,553[1]	59·0
99,602	16,229	49,701	288	264	14,492	200	7,629	14·5	29·1	17·1	3,844	USA
99,317	0	64,218	236	230	10,502	259	11,487	10·6	17·9	37·8	3,714	35·9
99,105	5,556	29,173	426	475	65	968	2,115	0·1	0·3	12·5	2,396	USA
99,022	4,096	24,357	471	461	4,942	427	3,871	5·0	22·0	19·6	3,449[1]	UQ
98,574	32,139	48,883	291	299	11,983	234	6,941	12·2	29·1	19·8	4,826[1]	FR
98,208	18,963	42,951	324	344	11,096	251	9,429	11·3	32·1	30·6	5,853[1]	66·9
98,196	5,500	33,452	387	351	5,634	383	2,810	5·7	16·7	8·7	6,090	7·2
97,882	631	59,343	253	273	15,127	195	11,522	15·5	29·9	¶22·8	4,351[1]	59·2
97,162	7,269	38,534	345	404	6,656	353	4,554	6·9	24·0	19·0	3,677	24·9
96,752	12,293	44,219	315	—	6,705	350	6,561	6·9	16·6	¶16·2	5,886[1]	UQ
96,607	—	2,256	972	978	556	907	301	0·6	35·8	13·2	239[1]	UQ
96,345	16,400	46,682	301	295	9,101	284	8,043	9·4	21·0	29·1	8,101[1]	SW
95,694	303	46,918	299	305	5,854	375	3,930	6·1	14·5	13·6	2,498	66·8
94,889	7,693	8,585	809	903	1,391	805	803	1·5	28·9	16·7	—	FR
93,344	1,113	34,007	381	417	7,414	327	5,940	7·9	28·0	27·0	3,580	44·1
92,915	957	7,641	850	827	2,286	680	1,573	2·5	32·4	20·8	1,562	USA
91,354	4,273	54,716	272	263	13,189	217	11,468	14·4	26·4	24·2	9,562	38·4
90,798	0	11,666	721	737	2,092	711	2,580	2·3	21·7	31·1	2,435	6·9
90,150	8,710	41,114	335	322	6,857	346	7,333	7·6	18·1	20·9	6,894	13·5
90,123	1,509	47,910	296	281	8,816	290	6,328	9·8	18·9	17·1	820[1]	24·6
89,664	26	16,701	605	622	2,093	710	1,910	2·3	15·5	15·8	2,628	7·8
89,313	—	62,243	239	215	13,867	208	9,433	15·5	21·6	16·1	5,023[1]	60·2
89,252	24,224	69,852	226	217	14,456	201	12,071	16·2	22·9	20·3	6,973	49·0
89,223	5,286	55,017	270	277	8,975	285	7,731	10·1	19·4	19·4	6,955	28·6

The following letters in the Market Capitalisation column denote unquoted companies and country of control: AUS = Australia.   CAN = Canada.   CI = Channel Islands. FR = France.   H = Holland.   LU = Luxembourg.   MAL = Malaysia.   PAN = Panama.   SW = Sweden.   UQ = Unquoted.   USA = United States of America.

Rank by turn-over	COMPANY	Main activity	Chairman and Managing Directors (in italics) §‖	Accounting period ended
351 (383)	Pirelli General Cable Works	Electrical Wire & Cable Manfrs.	Lord Thorneycroft, *A. C. Essex*	31–12–77
352 (368)	Hunting Assoc. Industries	Aviation Support, Eng., Tech. Survey, etc.	L. C. Hunting	31–12–77
353 (314)	Sperry Rand	Engineering, Business Machines, etc.	Sir Alan Dawtrey	31– 3–75
354 (352)	Rugby Portland Cement Co.	Cement Manufacturers	Lord Boyd-Carpenter, *M. Jenkins*	31–12–77
355 (394)	Electronic Rentals Group	Retail, Rental of T.V. & Elect. Goods	M. A. Fry	31– 3–77
356 (309)	Molins	Tobacco, Paper & Packaging Mchy. Mfrs.	H. R. Moore, *J. A. Mills*	31–12–77
357 (267)	Arthur Bell & Sons	Scotch Whisky Distillers & Blenders	R. C. Miquel (M.D.)	30– 6–77
358 (388)	LRC International	General Rubber Products	Sir Edward Howard, *M. M. Sellers*	31– 3–77
359 (346)	Fyffes Group	Fruit Importers	J. A. Taylor, *A. J. Ellis*	31–12–76
360 (427)	Kaye Organisation	Materials Handling Equipment	Sir Emmanuel Kaye	30– 4–77
361 (592)	Dunbee-Combex-Marx	Manfrs. of Toys, Plastics, Toiletries	Lord Westwood, *R. J. Beecham, B. S. Feldman*	31–12–76
362 (321)	Adams Food	Mktg., Distbn. Packg. of Food Products	J. H. Adams, *B. A. Joyce*	3– 7–76
363 (378)	Union Carbide UK	Metals, Chemicals, Eng., Carbon Prods.	R. Wilson, *J. T. Harvey*	31–12–77
364 (398)	Turner Curzon	Forest Products, Engineering, etc.	J. Wakenham (M.D.)	31– 3–77
365 (411)	Fiat Motor Co. (UK)	Fiat Car Distributors	*E. Spinelli*	31–12–76
366 (404)	Wm. Morrison Supermarkets	Supermarket Proprietors	K. D. Morrison (M.D.)	28– 1–78
367 (359)	Bestobell	Fluids Engineering, Insulation, etc.	Sir Humphrey Browne, *D. Spencer*	31–12–77
368 (323)	Howden Group	Engineers, Gas & Air Handling Plant	Sir Norman Elliott, *J. D. Hume*	30– 4–77
369 (351)	Ransome Hoffmann Pollard	Ball & Roller Bearings Mfrs., etc.	J. Eccles, *W. H. Holmes, R. F. Morgan, I. H. Owen*	30– 9–77
370 (328)	Burroughs Machines	Computational Equipment	*R. W. Akers*	30–11–76
371 (416)	Hartwells Group	Vehicle Distributors, etc.	F. S. Huggins	28– 2–78
372 (376)	Honeywell	Computers, Indl. & Medical Instruments	L. R. Price	31–12–76
373 (334)	Owen Owen	Department Stores	J. A. H. Norman (M.D.)	28– 1–78
374 (512)	Fredk. H. Burgess	Agricultural Engineers	H. F. Burgess, *A. F. Burgess*	31–12–77
375 (332)	CPC (United Kingdom)	Food, Glucose Syrups, Starches, etc.	W. G. Redley, *P. M. Ware*	30– 9–76
376 (499)	Comet Radiovision Services	Retailers of Electrical Goods, etc.	M. J. Hollingbery, *M. J. Foster*	27– 8–77
377 (395)	Dawson International	Cashmere, Camelhair & Wool Manfrs.	A. Smith	25– 3–78
378 (365)	Coates Bros. & Co.	Print. Inks & Indl. Surface Coatings	Sir Richard Meyjes	31–12–77
379 (354)	London Merchant Securities	Investment Holding Co.	Lord Rayne	31– 3–77
380 (390)	Morris & David Jones	Grocers & Provision Merchants	J. G. Gulliver	31–12–76
381 (357)	Alexander Howden Group	Insurance Brokers, Shipping Agents	K. V. Grob	31–12–77
382 (362)	Kraft Foods	Food Manufacturers	*V. W. Hill*	25–12–76
383 (386)	Baker Perkins Holdings	Machinery Manufacturers	I. H. G. Gilbert, *J. F. M. Braithwaite*	31– 3–77
384 (396)	Harp Lager	Mfr. & Sale of Harp Lager	C. E. Guinness (M.D.)	30– 9–77
385 (371)	Alcoa of Great Britain	Smelters & Fabricators of Aluminium	O. R. Norland	31–12–77
386 (706)	John Swire & Sons	Shipowners, etc.	J. A. Swire	31–12–76
387 (347)	Pegler-Hattersley	Manfrs. of Taps & Valves, etc.	J. M. Harrison, *A. L. Louden*	2– 4–77
388 (N/A)	Ceres (UK)	Grain Dealers & Merchants	A. J. Sear	31–12–76
389 (402)	Kellogg Co. of Gt. Britain	Cereal Food Manufacturers	G. D. Robinson (M.D.)	31–12–76
390 (466)	Dow Chemical Co.	Chemicals & Plastics	C. H. Boyd, *E. H. Huggins*	31–12–76
391 (417)	SGB Group	Building Equipment & Services	N. L. Clifford-Jones (J.M.D.), *C. Beck*	24– 9–77
392 (313)	Industrial Specialty (I & S)	Metal Merchants	G. S. Panchaud	31– 3–76
393 (468)	Bejam Group	Rtlrs. of Frozen Food & Deep Freezers	J. D. Apthorp, *L. Don, A. W. Perry*	2– 7–77
394 (382)	Lindustries	Engineering, Polymer and Textiles	W. E. Luke, *P. A. Rippon*	2– 4–77
395 (363)	Vantona Group	Household Textiles, etc.	J. D. Spooner	2–12–77
396 (409)	William Jackson & Son	Bakers, Confectioners, Meat Products	P. B. Oughtred (J.M.D.), *B. N. Oughtred*	30– 4–77
397 (397)	Bath & Portland Group	Minerals, Agric., Bldg., Civil Eng.	Sir Kenneth Selby	31–10–77
398 (391)	Serck	Control Equip., Heat Transfer, Valves	R. G. Martin	30– 9–77
399 (N/A)	Smurfit	Mfr. & Sale of Paper Prodts, Printing	M. W. Smurfit	31– 1–77
400 (375)	Oriel Foods	Distbn. & Processing of Foodstuffs	J. C. Page	31–12–76

NOTES: *Total tangible assets less current liabilities (other than bank loans and overdrafts and future tax). †As percentage of capital employed at beginning of the year. ‡As at 14 July 1978. §Appendix on page 70 gives list of Managing Directors which cannot be fitted into the main text. ‖M.D. = Managing Director; J.M.D. = Joint Managing Director; A.C. = Acting Chairman. ¶As percentage of capital employed at the end of the year. N/A Not available. ¹UK only.

TURNOVER		*CAPITAL EMPLOYED			NET PROFIT BEFORE INTEREST AND TAX						**No. of employees	‡Equity market cap. £M.
Total £000	Export £000	£000	Rank Latest year	Previous year	Latest year £000	Rank	Previous year £000	% to turnover Latest year	†% to capital employed Latest year	Previous year		
89,181	19,366	45,772	307	282	8,662	296	5,633	9·7	19·2	14·8	4,232[1]	IT
88,538	19,976	25,573	454	471	5,583	385	4,787	6·3	26·5	30·1	4,226[1]	15·5
87,874	25,773	58,965	254	229	5,217	411	2,608	5·9	13·0	7·8	6,946	USA
87,837	871	90,776	188	163	15,116	196	14,013	17·2	17·0	18·1	3,160[1]	70·9
87,513	2,639	73,799	220	221	14,804	198	10,484	16·9	20·6	¶14·6	6,986	88·6
87,430	46,700	73,590	221	193	10,350	261	12,969	11·8	13·9	20·9	7,460	37·2
87,324p.a.	11,802p.a.	54,853	271	248	10,352p.a.	260	10,496	11·9	18·6p.a.	23·0	1,839[1]	77·3
87,259	17,174	47,928	295	278	10,023	269	7,221	11·5	21·7	17·0	8,475	33·1
86,798	—	29,237	425	378	Loss 183	980	558	—	—	1·7	2,053[1]	USA
86,791	17,293	34,488	378	449	8,026	310	5,832	9·2	28·9	25·7	5,047[1]	UQ
86,490	6,436	36,092	362	530	8,481	299	4,393	9·8	¶23·5	26·6	3,859[1]	32·1
86,489	1,293	8,504	812	775	1,670	773	1,549	11·9	32·8	39·7	2,290	I
86,215	13,564	45,868	306	396	7,489	325	7,754	8·7	17·7	27·2	2,310[1]	USA
85,749	316	8,926	797	769	1,666	775	1,642p.a.	1·9	19·4	20·3p.a.	706	2·4
85,723	915	33,501	385	463	3,069	588	2,785	3·6	14·1	13·6	544[1]	IT
85,669	0	10,241	765	734	3,290	560	2,047	3·8	33·7	32·0	2,940	18·5
85,615	7,988	34,494	377	379	6,190	365	5,901	7·2	20·7	23·8	5,763	20·6
85,313	7,107	41,589	333	313	6,346	359	5,979	7·4	16·1	22·7	4,813	10·6
84,915	16,952	60,360	246	291	6,344	360	6,343	7·5	14·4	17·3	10,576	14·4
84,708	29,252	79,154	211	185	312	948	3,335	0·4	0·5	6·6	5,715[1]	USA
84,642	12	15,422	627	623	2,445	656	1,566	2·9	18·2	18·7	1,690	6·7
84,183	25,449	42,859	325	289	11,202	247	Loss 765	13·3	25·2	—	4,993[1]	USA
83,185	170	27,095	439	424	3,009	598	3,059	3·6	11·6	13·1	4,407[1]	7·8
83,086	5,605	30,607	410	609	4,686	447	2,804	5·6	26·7	20·0	2,760[1]	UQ
83,008	3,772	35,074	372	342	3,717	518	1,808	4·5	12·8	7·3	3,066	USA
82,915	785	10,887	743	868	3,870	504	1,484	4·7	62·9	21·2	1,982	23·8
82,597	37,200	39,596	341	421	16,268	180	11,880	19·7	62·7	59·0	5,521[1]	28·1
82,142	13,752	45,024	312	293	9,883	272	9,935	12·0	22·7	27·9	3,150	28·3
82,109	7,534	134,255	137	113	13,177	218	12,468	16·0	9·4	8·1	3,948	53·8
81,974	0	14,474	647	724	1,052	852	1,706	1·3	10·4	19·4	2,019[1]	USA
81,541	—	54,177	276	304	21,940	144	19,358	26·9	54·0	89·8	2,804[1]	149·0
81,457	3,915	32,630	397	394	1,833	748	1,250	2·3	6·4	5·3	4,069	USA
81,418	26,914	44,217	316	316	9,123	283	5,765	11·2	23·5	14·7	6,571	22·4
81,097	17	36,609	358	403	7,850	314	7,498	9·7	28·3	29·7	409[1]	UQ
81,078	5,357	74,163	218	210	430	931	Loss 445	0·5	0·6	—	1,931[1]	USA
80,987	—	120,331	153	183	21,037	149	11,742	26·0	26·4	18·2	—	UQ
80,189	19,700	68,618	229	209	18,763	164	15,152	23·4	32·4	36·4	7,076	46·6
80,030	70	5,552	904	—	451	927	212	0·6	12·8	¶ 6·0	—	H
80,012	3,368	34,693	375	406	8,968	287	7,213	11·2	32·5	34·4	2,785[1]	USA
79,901	14,422	30,010	418	555	3,748	512	3,329	4·7	21·8	18·4	537[1]	USA
79,736	7,419	46,189	303	303	9,976	270	6,862	12·5	24·5	18·6	5,421[1]	32·4
79,494	22,815	7,711	849	886	817	879	1,008	1·0	15·0	15·0	217[1]	SWZ
79,185	73	12,456	697	725	4,955	425	2,712	6·3	49·5	60·9	1,803	37·3
78,964	14,470	43,305	321	317	7,104	337	5,391p.a.	9·0	18·3	15·5p.a.	6,841[1]	25·0
78,834	11,473	35,471	371	369	7,655	320	7,402	9·7	24·6	25·8	8,068[1]	18·5
78,742	0	11,859	715	733	1,974	733	1,606	2·5	20·2	18·8	4,926	UQ
78,563	3,568	29,574	422	423	7,661	318	5,437	9·8	29·8	26·6	3,439[1]	11·4
78,387	16,200	37,295	355	354	10,117	268	7,897	12·9	30·3	28·7	5,550	35·1
78,164	843	27,779	434	—	6,559	356	3,391	8·4	¶23·6	¶27·1	4,032[1]	I
77,608	316	10,771	748	736	1,430	799	1,473	1·8	14·8	18·3	1,362[1]	USA

The following letters in the Market Capitalisation column denote unquoted companies and country of control: H = Holland.   I = Ireland.   IT = Italy.
SWZ = Switzerland.   UQ = Unquoted.   USA = United States of America.

Rank by turn-over	COMPANY	Main activity	Chairman and Managing Directors (in italics) §‖	Accounting period ended
401 (389)	Portals Holdings	Papermaking, Water Treatment, & Eng.	J. V. Sheffield, *J. W. Mather*	31–12–77
402 (469)	Britannia Lead Co.	Lead and Silver Refiners	R. H. Y. Mills, *K. R. Barrett*	3– 7–77
403 (387)	Green Shield Trading Stamp	Trading Stamp Dealers	G. R. F. Tompkins (M.D.)	6–11–76
404 (418)	Crown House	Glass Manfrs. Elec. & Mech. Engineers	P. Edge-Partington	31– 3–77
405 (461)	John Howard and Co.	Civil Engineering Contrs., etc.	Sir John Howard (M.D.)	31–12–76
406 (393)	Readicut International	Rug Making Kits, Carpets, Textiles	P. J. F. Croset, *G. M. L. Hirst, J. P. M. Denny*	31– 3–78
407 (412)	Geo. Bassett Holdings	Confectionery Mfg. & Distbn.	W. R. Mills, *C. J. Ede*	31– 3–77
408 (426)	Initial Services	Linen Supply, Cleaning, Light Eng. etc.,	A. F. R. Carling, *G. R. A. Metcalfe, E. F. Weston*	31– 3–77
409 (403)	NCR	Data Processing Eqpmt. Acctg. Machns.	C. E. Reynolds, *R. M. Fleet*	30–11–77
410 (401)	Norwest Holst	Civil Eng. & Building Contractors	S. E. Baucher	31– 3–77
411 (377)	Andrew Weir & Co.	Shipping, Insurance, etc.	Lord Inverforth	31–12–77
412 (463)	Borg-Warner	Engineering & Chemicals	R. O. Bass	31–12–77
413 (481)	Bayer UK	Marketing of Products of Bayer AG	Lord William Bentinck, *J. V. Webb*	31–12–76
414 (544)	Agricultural Holdings Co.	Electronics, Seeds & Commodities, etc.	P. Balint (M.D.)	30– 6–77
415 (384)	Howard Machinery	Farm Machinery Manufacturers	P. Coleclough	31–10–77
416 (423)	Sterling-Winthrop Group	Chemicals, Pharmaceuticals, etc.	E. E. Barber	31–10–76
417 (428)	Macarthys Pharmaceuticals	Wholesale & Retail Chemists, etc.	A. R. Ritchie, *A. L. Slow*	30– 4–77
418 (392)	Ingersoll-Rand Holdings	Engineers	F. I. H. Wood (M.D.)	31–12–77
419 (555)	Coutinho Caro & Co.	Steel, Chemicals, & Plant Suppliers	H. A. Oppenheimer, *H. Edmonds, R. D. Oppenheimer*	31–12–76
420 (432)	Wedgwood	Fine Bone China & Earthenware, etc.	Sir Arthur Bryan (J.M.D.), *P. Williams*	1– 4–78
421 (421)	J. H. Fenner & Co. (Holdings)	Power Transmission Engineers	J. Palmer	3– 9–77
422 (446)	General Motors Scotland	Earthmoving Equipment Manfrs.	G. B. Heaney (M.D.)	31–12–76
423 (450)	Bakelite Xylonite	Chemical & Plastics Mfrs.	B. Liden, *J. T. Harvey*	25–12–76
424 (N/A)	Interntl Synthetic Rubber	Synthetic Rubber Manfrs., etc.	D. A. Bennett	31–12–76
425 (451)	Firestone Tyre & Rubber Co.	Tyre Manufacturers	G. W. Webber (M.D.)	31–10–77
426 (462)	Robertson Foods	Food Industry	R. C. Robertson, *G. Cunliffe*	31– 3–78
427 (437)	Spar Food Holdings	Food Marketing	D. G. T. Linnel	30– 4–77
428 (414)	Black & Decker	Power Tool Manufacturers	J. C. Brooman	25– 9–77
429 (381)	European Grain & Shipping	Merchants & Brokers	H. André	31–12–76
430 (424)	Vernons Organisation	Pools Promoters, Financiers, etc.	V. Sangster, *G. R. Kennerley*	31– 7–75
431 (440)	Henry Boot & Sons	Construction Engineers, etc.	E. H. Boot (J.M.D.), *J. B. Parkinson*	31–12–77
432 (475)	Inveresk Group	Paper Manufacturers	T. S. Corrigan (M.D.)	31–12–77
433 (591)	C. Walker & Sons	Steel Stockholders	J. Walker, *J. Riley*	31– 5–77
434 (366)	Robert M. Douglas Holdings	Civil Eng. & Building Contractors	J. R. T. Douglas (M.D.)	31– 3–77
435 (379)	Cummins Engine Co.	Diesel Engine & Component Manfrs.	T. A. Lyon	31–12–76
436 (400)	Hall Engineering (Holdings)	General Engineering	R. N. C. Hall (M.D.)	31–12–77
437 (758)	Sheffield Smelting Co.	Precious Metals	D. Bryars	31–12–76
438 (484)	Capper-Neill	Process Plant & Pipework for Indsty.	W. P. Capper (M.D.)	31– 3–78
439 (459)	Hillards	Supermarket Operators	G. N. Hunter, *P. A. H. Hartley*	30– 4–77
440 (419)	Brown Boveri Kent	Industrial Instrument Makers, etc.	J. G. Vaughan	31–12–77
441 (480)	Shepherd Building Group	Building and Ancillary Activities	Sir Peter Shepherd	30– 6–77
442 (454)	Hickson & Welch (Holdings)	Manfrs. of Chemical Products, etc.	T. Harrington, *J. D. Horner*	30– 9–77
443 (542)	Armstrong Equipment	Vehicle Suspension Units, etc.	J. H. Hooper (M.D.)	3– 7–77
444 (476)	Harold Perry Motors	Ford Main Dealers	J. F. MacGregor (M.D.)	31–12–77
445 (974)	Badger	Managers, Consultants, etc.	A. J. Broggini, *M. J. Gordon*	30–11–76
446 (441)	Vaux Breweries	Brewers	P. D. Nicholson (M.D.)	1–10–77
447 (752)	Honda (UK)	Vehicle Importers	*K. Shimizu*	31–12–75
448 (519)	J. E. Sanger	Meat Traders	J. E. Sanger	31– 3–77
449 (767)	Ailsa Trucks	Commercial Vehicle Dealers	P. G. Gyllenhamer, *S. A. Olsen*	31–12–77
450 (430)	Bryant Holdings	Bldg. Contrs. & Civil Eng. Prop. Devpt.	A. C. Bryant (M.D.)	31– 5–77

NOTES: *Total tangible assets less current liabilities (other than bank loans and overdrafts and future tax). †As percentage of capital employed at beginning of the year. ‡As at 14 July 1978. §Appendix on page 70 gives list of Managing Directors which cannot be fitted into the main text. ‖M.D. = Managing Director; J.M.D. = Joint Managing Director; A.C. = Acting Chairman. ¶As percentage of capital employed at the end of the year. N/A Not available. ¹UK only. ³658% of turnover sold overseas

TURNOVER		*CAPITAL EMPLOYED			NET PROFIT BEFORE INTEREST AND TAX						**No. of	‡Equity
Total £000	Export £000	£000	Rank Latest year	Previous year	Latest year £000	Rank	Previous year £000	% to turnover Latest year	†% to capital employed Latest year	Previous year	employees	market cap. £M.
77,369	26,291	37,515	353	347	9,145	281	7,934	11·8	27·0	30·1	4,188	36·5
77,309	23,977	23,261	483	386	1,113	844	1,071	1·4	3·9	5·5	422	AUS
77,123	2	42,855	326	302	3,652	520	2,461	4·7	9·0	8·8	3,986[1]	UQ
76,965	8,897	14,823	638	626	2,872	606	2,557	3·7	21·6	18·2	6,376	12·3
76,812	69,510	29,076	427	416	2,786	613	1,620	3·6	10·5	¶ 6·1	1,579[1]	UQ
76,380	21,772	37,956	351	353	8,308	305	8,053	10·9	24·8	30·2	4,997[1]	26·9
75,888	6,429	13,739	664	681	3,359	555	2,751	4·4	30·0	25·6	5,041[1]	14·7
75,756	1,314	45,110	311	355	7,956	312	6,738	11·1	23·8	21·9	17,770[1]	31·7
75,690	22,500	45,934	304	245	4,689	446	3,516	6·2	¶10·2	6·2	4,800[1]	USA
75,682	0	12,541	695	732	3,719	517	3,121	4·9	34·5	23·2	4,712[1]	9·4
75,591	—	166,148	111	111	10,876	255	12,211	14·4	7·4	9·7	3,550	UQ
74,955	31,902	56,641	267	297	1,287	821	712	1·7	2·3	1·7	3,925[1]	USA
74,929	495	16,007	616	676	3,432	542	2,308	4·6	30·0	19·3	699[1]	G
74,847	9,797	18,646	573	675	4,322	472	2,817	5·8	31·9	20·3	1,152[1]	UQ
74,450	14,084	36,025	363	329	3,496	530	5,020	4·7	9·5	15·7	4,090	7·2
74,327	16,700	45,468	310	310	7,190	332	6,330	9·7	18·1	17·2	3,878[1]	USA
73,969	1,303	12,776	686	711	3,049	593	2,653	4·1	29·4	34·3	2,935	9·2
73,679	39,173	59,451	252	243	5,628	384	5,274	7·6	10·0	11·1	4,250[1]	USA
73,501	21,460	15,981	619	803	2,554	644	2,261	3·5	32·4	35·3	210[1]	UQ
73,443[36]	—	49,443	289	314	8,664	295	8,802	11·8	21·8	27·0	9,624[1]	40·3
73,009	11,580	41,053	336	311	9,560	276	7,942	13·1	25·4	26·4	7,212	37·3
73,002	29,013	45,522	309	352	7,717	316	7,034	10·6	23·0	25·3	2,074[1]	USA
72,825	13,257	53,771	278	276	4,230	478	Loss 832	5·8	9·0	—	5,059	USA
72,650	21,820	34,661	376	—	4,849	434	4,122	6·7	22·1	¶18·8	993[1]	UQ
72,412	7,667	32,699	396	387	267	952	Loss 1,206	0·4	0·9	—	4,939	USA
72,326	4,247	25,726	453	512	3,777	511	3,169	5·2	19·9	19·7	3,393[1]	12·7
71,855	—	34	1000	1000	13	974	6	—	38·2	17·6	—	UQ
71,544	37,291	33,030	394	341	8,833	288	7,787	12·3	25·1	22·2	3,487[1]	USA
71,389	26,681	2,303	971	933	452	926	618	0·6	13·2	11·8	57[1]	SWZ
71,129	136	21,248	518	548	4,111	484	5,080p.a.	5·8	20·2	29·4p.a.	3,410[1]	CI
70,966	4,204	19,322	562	503	2,181	694	2,676	3·1	11·3	16·1	3,844	8·4
70,815	3,762	26,354	447	443	3,168	572	2,042	4·5	13·7	11·6	3,158[1]	15·3
70,789	5,074	30,933	407	522	6,177	366	2,530	8·7	24·4	13·5	1,050[1]	UQ
70,648	3,640	14,696	641	639	3,064	589	2,574	4·3	24·0	24·7	3,483[1]	9·6
70,296	52,376	33,150	392	358	8,473	300	6,086	12·1	36·1	27·9	3,565	USA
69,312	4,312	30,091	417	392	5,494	393	4,365	7·9	19·2	17·4	2,632[1]	12·6
69,263	5,502	13,562	667	762	634	893	725	0·9	6·7	7·4	941[1]	USA
69,125	23,780	21,575	512	636	5,519	390	4,271	8·0	42·3	47·3	4,285	19·2
69,018	0	7,885	839	878	2,496	651	1,255	3·6	43·0	39·6	2,822	12·8
68,848	20,625	40,084	337	332	7,604	323	5,447p.a.	11·0	20·8	15·6p.a.	6,184	28·8
68,200	7,038	15,643	624	669	4,854	432	2,842	7·1	41·4	27·3	4,651	UQ
68,108	26,000	37,686	352	373	10,530	258	8,312	15·5	34·4	32·0	2,305[1]	37·7
67,427	5,810	39,179	342	385	7,384	328	4,966	11·0	25·1	25·6	3,977[1]	31·1
67,331	238	13,351	672	692	3,292	559	1,912	4·9	30·5	20·5	1,089	9·3
66,347	7,040	1,404	989	986	343	945	407	0·5	28·4	40·9	445	USA
66,247p.a.	6p.a.	48,389	293	286	7,049p.a.	338	5,564	10·6	15·7p.a.	13·3	7,510	31·0
65,520	—	8,524	810	881	3,275	563	1,968	5·0	57·5	47·6	130[1]	JAP
65,181	1,668	10,392	759	885	1,695	769	1,773	2·6	30·6	31·6	—	3·0
65,123	1,935	22,028	503	451	4,933	428	2,291	7·6	25·4	11·1	466	SW
65,000	1,416	21,324	517	558	3,116	580	2,954	4·8	18·2	17·6	2,237	9·0

The following letters in the Market Capitalisation column denote unquoted companies and country of control: AUS = Australia.   CI = Channel Islands.   G = Germany.
JAP = Japan.   SW = Sweden.   SWZ = Switzerland.   UQ = Unquoted.   USA = United States of America.

Rank by turnover	COMPANY	Main activity	Chairman and Managing Directors (in italics) §‖	Accounting period ended
451 (471)	A. Monk & Co.	Civil Eng. & Building Contractors, etc.	W. S. Whittingham (M.D.)	28– 2–77
452 (444)	Martin the Newsagent	Newsagents, Tobacconists, etc.	J. B. H. Martin (M.D.)	2–10–77
453 (447)	John Folkes Hefo	Eng., Merchanting, Housing	J. W. Hearnshaw	31–12–77
454 (467)	Giltspur	Industrial Services Group	M. Joseph, *T. E. D. Harker*	31– 3–77
455 (433)	Grampian Holdings	Construction, Trnspt., Plant Hire, Eng.	D. C. Greig	31–12–77
456 (477)	Hewden-Stuart Plant	Plant Hirers and Sellers	F. Jamieson	29– 1–78
457 (449)	Unicorn Industries	Grinding Wheels & Abrasives	B. G. Ball-Greene	31–12–77
458 (N/A)	Corrie Maccoll and Son	Commodity Dealers	D. F. Maccoll	30–11–76
459 (464)	Central & Sheerwood	Fin. Service, Eng., Printing, Publishing	F. A. Singer	31–12–77
460 (431)	F. H. Lloyd Holdings	Steel Founders & Mnfrs. of Eng. Prods.	R. H. Foster	2– 4–77
461 (548)	Uniroyal	Rubber, Plastic & Chemical Products	D. Beretta, *A. J. Stuart*	1– 1–78
462 (504)	Arthur Lee & Sons	Steel Manufacturing	H. P. Forder, *P. W. Lee*	30– 9–77
463 (443)	Lesney Products & Co.	Toys, Hobby Prods., Comm. Diecastings	P. M. Tapscott, *L. C. Smith*	29 –1–78
464 (—)	M. Golodetz	Produce Brokers	N/A	31–12–77
465 (487)	Raybeck	Retailers of Ladies' & Men's Wear	B. Raven, *A. Simons, H. Davies*	30– 4–77
466 (636)	Hecht, Heyworth & Alcan	Rubber Merchants	*D. A. E. Beech*	31–12–77
467 (435)	Ibstock Johnsen	Brick Manfrs. & Wood Pulp Agents	P. C. Hyde-Thomson	31–12–77
468 (438)	Matthews Wrightson Holdings	Insurance & Ship Brokers, etc.	E. J. G. Henry	31–12–77
469 (425)	Mersey Docks and Harbour	Operation of Port Facilities, etc.	Sir Arthur Peterson, *J. B. Fitzpatrick*	31–12–77
470 (465)	Ward White Group	Footwear Manfrs., Elect. & Mech. Engrs.	G. E. McWatters, *P. Birch*	31–12–77
471 (399)	Singer Co. (UK)	Sewing Machines, H/hold Elec., Eqpmt.	J. M. Wotherspoon	31–12–76
472 (533)	Telefusion	Renting, Retail Sale of Radio & T.V.	J. N. Wilkinson (M.D.)	30– 4–77
473 (422)	Westinghouse Brake & Signal	Electrical & Mechanical Engineers	L. E. Thompson, *D. Pollock*	1–10–77
474 (405)	Edward Billington & Son	Sugar Merchants, etc.	E. J. Billington	30– 4–76
475 (527)	Caravans International	Caravan Manufacturers	S. Alper, *E. J. B. Timlin*	31– 8–77
476 (478)	Tennants Consolidated	Chemical Manufacturers	K. A. Alexander	31–12–76
477 (514)	Polaroid (UK)	Photographic & Optical Eqpmt. Distbn.	*H. Allen*	31–12–76
478 (470)	Amos. Hinton & Sons	Retail Food Stores	D. A. Hinton, *W. P. C. Hinton*	4– 3–78
479 (436)	Brockhouse	Eng., Transport, Bldg. & Mtrls. Handlng.	R. J. H. Parkes (M.D.)	30– 9–77
480 (502)	Trident Television	Television Programme Contractors, etc.	G. E. Ward Thomas (M.D.)	30– 9–77
481 (472)	Kimberly-Clark	Cellulose Wadding Products	R. C. Ernest, *D. G. Croxon*	31–12–76
482 (429)	Allied Polymer Group[37]	Manfrs. of Rubber & Plastic Products	P. Fatharly	31–12–76
483 (495)	Godfrey Davis	Car Hire Specialists, Ford Main Dlrs.	C. A. Redfern (M.D.)	31– 3–77
484 (457)	A. J. Mills (Holdings)[33]	Food Importers & Distributors	A. J. Mills (M.D.)	29–10–77
485 (525)	Revertex Chemicals	Rubber Latex & Synthetic Resins	Sir Campbell Adamson, *D. W. Stutchbury*	31–12–77
486 (434)	Brown Brothers Corpn.	Motor Accessories, etc. Distbn. & Manf.	E. G. Spearing	31–12–76
487 (483)	Sedgwick Forbes Holdings	Insurance Brokers, Underwtg. Agents	P. T. Wright	31–12–77
488 (530)	Ductile Steels	Steel Production	R. Sidaway, *C. J. Baker*	2– 7–77
489 (511)	Lennons Group	Retail Foodstuffs, Wine & Spirits	D. P. Lennon, *J. W. Bolton*	2– 4–77
490 (528)	Sale Tilney & Co.	Industrial Plant Mfrs., Food Distbtrs.	T. J. King, *R. T. Allsop*	30–11–77
491 (490)	Scottish & Universal Invs.	Printing & Publishing, Whisky, etc.	R. W. Rowland	31– 3–77
492 (455)	HAT Group	Specialist Sub-Contrs. to Bldg. Ind.	Lord Harlech, *R. W. Wordley*	28– 2–77
493 (597)	Watson & Philip	Distribution of Foodstuffs	D. C. Greig, *H. V. Gardner*	28–10–77
494 (564)	United Baltic Corpn.	Shipowners & Merchants	Lord Inverforth	31–12–76
495 (561)	Whitworths Holdings	Food Products	W. A. George (J.M.D.), *H. Reynolds*	31– 3–76
496 (448)	Coalite & Chemical Products	Smokeless Fuel, Coal Oil, Coal Petrol	Viscount Ward of Witley, *C. E. Needham*	31– 3–77
497 (576)	Govan Shipbuilders	Shipbuilders	*A. Gilchrist*	30– 6–77
498 (531)	Sulzer Bros. (UK)	General Eng., Paper Mach., Pumping In.	*P. J. Strangeway, W. R. Walton*	31–12–77
499 (442)	George Wills & Sons (Hldgs.)	Importers & Exporters	J. Reynolds	31–12–77
500 (458)	Hestair	Special Vehicles, Consumer Prodts, etc.	D. Hargreaves	31– 1–78

NOTES: *Total tangible assets less current liabilities (other than bank loans and overdrafts and future tax).   †As percentage of capital employed at beginning of the year.   ‡As at 14 July 1978.   §Appendix on page 70 gives list of Managing Directors which cannot be fitted into the main text.   ‖M.D. = Managing Director; J.M.D. = Joint Managing Director; A.C. = Acting Chairman.   ¶As percentage of capital employed at the end of the year.   N/A Not available.   ¹UK only.   ³Acting as principal £10.2m, acting as agent, £5.0m.   ³³Now a sub. co. of Antony Gibbs Ltd.   ³⁷Now a sub. co. of BTR Ltd.

| TURNOVER | | *CAPITAL EMPLOYED | | | NET PROFIT BEFORE INTEREST AND TAX | | | | | | No. of | ‡Equity |
Total £000	Export £000	£000	Rank Latest year	Rank Previous year	Latest year £000	Rank	Previous year £000	% to turnover Latest year	†% to capital employed Latest year	Previous year	**employees	market cap. £M.
65,000	9	12,294	706	712	2,738	621	1,150	4·2	26·4	15·2	4,106	9·2
64,957	0	8,893	800	871	3,033	595	2,217	4·7	50·5	46·9	10,530	14·4
64,940	4,635	21,453	516	509	4,001	492	5,116	6·2	20·8	32·5	3,313	13·1
64,929	1,436	24,969	460	410	3,488	533	2,422	5·4	12·9	10·3	3,105[1]	10·9
64,793	8,868	20,437	533	524	1,774	758	2,710	2·7	9·5	17·4	4,046	5·7
64,610	796	41,827	331	388	5,812	376	4,503	9·0	18·7	20·9	3,429	28·5
64,572	15,114	43,072	323	298	7,753	315	6,149	12·0	18·6	18·3	4,102	23·3
64,561	—	3,141	950	—	1,282	824	1,479	2·0	58·1	¶67·0	—	H
63,818	11,004	25,568	455	434	5,389	399	4,509	8·4	21·8	24·9	4,436	20·2
63,706	8,957	30,746	408	407	6,135	369	5,037	9·6	22·1	19·3	5,693	15·6
63,654	20,028	26,811	441	576	2,084	715	3,524	3·3	10·0	22·2	2,969[1]	USA
63,486	4,656	29,451	423	414	4,701	444	2,949	7·4	18·0	13·0	2,386[1]	6·8
63,339	31,226	43,301	322	324	8,657	297	10,797	13·7	23·1	37·7	5,290[1]	24·0
63,300	15,200[8]	7,243	855	—	2,889	604	1,152	4·6	61·0	36·9	—	UQ
63,115	3,942	16,948	601	614	4,665	450	3,907	7·4	34·0	38·0	3,790	30·9
63,029	10	8,918	798	902	627	896	522	1·0	12·7	10·4	—	FR
62,796	340	24,042	472	491	4,835	436	4,157	7·7	24·1	25·0	1,966	16·4
62,694	0	33,641	384	368	9,690	273	10,785	15·5	31·0	30·5	2,736[1]	27·3
62,661	—	97,350	176	159	8,833	289	9,164	14·1	9·6	10·1	8,275[1]	
62,617	7,739	20,595	530	506	4,279	475	2,693	6·8	22·3	16·4	5,144[1]	6·3
62,081	41,001	34,008	380	361	2,934	603	2,859	4·7	9·0	¶ 8·7	8,702	USA
62,011	350	22,402	494	504	3,952	498	1,998	6·4	20·4	11·4	3,004[1]	16·3
61,961	12,806	42,132	330	335	6,881	343	5,771	11·1	19·2	16·7	5,066[1]	20·5
61,745	2,781	3,734	941	944	492	916	561	0·8	17·4	17·1	533[1]	UQ
61,705	10,409	11,211	735	752	4,708	442	2,938	7·6	51·7	36·6	2,773	6·6
61,498	5,790	22,127	502	544	5,072	417	3,757	8·2	28·7	25·3	1,171	UQ
61,393	38,969	21,457	515	470	10,183	266	7,663	16·6	48·3	53·5	1,305	USA
61,056	—	6,614	876	883	1,788	755	1,406	2·9	31·6	26·0	2,535	4·0
60,772	6,578	30,721	409	384	3,422	545	3,976	5·6	11·6	14·5	3,692[1]	11·0
60,541	898	24,757	464	595	7,621	322	5,545	12·6	51·0	47·2	1,812[1]	23·5
60,405	4,438	26,173	449	466	5,407	398	3,805	9·0	25·2	19·0	2,356	USA
60,015	11,999	20,179	541	487	1,974	732	3,368	3·3	9·2	20·0	6,330	—[37]
60,012	0	19,945	548	462	3,901	502	2,609	6·5	17·9	12·9	2,240	11·2
60,000	107	6,951	862	872	1,174	839	959	2·0	19·7	19·7	193[1]	—[33]
59,508	6,575	20,327	538	560	3,491	531	3,828	5·9	20·5	32·1	1,172[1]	9·5
58,883	2,045	13,124	677	633	2,395	665	2,263	4·1	17·6	15·6	3,301[1]	11·5
58,613	—	33,463	386	397	23,387	138	17,021	39·9	82·4	74·0	3,945	126·3
58,555	2,426	28,763	430	465	6,169	367	4,677	10·5	28·7	30·3	1,826[1]	16·3
58,508	0	9,908	774	893	1,766	761	1,283	3·0	33·2	35·3	2,171	8·9
58,508	5,113	12,995	679	644	2,410	662	1,900	4·1	19·1	19·5	803[1]	5·8
58,339	6,283	43,649	319	331	4,735	441	4,985	8·1	12·9	12·3	4,328[1]	37·3
57,752	272	12,144	709	755	3,126	578	3,210	5·4	34·5	43·3	9,453	10·7
57,739	0	4,536	923	927	1,196	836	881	2·1	33·1	40·6	805	4·6
57,549	2,657	19,175	564	554	3,501	529	2,101	6·1	20·3	15·5	187[1]	UQ
57,515	525	15,040	633	590	2,307	676	2,317	4·0	14·7	14·8	1,499[1]	UQ
57,427	8,721	36,016	364	391	12,108	230	8,563	21·1	42·1	34·2	2,502	47·7
57,332p.a.	57,170p.a.	27,239	437	325	Loss 2,906p.a.	992	Loss 6,766	—	—	—	5,761[1]	UQ
57,261	7,235	14,588	645	601	977	867	847	1·7	4·9	5·8	2,115[1]	SWZ
57,200	8,200	4,790	916	917	1,206	833	756	2·1	29·6	20·0	178[1]	2·3
57,053	19,852	15,630	625	670	5,040	418	4,773	8·8	43·0	35·6	3,000[1]	18·6

The following letters in the Market Capitalisation column denote unquoted companies and country of control: FR = France.　　H = Holland.　　SWZ = Switzerland.　UQ = Unquoted.　　USA = United States of America.

Rank by turn-over	COMPANY	Main activity	Chairman and Managing Directors (in italics) §‖	Accounting period ended
501 (486)	Aberdeen Construction Grp.	Civil Engineering & Building	W. Tinch (M.D.)	31–12–77
502 (556)	Ward & Goldstone	Manfrs. of Cables, Elec. Access., etc.	S. Goldstone, *M. H. Goldstone*	31– 3–77
503 (453)	Combined English Stores Grp.	Multiple Specialist Retailing Group	M. Gordon (J.M.D.), *E. J. De Winter*	28– 1–78
504 (595)	Pride & Clarke[8]	Retail Motor Cars & Accessories	E. P. Heath, *A. T. Clarke, J. C. B. Pride*	30– 9–77
505 (496)	Central Manfg. & Trading Grp.	Asbestos, Rubber, Plastics & All. Prod.	N. N. Hickman, *N. A. Hickman*	31– 7–77
506 (492)	Ogilvy Benson & Mather	Marketing and Advertising	A. A. Ross	31–12–76
507 (507)	Amalg. Power Engineering	Steam Turbines, Diesel Engines, etc.	H. A. Whittall, *J. G. Ryder*	31–12–77
508 (568)	Donald Macpherson Group	Paint & Other Surface Coatings	R. Chester, *H. K. Cushing*	30–10–77
509 (536)	Quaker Oats	Grocery Products, Chemicals & Toys	R. G. Lagden, *J. B. Felter Jr.*	30– 6–77
510 (494)	Prestige Group	Domestic Houseware Manufacturers	D. J. T. Lawman (M.D.)	31–12–77
511 (518)	Aspro-Nicholas	Pharmaceuticals, Chemicals, etc.	R. R. Walker	30– 6–77
512 (452)	Augustus Barnett & Son	Wine & Spirit Merchants	B. L. Barnett	29– 1–77
513 (631)	Carlsberg Brewery	Brewers	A. W. Nielson, *M. C. Iuul*	30– 9–76
514 (645)	F. J. C. Lilley	Civil Eng. & Public Works Contrs.	J. Aitken, *T. M. Bisset*	31– 1–78
515 (493)	Selincourt	Textiles, Lace & Fashion Garments	L. L. Leighton, *D. V. Pick*	31– 1–78
516 (586)	Rush & Tompkins Group	Propty. Invest. Bldg. & Civil Eng., etc.	D. J. Palmar	31–12–77
517 (506)	Daily Telegraph	Newspaper Proprietors	Lord Hartwell, *H. M. Stephen*	31– 3–77
518 (489)	Alfred Herbert	Machine Tools Manfrs. & Distributors	Sir John Buckley	31–12–77
519 (571)	BASF United Kingdom	Chemical Products, etc.	F. Schuster	31–12–76
520 (500)	Y. J. Lovell (Holdings)	Building Contractors, etc.	P. E. Trench, *N. E. Wakefield*	30– 9–77
521 (488)	Drake & Scull Holdings	Elec., Mechanical & Constr. Engineers	M. C. Abbott	31–10–77
522 (508)	B. Elliott & Co.	Machine Tool Manufacturers	F. M. Russell, *M. J. Beer*	31– 3–77
523 (474)	M. J. Gleeson (Contractors)	Civil Eng. & Building Contractors	J. P. Gleeson (M.D.)	30– 6–77
524 (491)	Wm. Collins & Sons (Holding)	Publishers, etc.	W. J. Collins	25–12–77
525 (550)	Diamond Shamrock Europe	Chemicals for Industrial Purposes	F. A. Russell, *R. J. Kingsley*	28– 2–77
526 (734)	James Finlay & Co.	International Traders & Financiers	Sir Colin Campbell	31–12–76
527 (543)	Allied Retailers	Retailers of Carpets & Furniture	H. Plotnek	2– 4–77
528 (534)	Whitecroft	Textiles, Bldg. & Eng. Sup., Eng., Leather	J. Tavare (M.D.)	31– 3–77
529 (731)	Merck Sharp & Dohme (Hldgs.)	Manufacturing Chemists	H. Ekaireb	31–12–76
530 (516)	Millford Grain	Grain Merchants	C. J. Priday	31– 3–77
531 (549)	Laker Airways (Internl.)	Air Tour Operators, Hoteliers, etc.	Sir Freddie Laker (M.D.)	31– 3–77
532 (672)	Bison Group	'Bison' Structural Precast Concrete	Sir Kenneth Wood, *G. Wigglesworth*	31– 3–77
533 (553)	Senior Engineering Group	Traders in Engineering Products	R. Smith, *G. R. Deveson*	31–12–77
534 (524)	Sheepbridge Engineering	Engineering	Lord Aberconway, *H. Gunner*	31– 3–77
535 (545)	Travis & Arnold	Builders' Merchants & Timber Imptrs.	E. R. Travis, *E. R. A. Travis, C. G. Porter*	31–12–77
536 (539)	Star Diamond Co.	Dealers in Diamonds	S. Hirschel (M.D.)	24– 5–77
537 (479)	Petrola (UK)	Dealers in Crude Oil	S. J. Latsis, *J. F. Jarvis-Smith*	31–12–74
538 (420)	Humphreys & Glasgow	Engineers	A. Congreve, *F. W. Edwards, R. Langford, W. Richardson*	31– 3–77
539 (—)	Dentsply	Dental Apparatus Manfrs. & Merchants	P. L. Burgin	30–11–77
540 (520)	Dorada Holdings	Motor Sales & Service, Engineers, etc.	T. Kenny	31–12–77
541 (515)	Metal Closures Group	Metal & Plastic Packaging	J. Boden	31–12–77
542 (505)	Rentokil Group	Timber Preservation, Pest Control, etc.	W. H. Westphal, *B. McGillivray*	31–12–77
543 (574)	Lopex	A Marketing Communications Group	C. J. N. Sykes	31–12–77
544 (482)	Frank Fehr & Co.	Produce Merchants & Brokers	B. H. F. Fehr	31–c2–76
545 (501)	British Enkalon	Man-made Fibre Producers	J. M. Ritchie, *A. S. Lobban*	31–12–77
546 (577)	GEI International	Engineering	T. Kenny, *J. O. Sewell*	31– 3–78
547 (567)	Conder International	Construction of Pre-Fab Buildings	R. T. Cole	31–12–76
548 (532)	Foster Bros. Clothing Co.	Clothiers, Tailors & Outfitters	H. G. High, *B. G. Davison*	28– 2–78
549 (557)	Whessoe	Engineers, etc.	Lord Erroll of Hale	24– 9–77
550 (485)	A. Oppenheimer & Co.	Export Merchants & Agents	J. Levison, R. P. Adler (*Joint Chairman*)	31–12–75

NOTES: *Total tangible assets less current liabilities (other than bank loans and overdrafts and future tax). †As percentage of capital employed at beginning of the year. ‡As at 14 July, 1978. §Appendix on page 70 gives list of Managing Directors which cannot be fitted into the main text. ‖M.D. = Managing Director; J.M.D. = Joint Managing Director; A.C. = Acting Chairman. ¶As percentage of capital employed at the end of the year. N/A Not available. [1]U.K. only [8]Now a sub co. of Inchcape & Co. Ltd.

TURNOVER		*CAPITAL EMPLOYED			NET PROFIT BEFORE INTEREST AND TAX						**No. of employees	‡Equity market cap. £M.
Total £000	Export £000	£000	Rank Latest year	Rank Previous year	Latest year £000	Rank	Previous year £000	% to turnover Latest year	†% to capital employed Latest year	†% to capital employed Previous year		
57,018	0	18,648	572	567	3,961	496	4,590	6·9	24·0	31·8	3,730	9·9
56,956	11,045	25,514	456	488	4,511	461	3,645	7·9	22·7	18·9	6,196¹	12·8
56,904	89	17,154	597	592	4,055	488	4,535	7·1	27·1	35·8	3,979	19·7
56,709	1,813	6,823	865	842	2,100	708	822	3·7	31·1	14·7	519	—⁸
56,317	942	26,605	442	450	4,619	451	4,136	8·2	20·5	19·1	2,329¹	13·7
56,146	—	6,357	880	899	1,980	729	1,710	3·5	40·4	33·8	633¹	USA
56,145	23,574	27,499	436	474	6,867	345	4,035	12·2	33·8	21·3	3,656¹	19·2
55,728	3,229	22,166	501	563	3,903	501	2,961	7·0	23·3	24·6	2,656¹	10·4
55,682	4,752	20,068	544	589	2,331	672	3,165	4·2	15·0	26·6	1,665	USA
54,890	9,428	22,241	498	494	6,667	352	5,819	12·1	33·8	32·3	4,100	29·9
54,831	6,441	22,833	487	467	6,224	363	5,414	11·4	29·2	27·2	1,244¹	AUS
54,645p.a.	0	1,834	981	969	407p.a.	933	Loss 627p.a.	0·7	14·2 p.a.	—	532	SPN
54,624	—	38,298	346	448	5,083	416	5,049	9·3	22·3	29·0	676	DEN
54,567	2,400	13,869	662	781	3,165	573	2,558	5·8	37·7	37·3	2,069	11·2
54,476	6,419	22,873	486	490	5,436	394	4,529	10·0	27·0	28·5	3,818¹	126·8
54,441	0	39,863	339	357	2,554	645	2,348	4·7	7·7	7·5	1,858¹	12·6
54,412	1,862	8,031	833	790	1,310	819	Loss 905	2·4	16·0	—	3,266	UQ
54,299	12,786	54,593	273	260	1,734	763	1,682	3·2	3·4	5·0	6,009	UQ
54,229	0	21,623	510	549	1,731	764	783	3·2	10·0	5·4	657¹	G
54,111	187	18,440	574	641	2,201	691	1,878	4·1	17·4	20·2	2,276	5·8
54,089	5,985	2,628	963	931	2,624	633	1,509	4·9	74·6	15·9	2,376¹	3·7
54,068	5,233	19,985	547	545	4,705	443	3,781	8·7	27·5	23·9	1,991¹	18·9
54,000	930	9,476	782	779	1,438	797	1,409	2·7	17·1	17·9	3,004¹	4·0
53,756	11,498	42,560	327	339	4,414	468	6,230	8·2	12·5	19·5	2,998¹	17·9
53,466	18,571	18,177	578	638	2,267	682	2,254	4·2	17·5	22·2	1,264	USA
53,092	1,290	53,161	280	300	12,595	224	4,571	23·7	¶23·7	12·8	1,156¹	36·5
52,718	186	14,515	646	705	3,840	507	3,368	7·3	36·5	42·7	2,084	23·7
52,526	3,564	26,486	445	405	5,993	372	3,652	11·4	21·7	16·1	4,353¹	18·2
52,303	15,538	54,345	274	505	10,341	262	8,082	19·8	27·6	¶21·6	1,165¹	USA
51,987	1,304	174	998	998	44	971	36	0·1	29·7	28·8	—	UQ
51,897	—	25,425	458	401	3,077	586	3,308	5·9	11·0	11·4	1,008	UQ
51,770	126	15,098	632	817	3,079	585	1,765	5·9	¶20·4	27·3	3,219	SAR
51,629	4,112	25,806	452	447	5,425	396	4,817	10·5	23·8	26·6	3,639¹	17·1
51,597	11,464	22,433	492	495	5,429	395	4,319	10·5	27·6	24·4	5,378	24·1
51,561	—	25,190	459	476	3,949	499	4,425	7·7	19·0	28·4	1,784	10·8
51,526	47,063	5,331	909	797	378	940	153	0·7	8·5	3·8	—	UQ
51,433	—	144	999	999	14	973	30	—	9·5	25·6	—	LU
51,225	20,191	5,421	907	915	1,860	743	1,497	3·6	45·2	51·5	1,952¹	UQ
51,185	7,555	19,155	565	—	2,568	643	2,072	5·0	7·9	¶ 6·4	2,268¹	USA
51,056	1,062	10,300	761	717	1,696	768	1,190	3·3	16·5	14·2	1,641	3·3
50,943	4,073	26,302	448	442	5,553	389	4,911	10·9	23·4	25·0	3,065¹	19·5
50,834	2,419	23,606	475	847	8,775	293	7,454	17·3	42·6	43·3	2,929¹	53·9
50,757	—	8,247	826	772	1,958	734	1,380	3·9	22·9	17·7	675¹	UQ
50,687	20,791	2,667	960	956	632	894	879	1·2	25·8	42·5	—	UQ
50,547	7,793	27,148	438	364	Loss 164	979	Loss 1,128	—	—	—	2,945	5·9
50,480	5,844	26,580	443	464	5,988	373	4,817	11·9	27·8	25·4	2,652¹	22·8
50,281	13,561	8,697	806	820	2,017	727	1,662	4·0	28·0	24·7	1,761¹	UQ
50,195	155	21,930	505	499	5,234	409	4,061	10·4	26·8	23·0	3,865	29·0
49,973	9,380	22,423	493	493	4,060	487	3,618	8·1	20·5	16·2	4,605	6·3
49,794	1,569	16,157	612	570	4,603	452	3,902	9·2	33·3	39·2	1,349	UQ

The following letters in the Market Capitalisation column denote unquoted companies and country of control: AUS = Australia.   DEN = Denmark.   G = Germany. LU = Luxembourg.   SAR = Saudi Arabia.   SPN = Spain.   UQ = Unquoted.   USA = United States of America.

Rank by turn-over	COMPANY	Main activity	Chairman and Managing Directors (in italics) § ‖	Accounting period ended
551 (439)	Usborne & Son (London)	Grain Importers	D. W. Frame	31– 3–77
552 (600)	Scott Lithgow	Shipbuilders	M. A. Sinclair Scott, *A. R. Belch*	31–12–76
553 (521)	McCorquodale & Co.	Printers & Stationers	A. McCorquodale, *J. L. Wood*	30– 9–77
554 (473)	Edgar Allen, Balfour	Steel Makers & Engineers	J. D. Oakley, *G. W. Wise*	2– 4–77
555 (587)	Gonzalez Byass & Co.	Wine & Spirit Producers & Shippers	G. W. Hawkings-Byass	31–12–76
556 (614)	Wm. Low & Co.	Supermarket Operators	A. M. Drysdale	3– 9–77
557 (582)	Lockwoods Foods	Fruit & Vegetable, etc., Canners	P. B. Lockwood, *W. P. Lockwood, N. G. Horton-Mastin*	31– 5–77
558 (547)	Gillette Industries	Razor & Blade Manufacturers, etc.	R. H. Burton, *R. S. Mills*	30–11–76
559 (559)	H. & R. Johnson-Richards Tiles	Ceramic Tile Manufacturers	J. A. Done	31– 3–77
560 (575)	United Newspapers	Newspaper Proprietors	Lord Barnetson (M.D.)	31–12–77
561 (538)	R. H. Thompson Group	Provision Merchants	D. J. N. Thompson, *R. M. Thompson, J. S. C. Tidmarsh*	29– 1–77
562 (498)	Crane Fruehauf	Commercial Vehicle Body Manfrs.	W. E. Grace, *P. Croft*	1– 1–77
563 (584)	Barr & Wallace Arnold Trust	Holidays & Travel, Motor Dlrs., etc.	J. M. Barr	31–12–77
564 (570)	Texas Instruments	Electronic Component Manufacturers	J. W. W. Peyton	31–12–76
565 (659)	May & Hassell	Timber Importers	J. H. B. Atley, *P. J. Atley*	31– 3–77
566 (569)	Courts (Furnishers)	Retailers of House Furniture, etc.	E. G. Cohen, *P. C. Cohen, B. J. R. Cohen*	31– 3–77
567 (585)	J. Gerber & Co.	Confirming House	K. P. Van Ek	31–12–77
568 (565)	Proprietors of Hay's Wharf	Goods Handling & Distribution, etc.	Sir David H. Burnett, *D. S. Clarabut*	30– 9–77
569 (618)	LEP Group	Intnl. Transport & Travel Agents, etc.	R. J. D. Leeper (M.D.)	31–12–76
570 (535)	Thomas Roberts (Westminster)	Timber, Road Materials, etc.	Mrs. P. M. Roberts, *B. Kilpatrick*	31– 3–77
571 (603)	Cameron Iron Works	Mrfs. of Valves, Oilfield Eqpt., etc.	H. Allen	30– 6–77
572 (560)	Dexion-Comino International	Storage & Materials Hndlg. Eqpmt.	S. Hinchliff (M.D.)	24–10–76
573 (730)	Fodens	Commercial Vehicle Manufacturers	L. J. Tolley, *D. C. Foden, S. P. Twemlow*	2– 4–77
574 (583)	NSS Newsagents	Retail Newsagents	P. H. Byam-Cook, *V. E. G. Tagliavini*	2–10–77
575 (503)	Lilly Industries	Pharmaceuticals, etc.	Dr. M. Perelman, *C. Birkett*	31–12–76
576 (546)	SKF (UK)	Ball & Roller Bearing Manfrs.	J. L. King, *C. O. Blomberg*	31–12–76
577 (563)	British Bata Shoe Co.	Footwear Manufacturers	T. J. Bata	31–12–76
578 (637)	Marshall's Universal	General Industrial Group	R. L. Doughty, *J. A. Oliver*	31–12–77
579 (579)	Liverpool Daily Post & Echo	Newspaper Printing & Publishing	H. B. Chrimes, *I. G. Park*	31–12–77
580 (718)	Roche Products	Chemical Manufacturers	A. W. Jann, *W. W. Gerard*	31–12–76
581 (509)	H. Samuel	Multiple Retail Jewellers	R. R. S. Edgar (J.M.D.), *R. Collingwood*	29– 1–77
582 (622)	Gibbons Dudley	Engineering, Refractories, etc.	R. D. Turner	31–12–77
583 (727)	Air Products	Industrial Gases & Equipment Manfrs.	A. W. Walker	30– 9–76
584 (581)	Alfred Preedy & Sons	Wholesale & Retail Tobacconists	H. L. Preedy	26– 3–77
585 (513)	British Olivetti	Business Machinery & Systems Mfrs.	G. Fei, *N. Colangelo*	31–12–76
586 (632)	Chamberlain Phipps	Shoe Components and Plastics, etc.	W. R. F. Chamberlain	31– 3–77
587 (517)	Federated Chemical Holdings44	Chemicals & Pharmaceuticals	G. T. Pryce, *R. A. Pargeter*	31–12–76
588 (699)	Lummus Co.	Refinery Engineers	R. E. Wise, *G. R. Lawrence*	31–12–76
589 (742)	T. C. Harrison	Ford Vauxhall, Bedford, JCB Main Dlrs.	T. C. Harrison, *E. Harrison, J. F. Harrison*	31–12–77
590 (606)	Cosmos Air Holidays	Tour Operators	Sir John Hornung	30–11–76
591 (540)	Pritchard Services Group	Bldg. Maint. & Security Services, etc.	P. R. Pritchard (M.D.)	1– 1–78
592 (965)	Lee Cooper Group	Casual Clothing Mfrs. & Distributors	H. C. Cooper, *P. Pouillot*	31–12–77
593 (624)	Charles Hurst	Vehicle Distbn. & Service	C. T. Hurst, *C. A. Stuart, S. Magowan*	31–12–77
594 (526)	Wilkins & Mitchell	Power Presses and Domestic Applnces	H. R. Wilkins (J.M.D.), *E. W. Wilkins*	2– 4–77
595 (626)	Jonas Woodhead & Sons	Vehicle Suspension Specialists	E. S. Simpson (M.D.)	31– 3–77
596 (729)	Newman Industries	Electrical, Foundries & Gen. Eng., etc.	A. F. Bartlett	31–12–77
597 (—)	Elbar Industrial	Vehicle Distbn., Agricultural Mchy., etc.	A. L. Hood, *K. Williams*	31–12–77
598 (650)	Rohm & Haas (UK)	Chemical Manufacturers	J. P. Mulroney, *E. J. Cullen*	31–12–76
599 (655)	Scapa Group	Paper-Machine Clothing Mfrs., etc.	T. D. Walker, *R. W. Goodall, J. Haythornwaite*	31– 3–77
600 (665)	Readson	Textile Manufacturers	E. Dodson, *T. Weatherby*	31– 3–77

NOTES: *Total tangible assets less current liabilities (other than bank loans and overdrafts and future tax). †As percentage of capital employed at beginning of the year. ‡As at 14 July 1978. §Appendix on page 70 gives list of Managing Directors which cannot be fitted into the main text. ‖M.D. = Managing Director; J.M.D. = Joint Managing Director; A.C. = Acting Chairman. ¶As percentage of capital employed at the end of the year. N/A Not available. 1UK only. 279-month period—including results of all trading subs for one year. 44Now a sub. co. of Dalgety Ltd.

| TURNOVER | | *CAPITAL EMPLOYED | | | NET PROFIT BEFORE INTEREST AND TAX | | | | | | **No. of employees | ‡Equity market cap. £M. |
Total £000	Export £000	£000	Rank Latest year	Previous year	Latest year £000	Rank	Previous year £000	% to turnover Latest year	†% to capital employed Latest year	Previous year		
49,604	—	3,165	949	962	380	939	373	0·8	17·1	22·2	—	UQ
49,353	29,002	19,558	557	539	Loss 346	983	766	—	—	4·2	8,101¹	UQ
49,224	4,094	29,658	420	398	3,744	513	1,987	7·6	13·2	7·6	4,618¹	13·2
49,130	9,109	36,959	357	333	1,931	738	4,598	3·9	5·2	¶12·7	4,758¹	9·5
49,115	241	33,359	389	389	2,346	670	1,815	4·8	8·1	10·3	135¹	BAH
48,776	0	6,769	868	887	1,833	749	1,142	3·8	33·7	23·8	2,916	8·0
48,675	1,142	18,085	579	517	3,479	534	3,328	7·1	18·0	22·4	2,364¹	5·9
48,556	—	28,466	432	411	1,774	757	2,465	3·7	6·6	9·5	—	USA
48,368	8,372	33,926	382	371	4,819	437	4,659	10·0	15·6	16·0	4,112	20·9
48,327	559	24,740	465	455	5,576	386	3,935	11·5	25·0	19·3	5,453	23·1
48,158	188	3,520	945	921	535	909	296	1·1	14·1	9·9	461¹	UQ
47,656	10,250	14,673	642	598	2,636	631	827	5·5	18·3	5·5	2,499¹	USA
47,589	25	11,021	739	822	1,923	739	1,328	4·0	26·5	23·7	1,706	4·2
47,504	17,404	20,675	527	523	1,773	759	2,255	3·7	¶ 8·6	8·9	2,797¹	USA
47,364	106	32,027	400	472	2,952	602	2,629	6·2	14·0	14·7	1,691¹	4·2
47,345	0	24,005	473	515	5,324	401	5,754	11·2	28·5	38·5	2,077¹	15·6
47,300	—	4,558	922	911	1,218	831	1,140	2·6	27·8	35·6	—	UQ
47,300	179	43,355	320	258	4,947	426	4,125	10·5	9·7	7·4	3,105¹	24·7
47,287	0	35,549	369	419	4,700	445	3,181	9·9	18·0	14·4	5,712	15·3
47,200	250	19,934	549	553	2,179	695	430	4·6	12·6	2·0	2,150	UQ
47,168	35,718	38,000	362	349	8,689	294	7,926	18·4	25·7	30·9	1,792	USA
47,164	7,603	17,822	585	557	4,595	453	2,692	9·7	26·8	19·7	1,432¹	USA
47,150	10,225	14,919	635	577	3,139	575	358	6·7	19·8	2·5	2,962¹	5·0
47,089	0	8,760	803	825	3,264	565	2,399	6·9	46·1	40·5	3,446	18·2
47,068	25,572	31,370	404	366	10,332	263	7,143	22·0	34·6	29·0	2,344	USA
46,990	17,951	44,929	313	319	Loss 277	982	3,805	—	—	13·1	4,160	SW
46,898	4,929	20,591	531	587	4,862	430	3,448	10·4	32·3	¶22·9	2,873¹	UQ
46,872	146	13,924	661	657	3,822	509	2,922	8·2	39·6	33·5	2,038	7·9
46,718	179	20,402	536	520	4,133	482	3,962	8·8	22·0	21·0	2,989¹	14·6
46,325	17,549	49,093	290	315	Loss 14,674	998	Loss 8,637	—	—	—	1,763	SWZ
46,261	1,118	31,004	406	370	9,127	282	8,805	19·7	33·4	41·3	4,243	63·4
46,206	2,699	28,891	429	435	4,288	474	3,948	9·3	17·5	19·0	2,768¹	16·4
46,096	13,969	34,255	379	374	8,082	309	3,968	17·5	26·5	15·0	2,153¹	USA
46,058	0	5,864	895	897	1,244	828	980	2·7	24·2	23·1	1,932	6·7
46,006	19,410	20,583	532	479	1,589	784	721	3·5	10·0	5·0	2,598	IT
45,889	7,240	12,745	688	665	2,683	627	1,213	5·8	23·3	8·5	2,827	9·4
45,819	4,519	15,285	629	584	3,405	550	1,007	7·4	29·8	8·7	526	—⁴⁴
45,695	3,244	2,002	978	988	2,287	679	903	5·0	192·8	93·6	1,019	USA
45,637	75	12,416	701	847	2,619	635	1,378	5·7	39·2	22·7	1,264	8·3
45,631	2,786	1,949	979	968	220	955	589	0·5	11·9	¶31·8	1,037¹	L
45,391	—	8,125	830	819	2,730	623	2,215	6·0	37·8	33·1	15,248¹	7·8
45,362²⁷	1,320²⁷	14,397	650	831	4,533²⁷	458	3,143	10·0	38·0	45·0	2,292	9·3
45,332	89	8,782	802	844	1,443	796	1,030	3·2	21·5	¶15·3	953	1·7
45,265	3,321	7,258	854	740	43	972	Loss 721	0·1	0·5	—	2,952	3·0
45,200	4,916	23,130	484	527	5,252	407	2,534	11·6	28·4	13·7	3,802¹	12·7
45,130	21,204	24,821	462	469	5,291	402	3,010	11·7	24·9	18·9	5,193¹	11·0
45,014	1,141	11,657	722	—	2,640	630	1,179	5·9	42·5	22·1	1,255	8·3
44,855	23,865	28,561	431	377	4,397	470	1,478	9·8	14·6	5·0	842¹	USA
44,835	10,285	35,998	365	375	8,374	303	4,992	18·7	27·9	19·5	4,100	24·8
44,528	3,047	14,812	639	686	3,278	562	2,510	7·4	30·0	24·8	2,978	UQ

The following letters in the Market Capitalisation column denote unquoted companies and country of control: BAH = Bahamas.　IT = Italy.　L = Liechtenstein. SW = Sweden.　SWZ = Switzerland.　UQ = Unquoted.　USA = United States of America.

Rank by turn-over	COMPANY	Main activity	Chairman and Managing Directors (in italics) §‖	Accounting period ended
601 (668)	H. & J. Quick Group	Passenger & Commercial Vehicle Dlrs.	N. Quick (M.D.)	31–12–77
602 (616)	Hewlett-Packard	Electronic Apparatus Manufacturers	F. Mariotti, *D. P. Taylor*	31–10–77
603 (598)	Sandvik	Steel Products	G. V. L. Ollen	31–12–76
604 (599)	Willis Faber	Insurance Brokers	A. R. Taylor	31–12–77
605 (605)	British Vita Co.	Manfrs. of Polymeric Products, etc.	F. A. Parker	31–12–77
606 (670)	Corning	Glass Manufacturers	O. Ames	28–11–76
607 (611)	Blagden & Noakes (Holdings)	Steel Drum Manfrs. & Reconditioners	J. K. Noakes	1– 1–78
608 (537)	Westminster Dredging Group	Dredging Contractors	J. Kraaijeveld Van Hemert (*Chief Executive*)	31–12–74
609 (541)	Staflex International	Manfrs. of Fusible Interlinings, etc.	*W. P. Rao*	31–12–76
610 (406)	Holco Trading Co.	Produce Merchants	W. A. Davies, *I. E. J. Foster, C. C. B. Morris*	31–12–76
611 (594)	Howard Tenens Services	Distribution & Eng. Services	J. F. Swanborough, *D. F. F. Barrett*	31– 3–77
612 (678)	Lookers	Motor Vehicle Distbs. and Engineers	R. E. Tongue, *W. K. Martindale*	30– 9–77
613 (661)	Hollis Bros. & ESA	Timber, Sawmillers, Flooring Contrs.	G. S. Mitchell (M.D.)	31– 3–77
614 (580)	K Shoes	Manufacturers & Sale of Footwear	S. Crookenden, *G. O. Probert*	30– 9–77
615 (736)	St. Regis International	Cartons, Cases, Paper, etc.	Lord Robens, *H. L. Hazell*	31–12–77
616 (N/A)	E. G. Cornelius & Co.	Commodity Merchants	W. R. Pick	30– 6–75
617 (529)	Cruden Investments	Building Contractors	A. C. Bennett, *M. R. A. Matthews*	31– 3–77
618 (676)	Ruston-Bucyrus	Manfrs. of Excavators and Cranes	E. P. Berg, *W. B. Winter*	31–12–76
619 (633)	Saatchi & Saatchi Compton	Advertising Agency	J. K. Gill	30– 9–77
620 (629)	Adwest Group	Engineers, etc.	F. V. Waller (M.D.)	30– 6–77
621 (623)	Seddon Diesel Vehicles	Vehicle Manufacturers	H. Redmond, *G. J. Redmond, D. W. Redmond*	30– 6–76
622 (621)	Myson Group	Heating, Ventilating & Air Conditng.	R. E. Myson (M.D.)	31–12–77
623 (644)	James Miller & Partners	Bldg. & Civil Engineering	J. Miller (M.D.)	31–12–76
624 (662)	James Neill Holdings	Tool Manufacturers, General Engineers	J. H. Neill	31–12–77
625 (552)	Otis Elevator Co.	Lift & Escalator Manfrs.	G. N. Jennings, *J. N. Cunningham*	30– 9–76
626 (797)	Peugeot Automobiles UK	Motor Vehicle Distributors	P. Peugeot, *H. Hassid*	31–12–76
627 (596)	Hardy & Co. (Furnishers)	Retail House Furnishers	E. L. Datnow	2– 4–77
628 (554)	Reuters	International News Organisation	Lord Barnetson, *G. Long*	31–12–76
629 (660)	Fine Art Developments	Greeting Card Mfrs., Mail Order, etc.	F. R. Kerry, *D. T. Barnes*	31– 3–78
630 (619)	Pentos	Publishing, Building, Eng., etc.	T. A. Maher	31–12–77
631 (641)	Wolverhampton & Dudley Brws.	Brewers	E. J. Thompson (M.D.)	30– 9–77
632 (658)	Napier Brown & Co.	Sugar & Dried Fruit Merchants	F. Ridgwell	31–12–76
633 (814)	Marshall of Cambridge (Enrg.)	General Engineering	Sir Arthur Marshall	31–12–76
634 (643)	A. C. Cossor	Electronic Equipment, etc.	Lord Sherfield	30–11–76
635 (640)	Redfearn National Glass	Glass Container Manufacturers	J. L. C. Pratt (M.D.)	2–10–77
636 (523)	Barker & Dobson	Confectioners, Tobacconists, Grocers	R. W. Aitken	2– 4–77
637 (634)	BPM Holdings	Printers & Publishers	Sir Michael Clapham	2– 7–77
638 (681)	Parker Timber Group	Timber Mchts., Manfrs. of Timber Prods.	K. Whitby, *H. Sherwood*	31– 3–77
639 (562)	Clayton Dewandre Holdings	Vehicle Equipment Manufacturers, etc.	Lord Orr-Ewing, *J. W. Kinchin*	31–12–76
640 (613)	Barton & Sons	Tubing Manufacturers & Engineers	J. M. Wardle	31–12–77
641 (647)	Armour Foods (UK)	Meat and Food Importers	A. S. Drain, *J. G. Harlow*	31–12–77
642 (589)	Butterfield-Harvey	Engineering, Factoring, Processing	T. F. Honess	2– 4–77
643 (711)	A. Cohen & Co.	Metal Refiners, Non-ferrous Alloys	R. H. Cohen, *M. Pylkkanen, C. A. Cohen*	31–12–76
644 (590)	Ratcliffs (Great Bridge)	Brass & Copper Rolled Strip Manfrs.	F. R. Ratcliff (J.M.D.), *E. H. Ratcliff*	31–12–77
645 (615)	Associated Octel Company	Manfrs. & Sale of Antiknock Compounds	*W. C. Greaves*	31–12–76
646 (566)	Harland & Wolff	Shipbuilders & Engineers	Viscount Rochdale	31–12–74
647 (612)	G. D. Searle & Co.	Ethical Pharmaceuticals	W. M. Dixon Jnr.	31–12–76
648 (608)	Anderson Strathclyde	Mining & Industrial Eqpt. Mfrs.	R. H. Thorpe (M.D.)	31– 3–77
649 (675)	Christie-Tyler	Manfrs. of Furniture & Upholstery	G. M. Williams (M.D.)	30– 4–77
650 (510)	Mears Bros. Holdings	Civil Eng., Bldg. Contrs.	Sir George Middleton	30– 9–77

NOTES: *Total tangible assets less current liabilities (other than bank loans and overdrafts and future tax). †As percentage of capital employed at beginning of the year. ‡As at 14 July 1978. §Appendix on page 70 gives list of Managing Directors which cannot be fitted into the main text. ‖M.D. = Managing Director; J.M.D. = Joint Managing Director; A.C. = Acting Chairman. ¶As percentage of capital employed at the end of the year. N/A Not available. ¹UK only. ⁴⁵Work carried out for customers outside UK.

TURNOVER Total £000	Export £000	*CAPITAL EMPLOYED £000	Rank Latest year	Rank Previous year	NET PROFIT BEFORE INTEREST AND TAX Latest year £000	Rank	Previous year £000	% to turnover Latest year	†% to capital employed Latest year	Previous year	**No. of employees	‡Equity market cap. £M.
44,374	13	5,727	900	865	1,376	808	875	3·1	33·7	24·9	975	2·3
44,204	11,622	17,707	588	581	5,014	421	6,150	11·3	32·6	56·2	1,144	USA
44,100	5,195	24,887	461	444	3,522	526	2,831	8·0	15·3	13·9	2,146	SW
44,071	—	66,281	233	246	20,665	153	17,507	46·9	37·1	43·7	2,728[1]	104·0
44,042	1,848	21,123	521	574	6,679	351	4,504	15·2	42·0	34·3	2,635[1]	16·0
43,918	16,377	28,134	433	484	3,414	549	2,126	7·8	16·8	11·2	4,253[1]	USA
43,835	2,069	18,329	575	658	4,273	476	3,774	9·7	35·1	37·4	2,337[1]	13·6
43,790	—	44,167	317	290	79	965	2,923	0·2	0·2	9·0	2,703	H
43,551	5,242	16,909	602	561	4,441	466	3,119	10·2	34·6	23·7	1,568	1·3
43,423	—	2,173	973	970	500	915	371	1·2	28·2	26·9	—	H
43,365	452	17,823	584	529	442	929	Loss 234	1·0	2·4	—	2,831	3·7
43,280	162	9,882	776	854	1,726	765	1,365	4·0	26·9	25·0	1,090	5·0
43,226	1,653	18,231	576	663	3,303	558	1,840	7·6	27·4	11·7	2,649	5·4
43,147	3,527	17,998	583	571	2,414	660	2,099	5·6	15·0	15·7	5,680[1]	9·8
43,081	1,517	36,533	359	383	8,972	286	5,030p.a.	20·8	26·0	17·1p.a.	2,526	USA
43,060	25,382	1,678	988	—	468	924	524	1·1	23·8	¶26·7	—	UQ
42,961	—	3,851	938	923	1,448	795	839	3·4	38·9	21·3	2,888[1]	UQ
42,741	25,195	32,125	399	420	8,470	301	6,832	19·8	¶26·4	33·0	2,032	USA
42,627	—	1,780	983	981	1,211	832	1,015	2·8	83·1	¶69·6	521	5·7
42,461	5,800	21,551	513	533	6,020	371	4,690	14·2	32·9	32·0	3,694[1]	22·3
42,440	3,739	12,913	683	604	255	953	973	0·6	1·8	8·5	2,102[1]	USA
42,244	4,994	20,114	543	501	1,588	785	2,070	3·8	8·2	12·2	2,728[1]	6·2
42,208	—	14,286	653	704	3,213	567	2,428	7·6	28·3	27·0	2,496	UQ
42,140	15,058	42,201	329	326	5,255	406	3,575	12·5	14·1	10·9	4,580	17·9
42,108	10,619	17,143	599	556	4,321	473	4,074	10·3	23·2	38·3	3,765	USA
42,053	—	3,845	939	979	2,262	683	1,043	5·4	146·7	39·7	—	FR
41,928	0	24,459	468	441	905	873	2,285p.a.	2·2	3·8	11·1p.a.	2,577	6·4
41,921	—	10,854	745	688	2,781	614	1,293	6·6	35·2	18·3	2,203	UQ
41,869	2,000	19,691	555	606	5,342	400	4,239	12·8	37·5	33·6	2,800[1]	24·3
41,800	6,594	15,846	622	596	4,060	486	3,756	9·7	27·5	32·3	2,938[1]	13·5
41,762	0	30,152	416	439	5,949	374	5,268	14·2	24·7	24·4	4,742	33·5
41,600	14	606	993	997	187	958	122	0·4	50·8	18·1	—	UQ
41,348	3,072	11,351	732	804	1,149	842	989	2·8	12·1	12·6	2,718[1]	UQ
41,240	11,238	17,622	589	546	3,415	548	2,455	8·3	19·0	16·6	3,544[1]	USA
41,199	413	15,943	620	627	4,852	433	3,310	11·8	40·7	30·8	2,702	17·6
41,146	2,795	5,169	910	814	Loss 117	978	Loss 1,821	—	—	—	3,356	7·7
41,063	47	10,820	746	730	2,023	725	1,325	4·9	20·2	13·5	3,748[1]	6·7
41,062	153	16,617	606	685	3,051	592	2,198	7·4	27·9	24·2	1,391	5·8
40,946	4,366	19,652	556	496	3,069	587	3,332	7·5	18·2	20·2	4,472[1]	USA
40,865	2,138	20,645	528	492	3,964	495	3,731	9·7	19·9	24·4	2,663	10·5
40,769p.a.	201p.a.	6,323	882	874	530p.a.	911	544	1·3	8·3p.a.	13·6	169	USA
40,691	4,248	20,064	545	497	2,188	693	2,208	5·4	11·1	11·8	3,429[1]	8·6
40,667	4,597	12,485	696	748	2,539	·647	2,138	6·2	27·3	21·7	2,000	2·7
40,546	11,549	9,948	772	706	1,684	771	1,304	4·2	16·0	15·8	790[1]	4·2
40,423	—	32,021	401	367	7,197	331	5,822	17·8	23·0	16·7	2,782	UQ
40,345	6,220[45]	18,906	568	514	Loss 15,677	999	Loss 32,196	—	—	—	9,947	UQ
40,304	16,769	35,714	368	359	2,088	712	3,662	5·2	6·4	13·9	2,938	USA
40,254	9,034	27,728	435	425	3,629	522	3,995	9·0	14·2	17·0	4,267[1]	21·8
40,154	749	5,629	903	908	2,631	632	3,260	6·6	58·5	106·2	2·642	6·7
40,080	1,343	7,893	838	848	386	937	1,224	1·0	5·8	23·1	1,348	1·0

The following letters in the Market Capitalisation column denote unquoted companies and country of control: FR = France. H = Holland. SW = Sweden.
UQ = Unquoted. USA = United States of America.

Rank by turn-over	COMPANY	Main activity	Chairman and Managing Directors (in italics) §‖	Accounting period ended
651 (823)	Favor Parker	Animal Feed Manufacturers	H. G. Parker	31–12–76
652 (573)	M & R-Martini & Rossi	Wine Merchants	I. G. Cottle (M.D.)	31–12–75
653 (663)	Bemrose Corporation	Packaging, Printing & Publishing	G. C. Brunton	31–12–77
654 (578)	W. R. Grace	Manfrs. of Chemical Products	*P. R. Johnston*	31–12–76
655 (639)	Waring & Gillow (Holdings)	Retail Furnishers, Clothing Manfrs.	M. Cussins, *J. R. Cussins*	31– 3–77
656 (620)	Matthew Clark & Sons (Hldgs.)	Wine & Spirit Shippers & Merchants	F. W. Gordon Clark	30– 4–77
657 (824)	Smith Kline & French Labs.	Pharmaceutical Manufacturers	J. M. Weaver, *L. N. A. Flockhart*	30–11–77
658 (656)	Bambergers	Timber, etc. Importers, Builders Mchts.	C. D. Woodburn-Bamberger (J.M.D.), *(see page 70)*	31– 3–77
659 (N/A)	Polygram Leisure	Gramophone Record, etc. Distributors	S L. G. Gootlieb	31–12–76
660 (654)	Airfix Industries	Toys, Gen. Housewares, Packaging, etc.	R. R. M. Ehrmann (M.D.)	31– 3–77
661 (652)	British Tissues	Paper Manufacturers	R. V. Olsen, *F. Wilson*	1– 1–77
662 (677)	Sony (UK)	Distrbs. of Electrical Goods	*H. Okochi*	31–10–76
663 (689)	Pontin's[34]	Holiday Camp & Village Proprietors	Sir Fred Pontin (M.D.)	31– 3–77
664 (604)	Spear & Jackson Internl.	Mfrs. of Steel, Saws & Hand Tools	S. M. De Bartolome, *L. A. Grosbard*	31–12–77
665 (522)	Richardsons, Westgarth & Co.	Marine, Turbine, Electrical & Gen. Eng.	*G. E. Darwin*	31–12–77
666 (777)	Sidney C. Banks	Grain Merchants & Seed Specialists	J. B. Godber, *M. C. Banks, R. L. Banks*	31– 5–77
667 (653)	Walter Runciman & Co.	Shipping & Freight Agents, etc.	W. G. Runciman	31–12–77
668 (690)	Haverhill Meat Products	Bacon Curing	D. S. Sainsbury	6– 3–77
669 (702)	Silentnight Holdings	Bedding & Upholstery Manufacturers	T. Clarke, *H. Crowther, K. C. Murray*	28– 1–78
670 (786)	ERF (Holdings)	Commercial Vehicle Manufacturers	E. P. Foden (M.D.)	2– 4–77
671 (588)	R. G. Carter (Holdings)	Builders	S. H. Tuddenham (A.C.-M.D.)	31–12–77
672 (744)	Brown & Tawse	Steel & Tube Stckhldrs. & Engineers	S. D. Rae (M.D.)	31– 3–77
673 (723)	Reo Stakis Organisation	Hoteliers and Caterers, etc.	R. Stakis, *J. F. Loughray*	2–10–77
674 (648)	Samuel Osborn & Co.[48]	Special Steels, Eng. Tools, etc.	B. E. Cotton	30– 9–77
675 (724)	Batleys of Yorkshire	Cash & Carry Wholesalers	L. Batley, *A. R. G. McCullen*	30– 4–77
676 (601)	Sidlaw Industries	Jute Spinning & Manufacturing, etc.	Sir John Carmichael	30– 9–77
677 (781)	Black & Edgington	Mnfrs. of Tents, Marquees, Canvas Gds.	R. G. Duthie (J.M.D.), *D. G. Moodie*	31–12–77
678 (666)	Homfray & Co.	Carpet Manufacturers	D. E. Gillam, *C. Croft*	1–10–77
679 (694)	Consolidated Pneumatic Tool	Pneumatic Tool Manufacturers, etc.	K. Lall	31–12–76
680 (651)	Renwick Group	Motor & Fuel Disbn., Travel Agnts. etc.	C. W. Wilton, *K. E. Holmes*	2– 4–77
681 (799)	John Silver Holdings	Meat Importers & Wholesalers	J. Silver, *M. J. Silver*	3– 7–76
682 (664)	Colgate-Palmolive	Toilet & Domestic Cleaning Products	S. M. Ford (M.D.)	31–12–76
683 (773)	MAT Transport Intl Group	Transport & Ancillary Services	Sir Leonard Neal, *P. A. Kunzler*	30– 9–76
684 (638)	Carless, Capel & Leonard	Refiners of Hydrocarbon Solvents	J. T. Leonard	31– 3–78
685 (551)	Rionda, De Pass	Sugar Dealers	J. M. Fox, *R. M. Beatson*	31–12–76
686 (695)	Phoenix Timber Co.	Timber etc., Importers, Mchts, etc.	A. B. Gourvitch (M.D.)	31– 3–77
687 (757)	Leigh & Sillavan Group	Metal Merchants and Manufacturers	R. M. W. Tolson	31– 3–77
688 (682)	Ellis & Everard	Building Materials, Chemicals, Fuel	A. J. Everard	30– 4–77
689 (798)	T. Cowie	Motor Vehicle Dealers, Finance, etc.	T. Cowie (M.D.)	30– 9–77
690 (713)	William Grant & Sons	Distillers of Scotch Whisky, etc.	A. G. Gordon (M.D.)	31–12–77
691 (764)	Wigglesworth & Co.	Merchanting of Fibres & Machinery	J. Forsythe, *V. J. Landon*	30– 9–77
692 (669)	Bowthorpe Holdings	Electrical Engineers, etc.	*R. A. Parsons*	31–12–77
693 (725)	Collett, Dickenson, Pearce	Advertising Agency	J. W. Pearce, *F. B. Lowe*	31–12–77
694 (680)	Cam Gears	Motor Steering Gears	D. S. Leese, *R. A. Pinnington*	1– 1–77
695 (—)	J. Murphy & Sons	Building, Civil Engineering, etc.	J. Murphy, *J. Clifford*	31–12–76
696 (649)	United Gas Industries	Gas Appliances and Meters, etc.	H. T. Nicholson	3– 4–77
697 (835)	Moutafian Commodities	Commodity Merchants & Brokers	A. N. Moutafian	31–12–76
698 (778)	Siebe Gorman Holdings	Diving, Survival & Safety Eqpmt. etc.	G. C. D'Arcy Biss, *E. B. Stephens*	2– 4–77
699 (919)	York Trailer Holdings	Commercial Trailer Mfrs. & Marketers	F. W. Davies	31–12–77
700 (696)	Surridge Dawson (Holdings)	Newsagents, Booksellers, Stationers	G. P. C. Krayenbrink (*Board Chairman*) *(see page 70)*	2– 1–77

NOTES : *Total tangible assets less current liabilities (other than bank loans and overdrafts and future tax).   †As percentage of capital employed at beginning of the year.   ‡As at 14 July 1978.   §Appendix on page 70 gives list of Managing Directors which cannot be fitted into the main text.   ‖M.D. = Managing Director; J.M.D. = Joint Managing Director; A.C. = Acting Chairman.   ¶As percentage of capital employed at the end of the year.   N/A Not available.   ¹UK only.   ³⁴Now a sub. co. of Coral Leisure Holdings Ltd.   ⁴⁸Now a sub. co. of Aurora Holdings Ltd.

TURNOVER Total £000	Export £000	*CAPITAL EMPLOYED £000	Rank Latest year	Previous year	NET PROFIT BEFORE INTEREST AND TAX Latest year £000	Rank	Previous year £000	% to turnover Latest year	†% to capital employed Latest year	Previous year	**No. of employees	‡Equity market cap. £M.
40,031	—	4,623	919	950	1,371	809	546	3·4	52·7	22·5	258[1]	UQ
40,006	55	10,576	752	703	1,290	820	539	3·2	23·7	10·9	271	IT/SWZ
39,887	7,033	18,219	577	585	2,165	699	2,615	5·4	14·2	18·9	3,160[1]	7·8
39,811	15,919	12,392	703	650	7,362	330	4,372	18·5	64·8	41·2	1,351[1]	USA
39,779	804	16,091	614	605	3,097	581	2,860	7·8	21·6	24·6	3,512	15·3
39,735	235	9,317	786	821	2,229	688	1,869	5·6	31·1	25·7	296	6·2
39,661	10,214	24,714	467	599	11,103	250	3,739	28·0	76·0	30·2	1,034[1]	USA
39,520	0	12,832	685	708	2,403	663	1,243	6·1	22·9	13·6	818	4·8
39,477	1,965	9,423	784	—	359	941	1,359	0·9	3·8	¶14·2	1,618[1]	G
39,399	9,265	22,191	500	507	5,037	419	4,493	12·8	26·3	29·2	3,686	13·5
39,310	723	19,430	559	521	479	920	779	1·2	2·5	4·2	2,216[1]	UQ
39,070	2,347	8,272	825	787	1,668	774	1,042	4·3	20·2	16·5	760[1]	JAP
38,956	0	54,193	275	285	7,383	329	5,576	19·0	16·4	12·3	3,801[1]	—[34]
38,936	5,994	17,082	600	480	2,179	696	2,291	5·6	10·6	12·2	2,142[1]	6·4
38,805	1,726	15,869	621	572	2,152	703	2,528	5·5	13·4	17·0	2,835	8·0
38,680	474	3,972	932	951	644	891	579	1·7	25·3	29·0	144	2·3
38,650	2,762	45,637	308	301	5,024	420	4,084	13·0	12·5	13·5	1,924[1]	5·6
38,569	—	6,798	867	837	1,823	752	85	4·7	26·8	¶ 1·2	1,639	UQ
38,428	1,209	11,952	712	788	3,465	539	2,905	9·0	42·2	56·0	2,678	11·2
38,423	4,172	8,352	822	836	2,060	717	427	5·4	29·8	5·7	1,225[1]	7·9
38,280	130	5,703	901	896	440	930	970	1·1	8·6	21·9	2,905	UQ
38,112	119	15,984	618	677	3,630	521	2,611	9·5	31·9	24·8	1,041	9·6
38,108	0	12,947	681	701	1,943	736	1,616	5·1	17·9	16·0	4,212	10·6
37,971	5,119	30,447	411	426	4,491	464	3,892	11·8	17·6	19·1	1,795[1]	11·3
37,962	0	3,489	946	963	531	910	361	1·4	24·3	21·0	289	2·2
37,961	3,405	20,429	535	456	1,955	735	1,746	5·1	8·8	8·8	3,445[1]	5·0
37,928	5,838	22,623	489	580	3,399	551	2,391	9·0	21·7	21·2	3,306[1]	17·8
37,911	10,874	26,826	440	445	2,160	701	2,130p.a.	5·7	9·4	10·6p.a.	1,997[1]	6·9
37,849	10,211	32,009	402	430	6,627	354	5,753	17·5	25·7	27·3	1,903	USA
37,764	2,369	5,834	897	898	1,168	840	3	3·1	22·9	0·1	1,614[1]	2·2
37,704	3,104	2,040	976	985	757	881	415	2·0	55·5	¶30·4	160	UQ
37,661	6,324	16,066	615	618	2,231	687	2,556	5·9	16·4	16·5	1,302	USA
37,457p.a.	0	4,561	921	928	47p.a.	970	504	0·1	1·3p.a.	20·4	1,046[1]	UQ
37,386	5,702	11,595	725	722	2,053	719	3,084	5·5	20·2	35·2	332	12·6
37,342	0	1,770	985	845	1,024	859	1,177	2·7	15·4	26·0	—	USA
37,333	310	14,632	644	666	3,284	561	1,562	8·8	26·9	12·1	1,264[1]	4·4
37,224	2,199	3,681	942	960	250	954	329	0·7	8·4	14·4	152	UQ
37,157	295	10,603	751	774	1,424	801	1,328	3·8	16·7	16·5	1,063	6·1
37,054	0	12,093	710	727	2,311	674	1,739	6·2	23·4	18·9	915	4·7
36,919	12,571	38,030	348	395	7,014	340	5,406	19·0	21·8	18·9	812	UQ
36,885	692	4,485	924	914	1,059	851	1,045	2·9	24·9	33·0	—	UQ
36,881	6,351	22,344	495	510	6,158	368	5,680	16·7	32·3	36·4	2,081[1]	20·0
36,802	—	2,098	974	973	1,370	810	844	3·7	78·7	57·1	251[1]	1·8
36,782	14,896	8,005	834	652	4,775	439	3,681	13·0	38·8	27·2	2,385[1]	USA
36,707	—	8,407	817	—	965	869	1,385	2·6	11·0	¶15·8	3,153	UQ
36,662	3,988	16,099	613	579	2,085	714	1,818	5·7	13·3	11·8	3,522[1]	6·3
36,368	—	2,021	977	992	1,176	838	116	3·2	134·9	14·5	—	UQ
36,352	4,566	18,796	569	575	4,589	454	3,380	12·6	28·9	25·4	2,793	18·4
36,213	14,137	11,900	714	840	3,019	596	1,461	8·3	34·9	18·9	1,805[1]	6·3
36,192	—	2,904	954	961	1,145	843	863	3·2	48·8	47·2	819	UQ

The following letters in the Market Capitalisation column denote unquoted companies and country of control: G = Germany.   IT = Italy.   JAP = Japan.
SWZ = Switzerland.   UQ = Unquoted.   USA = United States of America.

Rank by turn-over	COMPANY	Main activity	Chairman and Managing Directors (in italics) §‖	Accounting period ended
701 (768)	Motherwell Bridge (Hldgs)	Heavy Engineering	A. B. Miller	31–12–76
702 (704)	Avon Cosmetics	Manufacturers of Cosmetics, etc.	H. Clark, *W. W. Wagner, B. D. Crosby*	31–12–76
703 (693)	Armitage Shanks Group	Sanitary Pottery & Fittings Mfrs.	K. Campbell, *K. L. Shanks, L. Clarke*	2– 4–77
704 (—)	Mothercat	Pipeline Contractors, etc.	N/A	31–12–76
705 (688)	Harris & Sheldon Group	Lifts, Kitchen Furniture, Advtg. Eqpmt.	J. D. Miller	31–12–77
706 (739)	John Waddington	Manfrs. of Games & Pastimes, Printers	V. H. Watson, *E. P. Rundle, J. Scott*	3– 4–77
707 (630)	Libby, McNeill & Libby	Canned Food Manufacturers	H. J. Thrall (M.D.)	3– 7–76
708 (610)	J. E. England & Sons (Wllgtn)	Produce Merchants & Growers	J. R. England (J.M.D.), *J. H. L. England*	31–12–77
709 (667)	Hopkinsons Holdings	Boiler Mountings, Valves etc. Manfrs.	I. G. Hopkinson, *J. F. Goulding*	27– 1–78
710 (816)	Ofrex Group	Office & Ed. Eqpt. Supplies, Indl. Fast.	G. Drexler, *A. G. Andrews*	31–12–77
711 (—)	Star Aluminium Co.	Mfrs. & Marketers of Aluminium Foil	Sir Richard Powell, *D. Fredjohn*	31–12–77
712 (942)	Esperanza Tde & Transport	International Services, Copper	Lord Kissin, *R. B. Loder*	31– 3–77
713 (700)	Hoveringham Group	Extraction & Processing of Aggregates	G. H. C. Needler	31–12–77
714 (674)	Ley's Foundries & Engrg.	Malleable Castings & Engineering	F. D. Ley	30– 9–77
715 (684)	Bentalls	Department Stores	J. D. Spooner, *L. E. Bentall*	28– 1–78
716 (982)	Burnett & Hallamshire Hldgs.	Constructions, Mining, Oil, etc.	N. F. Swiffen	31– 3–78
717 (635)	Brintons	Woven Carpet Manufacturers	Sir Tatton Brinton (J.M.D.) (*see page 70*)	3– 7–76
718 (628)	J. C. Bamford Excavators	Manfrs. of Hydr. Earth Moving Eqpmt.	A. P. Bamford (M.D.)	31–12–75
719 (715)	Joseph Stocks & Sons (Hldgs.)	Wholesale Provision Merchants	D. W. Ostenfeld	31– 3–77
720 (722)	Macmillan Bloedel Containers	Fibreboard Container Manufacturers	J. S. Adair, *R. B. Adamson*	31–12–76
721 (692)	Tilbury Contracting Group	Civil Eng., Bldg. & Public Wks. Contrs.	J. P. S. Edge-Partington, *C. Brand*	31–12–77
722 (642)	British Sidac	Transparent Cellulose Film Makers	P. S. C. Ellis, *F. Warren*	31–12–76
723 (831)	Anglo European Foods Group[35]	Frozen Food Wholesalers	C. I. Thompson	1– 1–77
724 (755)	Hanger Investments	Motor Dealers	P. D. Adams (M.D.)	31–12–77
725 (762)	Plantation Holdings	Light Eng., Scientific Inst., Plantations	K. R. Cork	31–12–77
726 (671)	Eaton	Engineers	Sir Leonard Crossland, *D. C. J. Grabham*	31–12–76
727 (N/A)	Pure Lard	Traders of Oil & Fat Products	I. S. Hutcheson	28– 3–76
728 (895)	Robinson & Sons	Surgical Dressing Manfrs. etc.	R. B. Robinson	1– 1–78
729 (—)	John M. Henderson & Co. (Hgs.)	Engineering	P. Alafouzo, *A. Jarratt*	30– 6–76
730 (701)	Ocean Wilsons (Holdings)	Shipping Services, Port Activities	Earl of Dartmouth	31– 1–77
731 (627)	Inver House Distillers	Whisky Distillers	K. J. Neuman	31–12–76
732 (772)	Agfa-Gevaert	Marketing of Sensitised Materials	A. Beken	31–12–76
733 (842)	Charles Barker ABH Intl.	Advertising Practitioners	J. V. Wellesley	31–12–77
734 (753)	Ault & Wiborg Group	Printer's Inks & Rollers, Paints, etc.	J. McLaren, *C. F. Strang, P. V. Clarke*	31–12–77
735 (883)	Van Leer (UK)	Packaging Manufacturers	P. J. Kleiweg de Zwaan, *J. C. Prichard*	31–12–76
736 (617)	Turriff Corporation	Engineering Contractors, etc.	W. G. Turriff, *P. S. Wormald*	31–12–77
737 (737)	UKO International	Ophthalmic Lens Mfrs. Catering Eqpmt.	G. C. D'Arcy Biss, *Sir Ian Morrow*	31– 3–77
738 (740)	J. Hepworth & Son	Multiple Tailors	R. E. Chadwick, *J. T. Rowlay*	31– 8–77
739 (920)	MFI Furniture Centres	Retailers of H'hold Furniture, etc.	A. C. Southon, *N. A. V. Lister, J. W. Seabright*	28– 5–77
740 (673)	Tunnel Holdings	Manfrs. of Cement & Allied Products	J. D. Birkin (M.D.)	27– 3–77
741 (698)	Galliford Brindley	Civil Engineering Contractors, etc.	P. Galliford	30– 6–77
742 (228)	Swan Hunter Group	Ship Repairers, Civil & Gen. Eng., Bldg.	Sir John Hunter, *T. McIver*	30– 6–77
743 (889)	Control Data	Computer Systems	J. H. Ward	30–11–76
744 (769)	Royal Worcester	Table & Ornamental Ware, Electronics	Sir Ronald Fairfield, *L. T. Davies, J. E. Herrin*	31–12–77
745 (763)	Corah	Mnfrs. & Distr. of Clothing & Fabrics	G. N. Corah (J.M.D.), *L. O. Helgeson*	30–12–77
746 (609)	Sena Sugar Estates	Sugar Production	Sir John Hornung	31–12–76
747 (687)	Austin Reed Group	Menswear Retailers & Manfrs.	B. St. G. A. Reed	31– 1–78
748 (780)	H. P. Bulmer Holdings[28]	Manufacturers of Cider, etc.	P. J. Prior, *G. B. Nelson*	29– 4–77
749 (828)	Reads	Metal Container Manfrs.	A. J. O. Axford	1–10–76
750 (790)	Siemens	Selling Org. for Siemens Products	H. M. Threlfall, *H. W. Vahl*	30– 9–77

NOTES: *Total tangible assets less current liabilities (other than bank loans and overdrafts and future tax). †As percentage of capital employed at beginning of the year. ‡As at 14 July 1978. §Appendix on page 70 gives list of Managing Directors which cannot be fitted into the main text. ‖M.D. = Managing Director; J.M.D. = Joint Managing Director; A.C. = Acting Chairman. ¶As percentage of capital employed at the end of the year. N/A Not available. [1]UK only. [28]Figures for latest and previous years relate to H.P. Bulmer Ltd. [35]Comparative figures are those of Anglo European Foods Ltd. [41]Excluding results of shipbuilding and marine engineering subs nationalised 1.7.77.

TURNOVER Total £000	Export £000	*CAPITAL EMPLOYED £000	Rank Latest year	Rank Previous year	Latest year £000	Rank	Previous year £000	% to turnover Latest year	†% to capital employed Latest year	Previous year	**No. of employees	‡Equity market cap. £M.
36,161	6,908	14,467	648	691	4,685	448	2,625	13·0	43·0	33·7	2,591[1]	UQ
36,149	5,327	9,113	791	765	4,416	467	5,280	12·2	44·3	46·8	2,180[1]	USA
36 120	4,653	21,036	523	534	2,779	615	3,227	7·7	15·2	18·9	3,138[1]	14·6
36,060	—	21,743	508	—	12,054	232	3,422	33·4	100·8	¶28·6	—	LEB
35,943	3,693	21,065	522	569	3,625	523	3,303	10·1	22·3	23·0	4,184[1]	13·1
35,814	2,240	19,190	563	586	3,863	505	2,117	10·8	25·4	15·2	3,238	11·9
35,526	1,502	11,327	734	679	1,085	850	Loss 63	3·1	8·1	—	774	SWZ
35,521	412	1,751	986	984	479	921	1,259	1·3	35·0	124·2	346	1·3
35,444	7,855	24,805	463	454	4,506	463	4,772	12·7	20·1	22·3	3,962[1]	11·8
35,434	8,110	20,706	526	610	4,096	485	2,323	11·6	29·4	18·8	2,569[1]	15·7
35,357	3,238	33,252	391	—	3,308	557	1,650	9·4	12·8	7·7	—	SWZ
35,242	3,653	13,707	666	719	5,726	379	3,097	16·2	56·1	56·2	1,329[1]	15·8
35,235	—	18,063	581	594	3,978	493	2,705	11·3	26·6	17·7	1,748	13·7
35,195	7,752	19,030	567	538	1,689	770	3,109	4·8	9·4	19·7	3,483	6·4
35,151	150	16,388	611	600	2,600	638	2,167	7·4	17·8	16·9	3,297	14·4
35,111	33	13,733	665	805	2,749	618	2,469	7·8	25·2	32·3	1,123	9·6
35,100	5,453	16,410	610	568	3,460	540	1,837	9·9	25·8	13·7	2,502	UQ
35,062	—	25,863	451	513	2,872	605	3,018	8·2	12·5	15·9	—	UQ
35,056	0	1,707	987	982	595	902	566	1·7	41·8	42·6	199	1·3
34,995	—	10,162	766	672	4,676	449	2,552	13·4	40·2	21·9	1,506	CAN
34,892	1,266	12,077	711	723	2,131	705	1,949	6·1	21·0	19·6	1,682	5·5
34,802	11,826	17,722	587	541	2,334	671	Loss 1,011	6·7	14·9	—	2,504[1]	B
34,684	—	2,399	967	989	576	903	381[35]	1·7	¶24·0	131·4	567	UQ
34,544	0	10,905	742	812	2,039	721	1,227	5·9	27·0	18·4	721	4·5
34,541	7,079	21,962	504	508	4,236	477	3,704	12·3	22·2	22·4	2,297[1]	3·3
34,433	19,512	30,208	415	408	4,739	440	2,780	13·8	17·4	11·5	4,884	USA
34,421	426	4,774	917	—	1,150	841	1,789	3·3	20·8	¶32·4	200	UQ
34,408	3,865	18,065	580	613	2,280	681	1,780	6·6	14·1	12·9	3,723	UQ
34,298	2,132	9,916	773	—	277	951	1,967p.a.	0·8	3·1	33·5p.a.	1,334[1]	USA
34,290	0	8,273	824	860	2,846	610	2,006	8·3	45·1	38·7	854	12·6
34,152	11,510	22,215	499	477	Loss 1,888	991	307	—	—	1·6	824	USA
34,133	—	11,202	736	678	1,045	856	675	3·1	9·2	6·4	847[1]	B/G
34,081	—	1,902	980	976	526	912	531	1·5	41·8	32·9	461[1]	UQ
33,928	2,001	12,299	705	716	2,441	657	2,248	7·2	23·6	23·4	1,617	7·4
33,906	3,281	11,055	738	735	3,054	591	129	9·0	31·1	1·3	1,963[1]	H
33,871	0	5,022	912	901	1,181	837	938	3·5	23·8	20·1	1,411[1]	3·2
33,737	3,257	21,897	506	547	4,977	423	3,682	14·8	28·7	24·5	3,440[1]	20·1
33,735	0	61,846	241	330	4,848	435	3,905	14·4	13·2	11·0	4,109	27·3
33,728	0	5,868	894	909	1,937	737	1,096	5·7	43·8	31·8	1,280	23·1
33,583	1,324	41,744	332	323	6,437	358	6,168	19·2	17·2	16·9	1,789	24·4
33,450	95	6,159	886	900	2,413	661	1,940	7·2	47·7	50·9	2,065	6·6
33,381[41]p.a.	3,432[41]p.a.	48,644	292	256	5,008[41]pa	422	4,633	15·0	9·6p.a.	8·2	3,500[1]	26·2
33,277	3,689	20,627	529	653	1,846	746	Loss 1,249	5·5	15·0	—	1,095	USA
33,177	7,111	21,709	509	481	1,599	783	2,331	4·8	7·8	16·5	4,599[1]	9·0
33,135	1,997	16,485	608	588	3,563	525	1,548	10·7	23·5	10·6	3,918	10·3
33,090	—	25,436	457	380	Loss 5,509	995	156	—	—	0·7	—	0·7
33,064	2,499	18,687	571	536	3,082	584	2,867	9·3	17·0	14·9	1,938	10·3
32,913	1,797	22,968	485	559	4,507	462	3,483	13·7	26·4	24·6	2,113[1]	12·6
32,695	230	15,985	617	659	2,818	611	770	8·6	23·2	6·6	—	USA
32,570	3,800	13,540	668	634	1,749	762	756	5·4	13·4	8·2	925	G

The following letters in the Market Capitalisation column denote unquoted companies and country of control: B = Belgium.   CAN = Canada.   G = Germany.
H = Holland.   LEB = Lebanon.   SWZ = Switzerland.   UQ = Unquoted.   USA = United States of America.

Rank by turn-over	COMPANY	Main activity	Chairman and Managing Directors (in italics) §‖	Accounting period ended
751 (N/A)	Colombo Commercial (Produce)	Produce Merchants		31–12–76
752 (789)	Booth (International Hldgs.)	Hide & Skin Merchants and Tanners	G. W. Wilks, *J. S. M. Booth*	31–12–77
753 (788)	Associated Paper Industries	Paper Manufacturers	K. L. Young, *J. A. Graham*	1–10–77
754 (697)	Richards & Wallington Inds.	Plant Hirers	W. R. Richards (M.D.)	31–12–77
755 (749)	Lister & Co.	Textile Manufacturers	I. E. Kornberg, *J. A. Kornberg, M. H. E. Dracup*	31– 3–77
756 (857)	Fenwick	Department Stores	J. Fenwick, *J. J. Fenwick*	28– 1–77
757 (782)	Greene, King & Sons	Brewers, Maltsters, Wine & Spirit Mchts	Sir Hugh Greene, *W. J. Bridge*	1– 5–77
758 (821)	Gieves Group	Motor Dealers, Tailoring, Book Manfg.	M. E. A. Keeling	31– 1–78
759 (—)	National Panasonic (UK)	Importers of Electrical Goods	A. Imura	20– 9–77
760 (708)	Reader's Digest Association	Publishers	*V. Ross*	30– 6–77
761 (602)	Rexmore	Textiles, Timber & PVC Products, etc.	A. Rosenblatt, *M. Rosenblatt*	31– 3–77
762 (750)	G. Percy Trentham	Building & Civil Eng. Contractors	G. D. Trentham	31–12–76
763 (776)	George Mellis & Son	Grocers	D. W. Mellis	30– 4–77
764 (—)	Akzo Chemie UK (Holdings)	Chemical Manufacturers	Dr. E. M. Hunt (M.D.)	31–12–76
765 (707)	Percy Bilton	Prop. Inv. & Devmt., Bldg. & Civil Eng.	P. Bilton (M.D.)	31–12–77
766 (801)	Frederick Parker	Engineers	F. W. H. Parker, *K. J. Parker*	30– 9–77
767 (827)	Concentric	Controls & Assemblies for Industry	D. F. Dodd	1–10–77
768 (683)	Ferguson Industrial Hldgs.	Bldrs' & Plumrs' Mchts., Ironmongery, etc.	D. S. Vernon	28– 2–77
769 (787)	LWT (Holdings)[14]	ITA Programme Contractors	J. Freeman	24– 7–77
770 (783)	Ruberoid	Bituminous Building Materials, etc.	T. Kenny, *J. A. Roberts*	31–12–77
771 (685)	Reed & Smith Holdings[47]	Paper Manufacturers, etc.	D. Harrison	31–12–76
772 (808)	Hercules Powder Co.	Chemical Manufacturers	*E. G. Bruce*	30–11–77
773 (735)	D. C. Thomson & Co.	Printers & Publishers	B. H. Thomson	31– 3–77
774 (754)	Weetabix	Manfrs. of Breakfast Cereal Foods	W. A. George (M.D.)	31– 7–77
775 (714)	Luncheon Vouchers	Luncheon Voucher Service	B. K. Beaumont, *J. R. Hack*	31–12–76
776 (858)	MK Electric Holdings	Manfrs. of Electric Plugs, Sockets, etc.	D. L. M. Robertson, *L. G. Hazzard*	2– 4–77
777 (859)	Arlington Motor Holdings	Motor Dealers, etc.	N. C. N. Housden, *J. M. Heywood*	31– 3–77
778 (998)	Aurora Holdings	General & Precision Engineers	R. Atkinson, *A. A. Watt*	31–12–77
779 (726)	Redman Heenan International	Specialised Engineering Products	A. Murray	30– 9–77
780 (925)	Lancer Boss Group	Fork Lift Truck Mfrs. & Distributors	G. N. Bowman-Shaw	31– 3–78
781 (807)	Ransomes, Sims & Jefferies	Machinery Manfrs. & Property Devlprs.	G. W. Bone, *R. L. Dodsworth*	31–12–77
782 (717)	Carborundum Co.	Mnfrs. of Abrasives, Resistant Mats.	K. A. Mack, *T. A. Egan*	31–12–76
783 (716)	Johnson & Johnson	Surgical & Baby Products Manfrs., etc.	*A. M. Quilty, P. McKenna*	2– 1–77
784 (738)	Derek Crouch	Opencast Mining, Civil Eng., Bldg. Cnst.	D. C. H. Crouch	31–12–77
785 (826)	Manganese Bronze Holdings	Castings, Components, Bldg. Prods., etc.	R. Dennis Poore	31– 7–77
786 (—)	W. J. Oldacre (Holdings)	Animal Feed Manufacturers	W. J. Oldacre	31– 5–77
787 (719)	Telephone Rentals	Communication & Alarm Equipment	E. H. Cooper, *R. A. Sly*	31–12–77
788 (497)	Walmsley (Bury) Group	Papermaking & Pulp Machinery Manfrs.	A. Green, *H. K. Horne*	30– 9–77
789 (921)	Garner Scotblair	Tanners & Leather Manfrs.	Sir Kenneth Newton (M.D.)	31– 1–78
790 (846)	Allied Textile Companies	Textiles	J. E. Lumb	30– 9–77
791 (745)	Textron	Manfr. of Ball Bearings, Zips, Pens, etc.	J. B. Collinson, *R. P. Straetz*	30–11–76
792 (785)	Henry Wigfall & Son	Multiple Shop Retlrs. of Elec. Goods	F. C. B. Morrell, *R. W. Morrell*	2– 4–77
793 (775)	Valor Co.	Makers of Heat Apparatus, Engineers	M. Montague, *R. J. Ing, K. R. Stockwell*	31– 3–77
794 (732)	Ellis & Goldstein (Holdings)	Wholesale Manfrs. of Coats, Costumes	W. Goldstein, *B. Barnett*	31– 1–78
795 (991)	Roussel Laboratories	Pharmaceutical & Chemical Products	J. G. Machizaud, *G. E. Powderham*	31–12–77
796 (791)	Bellway Holdings	Building, Devmt. & Property Invest.	J. Bell, *K. Bell*	31– 7–77
797 (849)	Towers & Co.	Wholesale Distrbs. of Meat & Poultry	J. B. Buxton	1–10–76
798 (—)	Montedison (UK)	Plastic Raw Materials, etc.	*F. G. Pace*	31–12–76
799 (705)	Citroen Cars	Vehicle Importers & Distributors	L. Garbe, *P. M. Belin*	31–12–75
800 (968)	Ryland Vehicle Group	Vehicle Distributors	W. J. Whale	30– 4–77

NOTES: *Total tangible assets less current liabilities (other than bank loans and overdrafts and future tax). †As percentage of capital employed at beginning of the year. ‡As at 14 July 1978. §Appendix on page 70 gives list of Managing Directors which cannot be fitted into the main text. ‖M.D. = Managing Director; J.M.D. = Joint Managing Director; A.C. = Acting Chairman. ¶As percentage of capital employed at the end of the year. N/A Not available. ¹UK only. ¹⁴Previous year figures extracted from statement for Stock Exchange purposes. ⁴⁷Now a sub. co. of St. Regis International Ltd.

TURNOVER Total £000	Export £000	*CAPITAL EMPLOYED £000	Rank Latest year	Previous year	NET PROFIT BEFORE INTEREST AND TAX Latest year £000	Rank	Previous year £000	% to turnover Latest year	†% to capital employed Latest year	Previous year	No. of **employees	‡Equity market cap. £M.
32,542	17	571	996	—	116	962	101p.a.	0·4	36·4	¶31·7p.a.	—	BAH
32,490	3,886	7,874	840	859	1,343	815	1,473	4·1	21·0	32·1	799¹	2·3
32,462	2,263	10,420	758	756	2,157	702	Loss 4	6·6	23·9	—	1,429¹	6·6
32,441	3,554	36,524	360	334	4,894	429	4,051	15·1	13·8	12·1	2,414¹	11·5
32,382	2,792	20,348	537	531	396	936	Loss 30	1·2	2·2	—	4,048¹	7·4
32,209	0	14,841	637	646	2,866	607	2,187	8·9	22·9	25·0	2,354¹	UQ
32,178	0	17,307	596	616	3,736	514	3,059	11·6	27·3	22·1	1,388	27·5
32,092	3,303	9,992	770	808	1,462	793	995	4·6	18·8	14·5	1,632¹	3·3
32,010	693	5,007	913	—	3,274	564	820	10·2	146·4	¶36·7	135¹	JAP
31,842	2,395	7,744	847	826	1,708	766	1,759	5·4	24·1	26·4	1,133¹	USA
31,831	3,014	8,677	807	789	1,620	781	1,917	5·1	19·7	20·4	1,616	5·5
31,781	—	6,706	871	879	871	876	1,298	2·7	14·4	27·1	1,679¹	UQ
31,731	9	3,888	936	935	603	900	498	1·9	18·0	23·7	790¹	UQ
31,697	12,800	14,398	649	—	3,035	594	768	9·6	43·9	13·0	809¹	H
31,692	0	60,270	247	235	7,453	326	6,991	23·5	12·8	12·7	1,041	64·6
31,633	23,143	19,816	550	565	5,290	403	5,896	16·7	31·9	56·5	1,667¹	UQ
31,540	3,531	9,645	779	786	2,438	658	2,193	7·7	29·4	29·7	2,398	7·9
31,468	270	9,081	793	753	1,580	787	1,103	5·0	21·4	24·5	1,247	7·9
31,453	1,558	20,432	534	526	5,642	382	4,714	17·9	30·5	¶25·5	1,339	19·3
31,440	2,038	8,293	823	816	986	864	834	3·1	13·4	12·2	1,670	3·8
31,406	835	9,886	775	729	736	883	213	2·3	7·8	2·6	1,572	3·4
31,392	8,117	13,033	678	744	3,430	544	3,000	10·9	36·4	41·1	406	USA
31,365	1,346	29,690	419	412	6,920	342	5,758	22·1	25·9	23·9	2,962	UQ
31,311	3,305	17,394	594	683	1,559	789	4,082	5·0	14·0	42·6	1,719¹	UQ
31,230	99	574	995	995	383	938	384	1·2	90·3	91·2	—	UQ
31,228	5,785	21,148	520	562	6,097	370	2,473	19·5	36·2	14·9	4,422¹	28·9
31,224	195	6,105	890	833	1,285	823	1,009	4·1	18·4	15·8	933	5·2
31,139	4,350	17,592	590	660	3,082	583	1,994p.a.	9·9	25·4	28·0p.a.	2,272	18·5
31,110	8,325	10,071	768	778	2,730	624	2,329	8·8	32·3	26·6	2,517¹	8·5
31,088	19,485	11,794	717	861	4,378	471	2,894	14·1	54·8	45·9	981¹	UQ
31,046	8,906	31,196	405	402	3,211	568	2,848	10·3	12·9	13·5	2,772¹	8·4
31,022	8,347	19,740	553	528	5,194	413	4,234	16·7	28·1	29·3	2,919	USA
30,940	6,266	19,785	552	551	3,176	571	2,506	10·3	18·4	17·1	2,300	USA
30,854	0	11,601	724	767	2,397	664	1,617	7·8	26·9	21·5	1,970	9·0
30,836	3,856	15,250	630	631	3,467	536	1,938	11·2	26·4	16·4	2,555	7·9
30,789	—	2,655	962	—	637	892	226	2·1	38·7	¶13·7	240	UQ
30,778	442	39,082	344	340	9,559	277	9,253	31·1	27·1	29·1	1,936¹	53·2
30,763	5,563	22,699	488	489	2,549	646	4,293	8·3	10·5	19·2	1,565¹	USA
30,759	11,200	8,429	814	856	1,586	786	1,378	5·2	24·7	38·0	886	4·1
30,697	7,965	12,429	699	694	3,002	599	2,126	9·8	27·9	21·7	2,370	9·7
30,683	9,127	25,940	450	438	2,391	666	3,226	7·8	9·9	16·2	3,750¹	USA
30,647	0	20,255	540	482	2,415	659	2,752	7·9	11·9	12·1	2,715	11·8
30,635	3,107	11,328	733	671	1,890	740	1,617	6·2	16·2	13·7	2,444¹	4·5
30,594	4,308	8,894	799	771	1,287	822	980	4·2	15·0	11·8	4,418	5·6
30,594	9,700	21,593	511	624	2,975	600	2,696	9·7	15·4	20·0	947¹	G
30,590	103	34,918	373	457	1,325	818	3,620	4·3	5·9	16·0	1,439¹	16·5
30,553	2,990	3,748	940	948	419	932	503	1·4	¶11·2	19·9	—	NZ
30,433	210	15,651	623	—	1,769	760	506	5·8	20·2	12·1	—	IT
30,336	621	8,408	816	780	600	901	Loss 827	2·0	10·7	—	237¹	FR
30,276	220	5,962	892	907	1,363	811	804	4·5	30·3	22·0	691	UQ

The following letters in the Market Capitalisation column denote unquoted companies and country of control: BAH = Bahamas. FR = France. G = Germany. H = Holland. IT = Italy. JAP = Japan. NZ = New Zealand. UQ = Unquoted. USA = United States of America.

Rank by turn-over	COMPANY	Main activity	Chairman and Managing Directors (in italics) §‖	Accounting period ended
801 (832)	W. Canning	Electrical & Mechanical Engineers	A. R. Houseman, *B. Tromans*	31–12–77
802 (886)	Carnation Foods Co.	Manfrs. of Evaporated Milk, etc.	A. L. Merry	30– 9–76
803 (892)	Highland Distilleries	Malt Whisky Distillers	J. A. R. MacPhail, *J. M. Goodwin*	31– 8–77
804 (712)	Cincinnati Milacron	Manfrs. of Machine Tools, etc.	C. R. Meyer, *J. G. Campbell*	1– 1–77
805 (743)	Alfred Booth & Co.	Builders and Developers, etc.	R. H. Amis	31–12–76
806 (796)	Walter Lawrence	Building Contractors, etc.	B. J. Prichard	30– 6–77
807 (709)	Lin-Pac Containers	Packaging Manufacturers	H. E. Cornish (M.D.)	31–12–75
808 (851)	J. & J. Dyson	Refractory Mats. & Fire Resisting Gd.	G. A. Lomas, *E. Bales, F. J. Houghton*	31– 3–77
809 (834)	Time Products	Horological & Assoc. Activities	M. J. Margulies	31– 1–78
810 (710)	Fluor (England)	Engineers & Constructors	H. W. Sorensen, *T. S. Arkell*	31–10 75
811 (833)	Crest Nicholson	Housing, Leisure & Engineering	D. L. Donne	31–10–77
812 (951)	Stanley Tools	Hand Tool Manufacturers	S. H. Davies (M.D.)	29–10–76
813 (803)	Sandoz Products	Dyestuffs, Chemicals & Pharmctls.	F. H. Talbot	31–12–77
814 (720)	Caffyns	Retail Motor Industry	Sir Edward Caffyn (*see page 70*)	31– 3–77
815 (721)	Star Paper	Paper Manufacturers	T.-E. Lassenius, *E. V. Olander*	31–12–76
816 (761)	Brittains	Fine Papermakers, etc.	K. R. Latchford, *S. Mallinson*	31–12–77
817 (853)	Unwins Wine Group	Off Licence Operators	M. A. Wetz, *R. J. A. Rotter, M. J. C. Wetz*	28– 2–77
818 (882)	Holt Lloyd International	Mfrs. of Car-Care Products, etc.	T. Heywood (M.D.)	25– 2–78
819 (795)	Spirax-Sarco Engineering	Specialists in Fluid Control Eqpmt.	A. C. Brown (M.D.)	31–12–77
820 (890)	Bullough	Engineering	B. P. Jenks, *D. B. Battle*	31–10–77
821 (837)	Parkland Textile (Holdings)	Worsted Combers, Spinners & Manfrs.	J. L. Hanson, *B. J. Spencer*	3– 3–78
822 (913)	Pfizer	Chemical & Pharmaceutical Mfrs.	F. Goulding (M.D.)	30–11–77
823 (875)	East Lancashire Paper Group	Paper Manufacturers, etc.	C. G. Seddon, *J. C. Seddon*	31–12–77
824 (779)	Pioneer Concrete (Holdings)	Concrete Manufacturers	R. F. Crocker (M.D.)	30– 6–77
825 (845)	Maynards	Confectioners	H. P. Salmon (J.M.D.), *R. W. Ramsdale*	25– 6–77
826 (843)	Letraset International	Type Transfer & Instant Lettering	W. Fieldhouse	30– 4–77
827 (806)	Laurence Scott	Elect. Machinery & Control Gear Mfrs.	P. M. Tapscott, *W. McCraith*	31– 3–77
828 (903)	Triplex Foundries Group	Foundries, Engineering, etc.	R. Harrison (M.D.)	31– 3–77
829 (746)	Short Brothers	Aircraft & Missile Manfrs.	D. Bryars, *H. G. Kirkman*	31– 8–76
830 (N/A)	Forth Wines	Wholesale Wine & Spirit Merchants	A. A. Muirhead, *P. T. Bell*	30– 9–76
831 (728)	Caltex (UK)	Petroleum Distributors	W. E. Tucker, *S. Hollin*	31–12–76
832 (805)	Guardian & Manchester Ev. Ns.	Newspaper & Magazine Publishers	P. W. Gibbings	2– 4–77
833 (861)	Addressograph-Multigraph	Office Machinery Manufacturers	*H. H. Egginton*	30– 6–77
834 (817)	Sketchley	Dry Cleaning, Overall Service, Textls.	G. Wightman	1– 4–77
835 (811)	Warburtons	Bakers, Manufacturing & Wholesale	H. D. Warburton, T. H. Warburton, *J. P. Speak*	24–09–77
836 (950)	P. Leiner & Sons	Gelatine Manufacturers	L. Leiner, *E. A. Osman, M. R. Leiner*	31–03–77
837 (741)	Robert Horne & Co.	Paper Merchants	K. E. Horne, *M. T. Bairstow, W. D. Musgrove*	30– 9–76
838 (—)	Prosper De Mulder	Animal By-Product Manufacturers	P. F. De Mulder	31– 3–77
839 (830)	Minet Holdings	Insurance Brokers	J. Wallrock	31–12–77
840 (862)	Clifford Motor Components	Component Manufacturers	L. J. Tebodo, *L. T. Davies, J. E. Herrin*	
841 (747)	Borden (UK)	Mfrs. of Synthetics	H. A. Collinson, *K. M. Cole*	31–12–76
842 (748)	Pattullo, Higgs & Co.	Agricultural Merchants	J. D. Langlands (M.D.)	30– 6–76
843 (904)	Aaronson Bros.	Veneer Merchants	Chairmanship rotates between certain Dirs.	30– 9–77
844 (774)	J. & W. Henderson (Holdings)	Building Trades' Merchants	G. L. Grant (J.M.D.), *J. Duncan*	31– 3–77
845 (952)	Macmillan	Publishers	M. V. Macmillan, *F. H. Whitehead*	31–12–76
846 (793)	Wagon Industrial Holdings	Materials Handling, Transport, Eng.	C. L. Smith	31– 3–77
847 (N/A)	E. M. Denny (Holdings)	Meat Importers, etc.	J. F. L. Denny	02–10–76
848 (840)	Mettoy Co.	Toy Manufacturers	A. Katz, *P. H. Katz*	31–12–77
849 (931)	Reardon Smith Line	Shipping	C. R. Chatterton	31– 3–77
850 (751)	Danepak	Bacon Processors	J. Esp. Sorensen, *B. Robinson*	27– 9–75

NOTES: *Total tangible assets less current liabilities (other than bank loans and overdrafts and future tax). †As percentage of capital employed at beginning of the year. ‡As at 14 July 1978. §Appendix on page 70 gives list of Managing Directors which cannot be fitted into the main text. ‖M.D. = Managing Director; J.M.D. = Joint Managing Director; A.C. = Acting Chairman. ¶As percentage of capital employed at the end of the year. N/A Not available. ¹UK only.

TURNOVER Total £000	Export £000	*CAPITAL EMPLOYED £000	Rank Latest year	Rank Previous year	NET PROFIT BEFORE INTEREST AND TAX Latest year £000	Rank	Previous year £000	% to turnover Latest year	†% to capital employed Latest year	Previous year	No. of **employees	‡Equity market cap. £M.
30,273	4,436	12,859	684	791	1,864	742	1,376	6·2	22·1	17·3	1,905	6·9
30,224	6,360	11,484	728	801	2,309	675	801	7·6	22·1	8·3	572	USA
30,200	1,161	23,550	477	535	3,830	508	2,868	12·7	21·1	17·4	291	33·3
30,178	11,612	21,835	507	473	2,864	608	3,094	9·5	13·7	15·4	2,365[1]	USA
30,117	178	6,135	889	862	1,605	782	1,766	5·3	25·6	32·6	2,209[1]	UQ
30,046	23	8,816	801	829	1,573	788	1,509	5·2	22·5	21·4	1,483[1]	3·5
30,007	545	16,538	607	566	4,118	483	3,074	13·7	36·3	40·2	1,540[1]	UQ
29,930	9,054	15,491	626	617	2,972	601	1,656	9·9	21·8	14·1	2,219	7·9
29,904	793	14,178	657	697	4,017	490	3,045	13·4	37·5	38·7	1,059[1]	24·2
29,807	1,080	5,874	893	875	3,224	566	1,872	10·8	135·3	71·9	898	USA
29,726	10,452	10,442	757	760	2,098	709	1,501	7·1	23·6	15·8	1,353[1]	8·9
29,660	10,766	19,137	566	543	3,399	552	2,523	11·5	19·2	17·3	2,169[1]	USA
29,503	3,759	12,401	702	654	2,359	668	1,723	8·0	19·2	15·8	901	SWZ
29,481	60	8,358	821	783	973	868	961	3·3	12·4	17·6	1,643	3·6
29,464	2,973	12,207	708	656	1,036	857	206	3·5	9·4	1·8	1,276	FIN
29,441	6,950	14,105	658	645	1,558	790	1,175	5·3	12·4	10·4	1,778	3·7
29,403	0	2,772	958	955	486	918	398	1·7	19·8	19·1	868[1]	UQ
29,393	3,311	8,376	819	851	3,017	597	2,185	10·3	46·1	37·7	708[1]	15·2
29,269	5,224	20,147	542	564	5,519	391	4,686	18·9	33·0	34·6	1,780[1]	32·8
29,227	4,328	12,685	691	714	3,210	569	2,268	11·0	31·0	31·7	2,061	12·5
29,194	7,493	13,809	663	693	2,742	619	2,357	9·4	25·4	31·9	1,918	4·8
28,972	9,543	35,780	366	381	3,465	538	3,552	12·0	11·4	11·9	1,507	USA
28,867	862	9,144	790	746	1,424	800	437	4·9	15·2	5·7	1,674	2·9
28,864	—	8,143	829	855	2,136	704	1,557	7·4	33·3	27·1	546	AUS
28,687	1,277	6,492	878	880	1,650	779	1,098	5·8	28·8	21·8	1,998[1]	6·0
28,671	5,820	12,761	687	700	6,819	348	4,697	23·8	64·2	58·7	1,205	41·6
28,613	3,816	16,737	603	611	3,087	582	1,617p.a.	10·8	22·2	11·6p.a.	3,987[1]	9·8
28,596	443	9,165	789	800	2,371	667	1,788	8·3	29·8	24·2	2,941	7·3
28,564	18,481	20,283	539	460	Loss 3,977	994	Loss 3,435	—	—	—	6,166[1]	UQ
28,547	—	577	994	—	172	960	85	0·6	49·4	29·2	—	UQ
28,439	7,587	7,776	845	777	Loss 228	981	Loss 254	—	—	—	152[1]	USA
28,239	731	7,152	857	785	73	966	597	0·3	0·9	6·8	2,622	UQ
28,185	7,300	14,792	640	635	Loss 64	977	Loss 1,157	—	—	—	2,652	USA
28,137	1	13,184	673	649	2,623	634	2,262	9·3	21·1	20·7	5,439[1]	16·5
28,120	75	7,110	859	850	1,087	849	1,443	3·9	16·5	22·3	3,476	UQ
27,892	14,197	12,627	694	818	1,975	731	1,781	7·1	21·6	24·4	734[1]	UQ
27,875	153	4,302	926	912	562	906	255	2·0	13·9	8·5	373	UQ
27,857	5	6,546	877	—	2,115	707	1,985	7·6	41·4	37·2	731	UQ
27,787	—	32,284	398	458	15,026	197	12,710	54·1	68·2	75·9	1,314	98·0
27,775	3,913	14,211	654	591	4,053	489	2,852	14·6	27·0	22·9	2,757	USA
27,752	4,218	12,698	689	640	2,174	697	1,389	7·8	27·9	20·7	1,356[1]	USA
27,746	1,381	3,532	944	929	292	949	366	1·1	10·1	17·9	231	UQ
27,612	6,286	18,004	582	593	3,417	547	2,751	12·4	22·8	21·1	874[1]	13·6
27,570p.a.	0	6,143	887	906	1,049p.a.	853	1,105	3·8	23·0p.a.	33·4	480	5·5
27,552	7,185	11,680	719	751	3,420	546	2,402	12·4	37·5	29·5	679[1]	UQ
27,548	6,068	13,158	674	674	2,740	620	2,824	9·9	24·1	22·9	2,205[1]	11·8
27,546	116	6,813	866	—	849	877	340	3·1	14·1	7·4	568	AUS
27,496	11,368	12,965	680	668	3,129	576	2,818	11·4	26·7	31·5	3,223	9·3
27,481[9]	—	80,854	208	244	Loss 857	986	1,702	—	—	4·6	514[1]	4·1
27,477	—	5,821	898	877	356	942	124	1·3	7·8	2·8	989[1]	DEN

The following letters in the Market Capitalisation column denote unquoted companies and country of control: AUS = Australia.　DEN = Denmark.　FIN = Finland.
SWZ = Switzerland.　UQ = Unquoted.　USA = United States of America.

Rank by turn-over	COMPANY	Main activity	Chairman and Managing Directors (in italics) §‖	Accounting period ended
851 (963)	Cowan, De Groot	Toy & Fancy Goods, Electrical Dealrs.	D. Cowan (J.M.D.), *I. Williams*	30– 4–77
852 (866)	Keep Brothers	Confirming House	P. G. Lloyd (M.D.)	30– 9–77
853 (924)	H. Brammer & Co.	Transmission Belting, Bearing Distbn.	J. E. Head	31–12–77
854 (947)	James Latham	Timber Importers & Merchants	E. M. L. Latham (*see page 70*)	31– 3–77
855 (829)	Bulmer & Lumb (Holdings)	Worsted Spinners	J. H. Nunnerley, *Sir William Bulmer*	02– 4–78
856 (929)	Cee-N-Cee Supermarkets	Supermarket Proprietors	J. A. M. Humphreys	31–12–76
857 (759)	CBS United Kingdom	Records & Music	*M. L. Oberstein*	31–10–75
858 (760)	Pork Farms	Manufacturers of Meat Products	D. C. Samworth, *G. B. Skelston*	26– 2–77
859 (907)	Brit. Steam Specialties Grp.	Pipeline Equipment Suppliers	Mrs H. P. Waudby, *R. Sellick*	31– 3–77
860 (860)	Deritend Stamping Co.	Forgings, Pressings, Castings, Elects.	C. W. Perry, *D. J. Mead*	28– 2–78
861 (—)	Strong & Fisher (Holdings)	Clothing & Fashion Leather Tanners	E. D. G. Davies, *R. J. Strong*	31– 5–77
862 (765)	Crane	Fluid Control Equip. Manfrs.	L. V. Chater, *J. M. Fraser*	31–12–76
863 (871)	City Electrical Factors	Electrical Wholesalers & Manfrs.	R. E. Priestley (M.D.)	31– 3–76
864 (914)	Cyanamid of Great Britain	Pharmaceutical Products	S. M. Peretz, *J. H. Taylor*	30–11–76
865 (949)	Walter Alexander	Coachbuilding, Fuel Oil Distbn., etc.	W. Alexander, *W. R. Alexander*	31– 3–77
866 (820)	Office Cleaning Services	General Cleaning Contractors, etc.	W. G. Goodliffe, *D. H. G. Goodliffe*	31– 3–77
867 (—)	Alfa Romeo (Great Britain)	Motor Car Importers & Distributors	G. De Bona, *C. Cattaneo*	31–12–77
868 (888)	LEC Refrigeration	Refrigerator Manufacturers	C. R. Purley (J.M.D.), *E. A. Cowen*	31–12–77
869 (985)	Martonair International	Pneumatic Control Equipment Manfrs.	G. Godwin (J.M.D.), *R. C. Cartwright*	31– 7–77
870 (973)	Tullis Russell & Co.	Paper Manufacturers	D. F. O. Russell	31– 3–77
871 (813)	Tremletts Holdings	Engineering, Timber & Furniture	R. Smith, *D. J. Eccleston*	31– 3–77
872 (770)	Mixconcrete (Holdings)	Concrete & Building Material Supps.	J. Mackaness	30–11–77
873 (901)	R. Hostombe	Metals, Alloys & Minerals	R. E. Hostombe, *A. W. Quick*	31– 3–77
874 (975)	Unitech	Electronics, etc.	P. A. M. Curry	28– 5–77
875 (969)	Twinlock	Business Information Systems, etc.	A. K. L. Stephenson	3– 3–78
876 (927)	Midland News Association	Newspaper Proprietors	M. Graham, *L. J. Stallard*	31–12–77
877 (—)	United Sterling Corpn.	Plastics Raw Materials	Lord Plurenden	31–12–76
878 (928)	Tecalemit	Engineering	N. J. Bennett, *J. M. Bennett*	31– 3–77
879 (—)	Argos Distributors	Retailers	G. R. S. Tomkins, *T. V. McAuliffe, J. M. Phillips, Jr.*	6–11–76
880 (818)	Blackwood, Morton & Sons (Hgs)	Carpet & Rug Manufacturers	K. M. Hamilton (M.D.)	30– 6–77
881 (839)	Nabisco	Cereal, Biscuit & Cake Mix Manfrs.	R. E. Woodcock	30–11–76
882 (940)	Edwards Williams Hldgs.	Engineers	F. B. Williams	02–10–76
883 (815)	Gordon & Gotch Holdings	Exporters of Periodicals, Books, etc.	Sir Anthony Percival, *C. C. Goodall*	31– 3–77
884 (784)	Frankipile	Foundation Engineers	W. R. Rowland (M.D.)	31–12–75
885 (939)	Leopold Lazarus	Metal Merchants	F. A. Lissauer	31– 7–76
886 (—)	Brunning Group	Advertising Agency, etc.	G. B. Brunning (M.D.)	31– 3–78
887 (—)	Scotia Investments	Leisure Industry, Insce. Broking, etc.	C. F. Braun, *A. T. Dembeniotis, P. Frohlich*	31– 7–75
888 (937)	Lonsdale Universal	Printers & Stationers, etc.	N. G. Ramseyer, *A. K. W. Edwards*	30– 9–77
889 (885)	A. H. Philpot and Sons	Farming and Agricultural Products	H. R. Philpot	30– 9–76
890 (—)	William Leech (Builders)	House-Building & Development	J. Adamson, *J. R. Adamson*	28– 2–77
891 (948)	Diploma Investments	Electnc. Compts., Engineering, etc.	A. J. C. Thomas	30– 6–77
892 (995)	Fuerst Day Lawson Holdings	Commodity Merchants	Mrs. E. D. Lawson, *R. V. Neal*	31–12–76
893 (855)	James Beattie	Retail Department Stores	James Beattie (M.D.)	31– 1–78
894 (—)	Motorola	Car Radio Manufacturers, etc.	M. W. Larkin	31–12–76
895 (967)	James Burrough	Gin Distillers	A. Burrough	28– 2–78
896 (856)	Bodycote International	Textiles & Industrial Clothing, etc.	J. C. Dwek (M.D.)	31–12–77
897 (944)	Braid Group	Vehicle Distributors, etc.	D. C. Bamford, *W. C. G. Cartwright*	30– 9–77
898 (766)	Oliver Rix	Motor Distrs., Factors of Parts & Acc.	A. K. L. Stephenson, *A. M. Struthers*	30– 9–77
899 (—)	Wrigley Co.	Chewing Gum Manufacturers	*G. T. Morgan*	31–12–77
900 (—)	Longton Transport (Hldgs.)	Road Transport, Steel Stkhg., Veh. Dist.	A. J. Dale	31– 3–77

NOTES: *Total tangible assets less current liabilities (other than bank loans and overdrafts and future tax).   †As percentage of capital employed at beginning of the year.   ‡As at 14 July 1978.   §Appendix on page 70 gives list of Managing Directors which cannot be fitted into the main text.   ‖M.D. = Managing Director; J.M.D. = Joint Managing Director; A.C. = Acting Chairman.   ¶As percentage of capital employed at the end of the year.   N/A Not available.   ¹UK only.   ¹⁵Including inter-group sales.   ²¹Quotation suspended.

TURNOVER Total £000	Export £000	*CAPITAL EMPLOYED £000	Rank Latest year	Rank Previous year	NET PROFIT BEFORE INTEREST AND TAX Latest year £000	Rank	Previous year £000	% to turnover Latest year	†% to capital employed Latest year	†% to capital employed Previous year	No. of **employees	‡Equity market cap. £M.
27,459	621	8,455	813	884	2,070	716	1,441	7·5	37·2	35·9	659	8·6
27,422	—	2,679	959	964	840	878	556	3·1	38·8	38·9	—	UQ
27,405	1,675	12,444	698	754	4,577	455	3,212	16·7	50·6	43·1	1,423[1]	21·4
27,368	46	11,151	737	757	2,057	718	1,122	7·5	22·8	13·2	502[1]	3·4
27,340	1,770	6,948	863	828	2,288	678	1,629	8·4	32·6	26·4	1,582	4·9
27,296	0	3,452	947	967	3,452	541	507p.a.	2·6	37·1	44·5p.a.	1,086	UQ
27,279	1,645	2,467	965	953	3,603	524	2,485	13·2	243·9	95·5	1,477[1]	USA
27,250	0	3,962	933	919	2,165	700	1,350	7·9	69·2	32·9	2,294	22·9
27,235	1,568	8,421	815	810	2,031	724	1,349	7·5	26·7	23·6	1,090[1]	8·4
27,235	2,026	11,510	727	726	1,830	750	1,342	6·7	18·4	14·6	2,275	5·3
27,179	8,351	11,631	723	—	2,472	655	1,811	9·1	34·9	33·8	1,270	2·9
27,144	8,344	13,489	670	608	1,857	744	821	6·8	13·2	5·8	3,721	USA
27,141	—	7,744	846	852	2,536	648	3,007	9·3	35·1	63·5	—	UQ
27,123	13,245	26,474	446	525	4,406	469	3,620	16·2	23·7	24·4	1,362	USA
27,088	1,845	10,469	755	807	2,085	713	1,390	7·7	26·7	18·8	1,688[1]	UQ
27,088	143	13,377	671	662	2,504	650	2,446	9·2	20·7	21·9	15,000	UQ
26,881	1,057	6,673	874	—	151	961	142	0·6	3·4	¶ 3·2	125[1]	IT
26,702	7,747	9,190	788	838	1,821	753	1,769	6·8	26·8	31·1	1,863	4·3
26,692	5,489	17,145	598	619	3,961	497	2,485	14·8	29·2	17·1	1,340[1]	19·3
26,674	4,952	29,024	428	437	2,666	628	1,301	10·0	11·0	5·8	1,561[1]	UQ
26,623	1,936	10,574	753	741	2,208	689	2,029	8·3	23·2	¶21·3	1,698[1]	DEN
26,595	85	7,436	853	843	1,435	798	1,400	5·4	21·3	19·1	1,038	5·8
26,578	947	3,942	934	936	1,047	855	546	3·9	¶26·6	12·8	—	UQ
26,574	1,650	8,229	827	839	2,574	642	1,786	9·7	38·0	28·0	1,850	16·4
26,565	4,696	10,469	756	673	1,661	777	1,051	6·3	14·4	9·0	2,313	UQ
26,562	0	8,185	828	792	2,757	617	1,950	10·4	33·7	27·6	1,619	UQ
26,516	5,827	9,086	792	—	1,816	754	629	6·8	22·1	7·3	918[1]	CI
26,432	3,637	14,034	660	661	3,143	574	1,587	11·9	26·0	14·3	2,585[1]	12·2
26,372	4	4,237	927	—	55	969	Loss 4p.a.	0·2	2·9	—	874[1]	UQ
26,369	5,328	14,392	651	625	622	897	1,143	2·4	4·8	10·1	2,937[1]	2·2
26,233	1,915[15]	6,317	883	866	743	882	826	2·8	12·1	13·1	2,090	USA
26,230	16,057	6,848	864	894	2,119	706	1,199	8·1	40·0	27·2	1,441[1]	UQ
26,218	20,946	5,731	899	889	991	863	995	3·8	18·3	22·1	507	3·6
26,178	15	10,988	740	684	1,099	846	1,207	4·2	13·0	18·0	586	B
26,154	9,571	7,734	848	857	995	862	1,337	3·8	15·5	25·5	—	SWZ
26,113	864	4,753	918	—	902	874	793	3·5	20·2	21·2	770	2·1
26,080p.a.	6p.a.	9,859	778	—	1,336p.a.	816	2,009	5·1	10·5p.a.	¶15·7	1,425	—[21]
26,019	892	9,867	777	702	1,880	741	1,344	7·2	17·8	19·1	2,454	5·8
26,015	8,897	2,822	956	983	178	959	73	0·7	12·6	4·8	—	UQ
25,943	0	17,345	595	—	3,366	554	2,893	13·0	28·1	29·7	2,097[1]	9·8
25,910	1,448	13,137	676	696	4,229	479	2,737	16·3	39·4	27·7	1,647	17·8
25,850	13,379	2,082	975	974	562	905	304	2·2	29·8	17·6	—	UQ
25,822	0	7,988	835	766	2,576	641	2,104	10·0	29·6	29·7	2,101	13·5
25,814	8,887	12,696	690	—	400	935	Loss 2,152	1·5	4·3	—	718	USA
25,812	15,838	10,258	763	776	3,127	577	3,224	12·1	33·1	37·9	520	UQ
25,703	391	11,366	731	707	2,249	684	1,999	8·7	21·4	20·2	1,703[1]	4·7
25,649	0	7,220	856	890	1,048	854	715	4·1	19·4	15·2	891	2·4
25,607	58	6,683	873	809	681	887	546	2·7	8·8	5·9	892	3·9
25,525	4,037	12,418	700	—	4,530	459	3,847	17·7	43·3	40·1	598[1]	USA
25,511	0	9,332	785	—	1,850	745	1,216	7·3	23·5	17·6	1,040	3·8

The following letters in the Market Capitalisation column denote unquoted companies and country of control: B = Belgium. CI = Channel Islands. DEN = Denmark. IT = Italy. SWZ = Switzerland. UQ = Unquoted. USA = United States of America.

Rank by turn-over	COMPANY	Main activity	Chairman and Managing Directors (in italics) §‖	Accounting period ended
901 (800)	Graylaw Holdings	Prop. Invest & Garage Proprietors	V. W. A. Gray	30– 6–75
902 (971)	Turner Manufacturing Co.	Commercial Gearbox Manufacturers	Sir Monty Prichard, *R. B. Dumbell*	1–10–77
903 (906)	Macpherson, Train & Co.	Food Distributors	Lord Macpherson	31– 5–77
904 (877)	William R. Warner & Co.	Manufacturing Chemists	W. J. Curtis	30–11–76
905 (978)	Wm. Donald (W'sale Meat Ctrs.)	Wholesale Meat Contractors, Farmers	W. S. Donald (M.D.)	31– 3–77
906 (893)	McConomy & Co.	Hide & Skin Traders	G. J. Potter (M.D.)	31–12–77
907 (934)	J. Saville Gordon Group	Metal Mchts., Processors & Engrs' Mch.	J. D. Saville	30– 4–77
908 (865)	Edrington Holdings	Scotch Whisky Industry	Miss E. G. Robertson	31–12–76
909 (771)	Francis Industries	Engineering	D. M. Saunders	31–12–77
910 (980)	United Continental Steels	Iron and Steel Merchants	A. L. J. Lamproye, *J. L. Cowley*	31–12–76
911 (810)	RCA	Electronic Engineers	P. Potashner, *J. M. Sheasby*	31–12–76
912 (N/A)	Gambia Produce Marketing Co.	Dealers in Groundnuts, etc.	M. B. O. Jallow, *K. H. B. Richards*	30– 9–77
913 (—)	Camford Engineering	General Engineering	L. J. Citroen, *D. Keech*	30– 9–77
914 (804)	Morgan Edwards	Food Distributors	M. A. Grant (A.C.), *R. E. Semark*	2– 4–77
915 (812)	Peek Holdings	Distbn. & Storage of Food Products	Viscount Slim	31–12–75
916 (847)	Boustead	Plantations, Eng., Metals, etc.	A. Charton	31–12–77
917 (976)	Crown Cork Co.	Mfrs. of Bottletops, etc.	A. H. F.Hayward (M.D.)	31–12–76
918 (819)	Ronson Products	Lighters, Razors & Domestic Applncs.	J. A. Goddard (M.D.)	31–12–76
919 (—)	Bell & Howell	Scientific Instrument Manfrs.	E. F. Wagner	1– 1–77
920 (863)	Laws Stores	Grocers	W. G. McClelland, *P. M. Kilby*	9– 4–77
921 (—)	Highams	Textile Manufacturers	W. M. Higham (J.M.D.), *J. H. F. Wilken*	1– 4–78
922 (841)	J. E. Lesser & Sons (Hldgs.)	Construction and Development	C. L. Lesser, *M. M. Lesser*	31–12–76
923 (836)	Ash & Lacy	Metal Stockholders & Perforators	J. F. Vernon (M.D.)	30–12–77
924 (—)	Fein & Co.	Fur & Skin Merchants		31– 5–77
925 (—)	Hogg Robinson Group	Insurers & Lloyds Brokers	M. P. Abbott (M.D.)	31– 3–77
926 (961)	Morgan-Grampian[6]	Publishers	G. V. Sherren	31– 3–77
927 (703)	Henry Stephens & Sons (Lon.)	Importers & Exporters	*J .E. Aldridge*	31– 7–76
928 (756)	Wates Construction	Building Contractors	A. Wates	26–12–76
929 (—)	Burco Dean	Manfrs. of Domestic Appliances, etc.	Lord Hewlett	30– 9–77
930 (825)	T.P.T.	Paper & Plastic Products Mfrs.	W. D. Grove (M.D.)	31–12–76
931 (879)	Leisure & General Holdings[31]	Leisure, Hotels, Bookmaking, etc.	J. G. D. Chapple, *G. H. Hall*	30– 4–77
932 (822)	Camrex (Holdings)	Specialised Coatings, Corrosion Engs.	R. Wake	31–12–77
933 (910)	P. Panto & Co.	Whsle, Tobacconists, Confectioners, etc.	P. Panto, *I. Panto* (M.D.)	23–12–77
934 (N/A)	Sotheby Parke Bernet Group	Fine Art Auctioneers	P. C. Wilson	31– 8–77
935 (958)	British Mohair Spinners	Combing, Dyeing & Spinning	T. W. Hibbert, *G. Litten*	31–12–77
936 (993)	Glass, Glover Group	Importers & Distb. of Fruit & Vegtbs.	H. Glass	30– 9–77
937 (970)	Alfa Laval Co.	Centrifugal & Agricultural Engineers	Sir Archibald Ross, *B. H. Kent*	31–12–76
938 (946)	Manders (Holdings)	Manfrs. of Paint & Printing Ink	G. Norman (M.D.)	31–12–77
939 (N/A)	Sanyo Marubeni (UK)	Distbn. of Electrical Consumer Prods.	*I. Megata*	31– 3–77
940 (954)	Clark Equipment	Constr. Machy. & Cargo Van Carriers	R. J. Smith	31–12–75
941 (964)	Kyle Stewart (Contractors)	Building Contractors	R. M. I. Stewart (J.M.D.), *S. H. Anderson*	30– 9–76
942 (956)	Leyland Paint and Wallpaper	Manfrs. of Paint, Wallcoverings, etc.	P. W. A. Simmonds, *B. Jones*	31–12–77
943 (—)	Stothert & Pitt	Engineers	Sir Ralph Bateman, *A. Cheetham*	02– 7–77
944 (916)	Thomas Witter & Co.	Floor & Wall Covering Manufacturers	H. Bowser, *J. Jackson*	30–11–77
945 (867)	Armstrong Cork Co.	Thermoplastic Flooring Manfrs.	J. H. Binns, *R. Kemp*	31–12–76
946 (—)	Warren Plantation Holdings	Tea & Coffee Plantations, etc.	H. J. R. B. Salmon, *C. D. Jakes*	31–12–77
947 (—)	Avana Group	Cake Manfrs., Bakers & Confectioners	Sir Julian Hodge, *J. S. Randall*	2– 4–77
948 (922)	Braby Leslie	Civil & Mechanical Engineering	E. R. Izod	31– 3–77
949 (986)	Tunnel Refineries	Starch Manufacturers, etc.	Earl Jellicoe, *B. J. Smartt*	28–18–76
950 (881)	Associated Book Publishers	Publishers & Booksellers	P. H. B. Allsop, *M. R. Turner*	31–12–77

NOTES: *Total tangible assets less current liabilities (other than bank loans and overdrafts and future tax).   †As percentage of capital employed at beginning of the year.   ‡As at 14 July 1978.   §Appendix on page 70 gives list of Managing Directors which cannot be fitted into the main text.   ‖M.D. = Managing Director; J.M.D. = Joint Managing Director; A.C. = Acting Chairman.   ¶As percentage of capital employed at the end of the year.   N/A Not available.   ¹UK only.   ⁶Now a sub. co. of Trafalgar House Ltd.   ²²Comparative figures for previous year not available.   ³¹Now a sub. co. of Ladbroke Group Ltd.

| TURNOVER | | *CAPITAL EMPLOYED | Rank | | NET PROFIT BEFORE INTEREST AND TAX | | | | †% to capital employed | | **No. of employees | ‡Equity market cap. £M. |
Total £000	Export £000	£000	Latest year	Previous year	Latest year £000	Rank	Previous year £000	% to turnover Latest year	Latest year	Previous year		
25,458	6	32,736	395	360	1,979	730	1,804	7·8	6·9	8·3	663[1]	UQ
25,440	5,777	12,916	682	742	3,475	535	2,291	13·7	36·6	37·0	2,015[1]	14·0
25,400	1,719	2,356	968	946	323	947	286	1·3	11·5	14·4	103	UQ
25,392	11,551	8,090	831	728	2,720	626	1,951	10·7	27·5	26·3	1,451[1]	USA
25,386	951	4,087	930	932	444	928	636	1·7	12·4	25·7	386	UQ
25,359	—	2,414	966	954	458	925	717	1·8	18·6	79·4	—	UQ
25,270	2	6,310	884	918	1,021	860	908	4·0	25·6	28·7	294	2·2
25,196	1,255	40,013	338	413	5,747	378	3,128	22·8	19·4	11·7	718[1]	UQ
25,195	841	10,246	764	739	2,033	723	1,794	8·1	21·3	20·3	2,221	5·1
25,192	6	5,533	905	938	291	950	161	1·2	9·5	7·7	—	B
25,131	6,207	8,367	820	782	1,456	794	Loss 200	5·8	21·3	—	1,536	USA
25,112	819	2,309	970	—	11	975	5	—	0·7	1·7	—	GAM
25,080	2,167	14,961	634	—	2,586	639	2,104	10·3	22·2	19·0	1,505	10·7
25,064	0	1,773	984	977	90	964	154	0·4	5·8	9·7	650	1·7
25,046p.a.	10p.a.	6,219	885	864	Loss 607p.a.	985	—[22]	—	—	—	1,086	0·3
25,041	1,065	12,673	692	651	2,201	690	2,066	8·8	18·4	17·8	—	5·7
25,012	2,378	11,550	726	749	1,410	803	1,238	5·6	14·6	15·1	958[1]	USA
24,987	9,827	10,124	767	743	1,279	825	992	5·1	13·5	10·0	3,059	USA
24,964	1,446	9,426	783	—	1,999	728	1,593	8·0	30·4	31·6	621	USA
24,909	—	3,344	948	947	472	923	101	1·9	17·8	4·0	1,222	UQ
24,776	968	7,785	844	—	1,378	807	1,387	5·6	19·2	20·9	2,159	3·0
24,620	5,862	14,298	652	602	1,095	847	1,629	4·4	7·6	17·0	1,311[1]	UQ
24,605	245	10,872	744	709	1,665	776	2,058	6·8	15·9	26·9	845	5·1
24,545	8,684	2,912	953	—	622	898	430	2·5	30·0	36·5	—	UQ
24,544	—	21,157	519	—	8,196	307	6,033	33·4	64·8	52·6	2,025[1]	41·7
24,490	1,123	11,672	720	682	3,431	543	2,364	14·0	30·7	20·0	949	—[6]
24,359	1,648	431	997	996	108	963	123	0·4	27·6	37·0	—	UQ
24,331	—	4,012	931	784	510	914	818	2·1	6·1	9·3	1,344	UQ
24,312	1,452	9,597	780	—	1,469	792	688	6·0	15·8	8·6	1,919	4·7
24,308	767	12,665	693	642	3,721	516	2,303	15·3	39·0	26·3	1,023[1]	USA
24,246	0	6,657	875	873	1,362	812	1,138	5·6	23·0	21·9	1,895	—[31]
24,209	8,716	10,057	769	745	2,492	652	2,555	10·3	26·4	22·6	1,643[1]	5·9
24,203	0	2,775	957	941	405	934	374	1·7	13·9	15·6	453	1·0
24,185	65	14,210	655	—	5,167	415	3,845	21·4	48·6	¶36·2	575[1]	32·2
24,132	8,929	14,036	659	643	2,724	625	2,362	11·3	21·6	25·1	1,860[1]	5·2
24,118	0	1,375	990	987	485	919	375	2·0	39·6	33·2	339	1·3
24,071	3,860	8,928	796	763	1,483	791	1,011	6·2	17·0	14·7	969[1]	SW
24,069	1,264	19,986	546	628	2,535	649	2,547	10·5	19·2	22·4	1,346[1]	13·4
24,036	357	2,521	964	—	573	904	536	2·4	26·7	¶25·0	245	JAP
23,900	11,702	7,920	837	738	Loss 11,598	997	Loss 1,607	—	—	—	954	USA
23,840	—	2,661	961	930	629	895	690	2·6	17·8	22·6	987	UQ
23,822p.a.	4,454p.a.	7,612	852	835	1,776p.a.	756	1,809	7·5	25·6p.a.	26·8	1,647	4·6
23,813	14,851	7,809	842	—	1,238	830	933	5·2	11·3	10·7	2,028	3·6
23,794	4,432	8,379	818	806	925	871	1,168	3·9	11·8	16·1	1,114[1]	4·4
23,747	1,010	24,411	469	516	Loss 1,015	987	Loss 832	—	—	—	1,493	USA
23,727	157	18,697	570	—	11,231	244	5,237	47·3	78·3	¶36·5	220[1]	9·7
23,698	285	10,795	747	—	2,017	726	1,275	8·5	29·7	17·3	1,611	8·0
23,659	3,540	6,420	879	892	1,651	778	1,609	7·0	30·0	34·9	1,401	6·8
23,647	834	10,264	762	841	2,795	612	1,897	11·8	41·4	34·0	455[1]	UQ
23,642	4,139	9,275	787	795	2,733	622	2,416	11·6	33·7	35·9	495[1]	8·1

The following letters in the Market Capitalisation column denote unquoted companies and country of control: B = Belgium.   GAM = Gambia.   JAP = Japan.
SW = Sweden.   UQ = Unquoted.   USA = United States of America.

Rank by turn-over	COMPANY	Main activity	Chairman and Managing Directors (in italics) §‖	Accounting period ended
951 (—)	Cosalt	Ships' Chandlery, Caravan Mfrs., etc.	J. M. T. Ross	1– 1–78
952 (870)	Francis Parker	Sand, Gravel, Concrete Products, etc.	R. K. Francis (J.M.D.), *C. Loveless*	31– 3–77
953 (—)	Biro Bic	Manufacturers of Ball Point Pens	M. L. M. A. Birch, *F. W. G. Bolt*	31–12–76
954 (1000)	R. H. Cole	Plastics, Chemicals and Electronics	P. H. Cole	31–12–77
955 (981)	Alexanders Holdings	Ford Main Dealers, etc.	J. B. T. Loudon, *H. Clayton, W. E. Burns*	30– 9–77
956 (887)	Gomme Holdings	Manfrs. of 'G' Plan Furniture	H. N. Sporborg, *D. L. Gomme*	29– 7–77
957 (872)	James Walker & Co.	Manfrs. of Packings & Jointings	D. Davies	31– 3–77
958 (—)	Sheffield Twist Drill & Steel	Manfrs. of Engineers' Small Tools	N. H. Waple	31–12–77
959 (—)	William Moss Group	Builders & Contractors	T. F. James	31–12–77
960 (957)	National Carbonising Co.	Producers of Smokeless Fuel, etc.	M. A. Gaze	31– 3–77
961 (966)	Davies Turner & Co.	Shipping & Forwarding Agents, etc.	U. G. E. Stephenson (J.M.D.), *K. A. Hewett*	31– 3–77
962 (909)	Manchester Ship Canal Co.	Operators of Manchester Ship Canal	D. K. Redford (M.D.)	31–12–77
963 (880)	Stern Osmat Group	Hardware Merchants, etc.	F. W. Stern (M.D.)	31–12–77
964 (—)	Evode Holdings	Mfrs. of Adhesives, Jointing Cmpns., etc.	H. Simon	1–10–77
965 (878)	Expanded Metal Co.	Expanded Metal Products, etc.	S. A. Field, *R. D. Scott*	31–12–77
966 (—)	Elliott Grp. of Peterborough	Mfrs. & Distbtrs. of Timber Products	A. W. Houston, *B. P. Dyer*	31– 3–77
967 (979)	Home Brewery Co.	Brewers	B. H. Farr	30– 9–77
968 (938)	Brookton	Supermarkets, etc.	A. M. G. Weston	2–10–76
969 (962)	Stocklake Holdings	Exporters, Importers, Steel Stkhldrs.	A. M. McKay	31– 3–77
970 (917)	William Pickles & Co.	Textile Manufacturers, etc.	D. S. Greensmith, *N. F. Garrett*	31–12–77
971 (868)	Linotype and Machinery	Engineers, Printing Machy.	P. J. Cope (A.C.-M.D.)	30– 9–76
972 (894)	Berry Bros. & Rudd	Wine and Spirit Merchants	A. A. Berry	31– 3–77
973 (932)	C. E. Heath & Co.	Insurance Brokers, U/W Agents	F. R. D. Holland	31– 3–78
974 (—)	Electrocomponents	Electronic Component Mfrs. & Disbtrs.	R. A. Marler	31– 3–77
975 (—)	Grundig International	Marketing of Electronic Equipment	W. Scheller, *H. P. Spring*	2–10–76
976 (869)	Titaghur Jute Factory Co.	Manufacture of Jute Goods	H. J. Silverston	30– 6–77
977 (—)	Edbro (Holdings)	Engineers	L. V. D. Tindale, *G. S. Moss*	31– 3–77
978 (—)	Londis (Holdings)	Provision Merchants	J. A. Perkins, *J. Callaghan*	30– 1–76
979 (873)	Randalls Group	Distbs. to Bldg. Eng. Electl. Industries	C. R. Randall, *O. W. Harvey*	31–12–76
980 (874)	Minter Investment Co.	Building Contractors, etc.	R. H. Minter (M.D.)	31–12–75
981 (—)	H. E. Samson	Suppliers of Cut Steel	H. E. Samson	31– 3–77
982 (918)	Murco Petroleum	Petroleum Distributors	J. L. Reed	31–12–76
983 (—)	Colt International & Assoc.	Heating & Ventilation Equipment	I. J. O'Hea, *A. O'Hea*	31–12–76
984 (—)	C. G. Hacking & Sons	Produce Merchants	P. Manby, *C. G. Hacking*	30– 6–77
985 (977)	Atlas Express Group	Carriers, etc.	R. H. Farmer (M.D.)	31–12–76
986 (—)	D. B. Marshall (Newbridge)	Broiler Chicken Breeders	D. D. Marshall, *W. M. Marshall, D. E. Roberts, Jr.*	30– 9–76
987 (—)	Mills & Allen International	Advertising, Money Broking, Printing	Sir Ian Morrow, *C. R. Hollick*	30– 6–77
988 (902)	Yorkshire Chemicals	Manfrs. of Dyestuffs & Chemicals	T. McDonald, *S. Fowler*	31–12–77
989 (—)	Home Charm	Wallpaper, DIY, etc. Suppliers	H. E. Fogel (M.D.)	31–12–77
990 (—)	Johnson Wax	Manufacturers of Polish, etc.	S. C. Johnson, *J. D. Crabb*	1– 7–77
991 (—)	Champion Sparking Plug Co.	Spark Plug Manufacturers	R. A. Stranahan, Jr., *R. V. Senez*	31–12–76
992 (996)	H. A. Job	Milk Distributors, etc.	D. H. Roberts, *A. L. Roberts, S. Roberts*	30– 4–77
993 (—)	Carr's Milling Industries	Flour Millers, Bakers, etc.	I. C. Carr	3– 9–77
994 (844)	Melville, Dundas & Whitson	Bldg. & Civil Eng. Contractors	H. A. Whitson, *J. C. K. Murray*	31–12–77
995 (686)	Ridpath Brothers	Food Distributors, etc.	R. J. Collis	1– 4–77
996 (953)	Buitoni	Food Mfr. & Distribution	F. Buitoni, *G. E. Fairclough*	1– 1–77
997 (—)	Dart Industries	Mfrs. of Plastic & Cosmetic Products	J. Dart, *S. Brodie*	31–12–76
998 (—)	Norton Villiers Triumph	Motor Cycle Manufacturers	R. D. Poore	31– 7–77
999 (—)	Pitman	Publishers, Printers, College Proprs.	H. De B. Lawson Johnston, *D. C. Davis*	31– 3–77
1000 (—)	S. W. Wood Group	Non-Ferrous Metal Mchts., Processors	A. N. Bolsom, *S. W. Wood*	31– 3–77

NOTES: *Total tangible assets less current liabilities (other than bank loans and overdrafts and future tax). †As percentage of capital employed at beginning of the year. ‡As at 14 July 1978. §Appendix on page 70 gives list of Managing Directors which cannot be fitted into the main text. ‖M.D. = Managing Director; J.M.D. = Joint Managing Director; A.C. = Acting Chairman. ¶As percentage of capital employed at the end of the year. N/A Not available. ¹UK only. ²²Comparative figures for previous year not available.

| TURNOVER | | *CAPITAL EMPLOYED | | | NET PROFIT BEFORE INTEREST AND TAX | | | | | | **No. of | ‡Equity |
Total £000	Export £000	£000	Rank Latest year	Previous year	Latest year £000	Rank	Previous year £000	% to turnover Latest year	†% to capital employed Latest year	Previous year	employees	market cap. £M.
23,608	6,819	11,933	713	—	2,609	637	1,771	11·1	31·5	22·5	1,273	5·4
23,597	—	19,382	560	433	1,035	858	869	4·4	4·4	3·3	1,172	4·4
23,568	2,562	13,503	669	—	2,770	616	1,709	11·8	27·5	20·4	302	FR
23,564	1,983	8,523	811	869	1,381	806	1,039	5·9	22·7	22·6	517	3·2
23,561	—	4,345	925	924	695	884	427	2·9	18·8	10·9	583	3·1
23,551	460	10,637	749	773	2,235	686	2,647	9·5	26·2	39·8	1,929	8·1
23,525	4,678	19,339	561	552	3,489	532	3,841	14·8	18·0	27·0	2,341[1]	UQ
23,461	8,289	23,297	481	—	3,059	590	2,063	13·0	17·4	16·1	2,449[1]	SW
23,444	1,428	4,585	920	—	805	880	741	3·4	21·0	20·9	1,543	UQ
23,418	5,602	10,340	760	849	488	917	582	2·1	7·4	9·3	849	4·7
23,359	0	2,350	969	972	659	889	430	2·8	37·6	25·7	485[1]	UQ
23,340	—	51,499	282	262	2,664	629	4,218	11·4	5·3	8·8	3,395	8·8
23,223	1	4,986	914	895	556	908	536	2·4	10·7	10·7	1,027	UQ
23,218	1,432	7,790	843	—	1,634	780	1,566	7·0	27·8	28·4	1,011[1]	6·4
23,154	3,684	17,535	592	620	2,349	669	3,277	10·1	17·3	28·6	947	14·3
23,097p.a.	8,391p.a.	10,931	741	—	1,244p.a.	827	1,210	5·4	14·8p.a.	13·3	812	2·4
23,019	0	17,565	591	578	3,521	527	2,676	15·3	22·4	19·1	1,516	UQ
22,996	—	1,799	982	975	352	943	246	1·5	21·5	15·6	655[1]	UQ
22,927	10,921	7,086	860	858	2,190	692	1,652	9·6	34·3	22·5	145[1]	2·7
22,925	2,418	8,750	804	798	1,199	834	1,207	5·2	14·9	17·6	1,862[1]	3·3
22,897	12,842	12,254	707	655	2,486	654	2,291	10·9	22·3	24·4	1,759[1]	USA
22,873	20,674	7,118	858	853	653	890	477	2·9	10·1	7·5	—	UQ
22,866	—	24,403	470	519	14,448	202	11,318	63·2	76·7	97·0	1,238[1]	80·0
22,849	1,166	8,956	795	—	4,537	457	2,849	19·9	73·0	57·9	1,001	47·7
22,830p.a.	7,062p.a.	9,064	794	—	336p.a.	946	Loss 362	1·5	4·4p.a.	—	312[1]	G
22,783	288	5,493	906	870	Loss 1,294	990	91	—	—	1·3	18,634	0·1
22,737	8,610	11,372	730	—	3,699	519	2,722	16·3	49·0	36·2	1,484[1]	14·8
22,643	—	944	991	—	208	956	203	0·9	29·2	42·2	207[1]	UQ
22,625	616	5,680	902	882	948	870	781	4·2	20·6	18·9	1,204	1·7
22,586	319	2,988	952	940	525	913	Loss 75	2·3	17·3	—	1,321[1]	UQ
22,580	1,967	2,897	955	—	605	899	510	2·7	26·0	24·4	—	UQ
22,550	—	7,063	861	731	Loss 500	984	973	—	—	9·2	161	USA
22,502	1,977	11,762	718	—	3,466	537	1,349	15·4	38·9	14·5	1,134[1]	UQ
22,477	16,235	923	992	—	197	957	127	0·9	22·5	19·4	—	UQ
22,472	—	3,932	935	922	675	888	509	3·0	18·0	12·1	1,977[1]	UQ
22,465	337	11,400	729	—	1,198	835	1,661	5·3	13·3	26·5	1,789	UQ
22,444	627	5,063	911	—	4,212	480	2,404	18·8	87·4	24·7	945[1]	14·4
22,435	12,788	23,583	476	440	2,619	636	4,116	11·7	10·9	22·7	1,047[1]	9·6
22,334	546	4,181	928	—	1,360	813	1,014	6·1	44·5	48·6	764	6·6
22,243	5,857	7,929	836	—	1,828	751	1,059	8·2	27·7	18·0	763[1]	USA
22,194	8,319	7,827	841	—	4,179	481	2,601	18·8	49·9	36·8	1,450	USA
22,118	0	4,135	929	926	1,332	817	1,305	6·0	36·9	41·8	1,019	UQ
22,105	37	6,750	869	—	885	875	803	4·0	17·6	19·4	801	2·3
22,100	—	4,812	915	905	691	886	1,275	3·1	15·1	34·5	799	2·4
22,046	—	3,075	951	943	477	922	701	2·2	16·4	30·1	150	UQ
22,016	77	6,354	881	876	914	872	616	4·2	15·7	6·9	391[1]	IT
22,007	2,659	10,604	750	—	1,110	845	151	5·0	13·1	2·2	1,125	USA
22,007	10,441	3,681	943	—	2,034	722	—[22]	9·2	¶55·3	—	629	UQ
21,980	2,713	12,364	704	—	1,839	747	1,306	8·4	16·7	13·6	1,765[1]	UQ
21,977	891	5,402	908	—	73	967	678	0·3	1·2	13·7	299	2·3

The following letters in the Market Capitalisation column denote unquoted companies and country of control: FR = France.   G = Germany.   IT = Italy.
SW = Switzerland.   UQ = Unquoted.   USA = United States of America.

Appendix: Managing Directors

Rank in table	Company	Managing Directors
1	British Petroleum Co.	*J. Birks, C. C. F. Laidlaw, J. W. R. Sutcliffe, P. I. Walters, M. M. Pennell, R. W. Adam*
24	Inchcape & Co.	*Sir Michael Parsons, J. W. Ritchie, J. M. H. Millington-Drake*
26	Marks & Spencer	*M. M. Sacher, R. Greenbury, W. B. Howard, H. N. Lewis, Sir Derek Rayner*
47	EMI	*J. M. Kuipers, J. A. Powell, R. L. Watt*
151	British Sugar Corpn	*J. M. Beckett (Chief Executive)*
165	Croda International	*E. W. Tyerman, D. Mather, G. R. Hembrough, D. Jewsbury*
293	Illingworth Morris & Co.	*D. Hanson, P. Hardy, J. L. Hopkinson, J. D. P. Tanner*
334	Magnet & Southerns	*P. H. Doughty, P. T. Duxbury, C. E. Illingworth, G. A. B. Storey*
658	Bambergers	*L. A. Woodburn-Bamberger*
700	Surridge Dawson (Holdings)	*P. J. M. Surridge (Executive Chairman), P. G. Durance*
717	Brintons	*T. A. Tolley, H. F. Lowe*
814	Caffyns	*A. M. Caffyn, A. E. F. Caffyn, R. J. M. Caffyn*
854	James Latham	*C. G. A. Latham, D. R. Latham, J. M. Latham, R. H. Bridle*

2: The 50 largest acquisitions and mergers*

Rank (total consid-eration)	Acquiring company	Acquired company	VALUE OF CONSIDERATION FOR EQUITY NOT ALREADY OWNED			
			Total £000	Cash £000	Equity £000	Other £000
1	Coral Leisure Group	Pontin's	44,246	16,138	28,108	—
2	Générale Occidentale**	Cavenham	39,697	39,697	—	—
3	Northern Engineering Industries	Reyrolle Parsons	33,484	—	29,692	3,792
4	Seagram Investments Inc.	Glenlivet Distillers	33,354	33,354	—	—
5	Northern Engineering Industries	Clarke Chapman	29,519	—	29,519	—
6	Oce-Van Der Grinten Finance	Ozalid Group Holdings	25,047	11,309	—	13,738
7	Lonrho	AVP Industries	24,832	24,832	—	—
8	Fisons	A. Gallenkamp & Co.	24,341	8,234	16,107	—
9	Moore Business Forms Holdings UK[1]	Moore Business Forms	24,262	24,262	—	—
10	Turner & Newall	Storey Brothers & Co.	21,415	4,619	16,796	—
11	Coalite & Chemical Products	Charringtons Industrial Holdings	20,600	11,885	8,715	—
12	Trafalgar House	Morgan-Grampian	20,521	20,521	—	—
13	American Standard (UK)	Clayton Dewandre Holdings	19,421	19,421	—	—
14	BICC	Dorman Smith Holdings	18,797	18,797	—	—
15	H. P. Bulmer Holdings	H. P. Bulmer	15,911	—	14,540	1,371
16	European Ferries	English & Caledonian Investment Co.	14,796	—	14,796	—
17	Hawker Siddeley Group	L. Gardner & Sons	14,699	14,699	—	—
18	Coral Leisure Group	Centre Hotels (Cranston)	14,164	6,826	7,338	—
19	S. Pearson & Sons	Madame Tussaud's	12,925	12,925	—	—
20	Diamond Shamrock International Holdings	Diamond Shamrock Europe	12,484	12,484	—	—
21	Thomas Borthwick & Sons	Matthews Holdings	12,330	3,825	8,505	—
22	International Stores Holdings[2]	F. J. Wallis	12,074	12,074	—	—
23	Harrisons & Crosfield	Harcros Investment Trust	11,457	—	11,457	—
24	Dalgety	Federated Chemical Holdings	10,962	—	10,962	—
25	Trafalgar House	Beaverbrook Newspapers	10,881	10,881	—	—
26	NCI Investments (UK)	Bison Group	10,813	10,813	—	—
27	Fruehauf International	Crane Fruehauf	10,289	10,289	—	—
28	Inchcape & Co.	Pride & Clarke	9,864	—	9,864	—
29	BTR	Allied Polymer Group	9,403	9,403	—	—
30	MK Electric Holdings	EGA Holdings	9,227	3,629	5,598	—
31	Johnson & Firth Brown	British Rollmakers Corporation	8,767	—	8,767	—
32	Northern Engineering Industries	International Combustion (Holdings)	8,041	3,061	4,980	—
33	Richard Costain	Kwikform	7,177	7,177	—	—
34	Harrisons & Crosfield	Malayalam Plantations (Holdings)	7,055	—	7,055	—
35	Dowty Group	Ultra Electronic Holdings	5,930	—	5,930	—
36	Ladbroke Group	Leisure & General Holdings	5,923	5,923	—	—
37	Pilkington Brothers	Barr & Stroud	5,825	2,650	3,175	—
38	Ductile Steels	Newman Tubes	5,756	2,112	3,644	—
39	Ellerman Lines	Tollemache & Cobbold Breweries	5,692	5,692	—	—
40	Mann Egerton & Co.[3]	Lighting & Leisure Industries	5,651	5,651	—	—
41	Wedgwood	SPR Investments	5,646	60	5,586	—
42	Low & Bonar Group	GHP Group	5,527	—	3,006	2,521
43	Davy International	Herbert Morris	5,361	—	5,361	—
44	Blagden & Noakes (Holdings)	W. W. Ball & Sons	5,171	3,291	1,880	—
45	NFU Development Trust	FMC	5,056	5,056	—	—
46	Andrew Weir & Co.	Spink & Son	4,794	4,794	—	—
47	BTR	André Silentbloc	4,264	4,264	—	—
48	St. Regis International	Reed & Smith Holdings	4,093	4,093	—	—
49	Tootal	Slimma Group Holdings	4,046	—	4,046	—
50	B. Elliot & Co.	Newall Machine Tool	3,110	619	2,491	—

NOTES: *This table covers the fiscal year 1977/78 and includes companies listed in Table 1 of last year's *Times 1000*. Acquisitions of unquoted companies are not included and alternative offers have been ignored and consideration calculated on the basic offer.
**Générale Occidentale held some 40% of Cavenham prior to its offer to acquire one half of the remaining shares (under the terms of a subsequent Scheme of Arrangement, Cavenham became a wholly owned subsidiary of Générale Occidentale).
[1]Sub. co. of Moore Corpn. of USA (who held 52% of Moore Business Forms, formerly Lamson Industries, prior to the offer for the remaining shares).
[2]Sub. co. of BAT Industries.
[3]Sub. co. of Inchcape & Co.

3: Largest shareholdings table*

Rank in 1977/8 '1000	Company	Date	Nominal equity capital £000	Prudential Assurance %	Legal & General Assurance %	Britannic Assurance %	Norwich Union Life Ins. %	Pearl Assurance %	Co-Op. Ins. %	**Nominees %	Others %
1	British Petroleum Co.	9.3.78	386,518	1.71	—	—	—	—	—	—	(a) 30.87 / (b) 20.13 / (c) 1.57
2	"Shell" Transport & Trading Co.	31.3.78	138,104	2.9	—	—	—	—	—	—	—
3	BAT Industries	31.3.78	90,455	1.56	—	—	—	—	—	1.51	(d) 14.83
4	Imperial Chemical Industries	1.1.78	564,336	2.83	—	—	—	—	—	2.44	—
5	Unilever Ltd.	31.3.78	45,767	3.84	—	—	1.08	—	—	—	(b) 2.12 / (e) 18.45
6	Imperial Group	30.4.78	176,559	2.18	1.44	—	—	—	—	4.22	—
7	BL	30.3.78	129,637	—	—	—	—	—	—	—	(g) 95.1
9	General Electric Co.	31.12.77	137,175	5.95	—	—	—	—	—	—	(h) 1.09
10	Rio Tinto-Zinc Corpn	16.3.78	62,723	3.14	—	—	—	—	—	10.49	—
13	Bowater Corporation	2.6.78	149,759	3.00	—	—	—	1.45	—	10.69	(vv) 1.03
14	Courtaulds	31.3.78	68,309	2.03	—	—	—	—	—	4.72	—
15	Guest Keen & Nettlefolds	31.3.78	151,321	2.66	1.23	1.26	—	1.27	—	5.88	(j) 1.43 / (k) 1.01
16	Grand Metropolitan	2.5.78	220,901	2.57	1.08	—	1.12	—	—	5.16	—
17	Tate & Lyle	7.6.78	54,559	3.42	—	—	—	—	1.05	3.42	—
19	Dunlop Holdings	8.5.78	65,532	1.86	—	1.37	—	1.41	—	7.37	(n) 1.25
23	Marks & Spencer	31.3.78	162,251	6.37	—	—	—	—	—	1.56	—
24	Reed International	20.3.78	111,746	3.38	—	—	1.79	1.05	1.14	5.82	(p) 1.84
25	Amalgamated Metal Corpn	11.4.78	6,285	1.34	—	—	—	1.14	—	—	(q) 53.36 / (r) 1.27 / (s) 17.09 / (t) 2.27
27	Burmah Oil Co.	31.3.78	143,972	—	—	—	—	—	—	15.79	—
29	Hawker Siddeley Group	28.3.78	49,015	2.96	—	—	—	—	—	8.05	(u) 1.06
30	C. T. Bowring & Co.	3.1.78	26,492	—	—	—	—	1.18	—	5.24	(v) 1.20 / (w) 1.13
31	Ranks Hovis McDougall	30.4.78	68,303	2.74	1.41	—	—	1.53	—	17.82	(n) 1.09 / (x) 1.08 / (y) 2.51 / (z) 1.70
32	Inchcape & Co.	31.3.78	78,087	2.50	—	—	—	—	—	7.47	(aa) 1.54 / (bb) 3.90 / (cc) 1.18
33	Tozer Kemsley & Millbourn	31.3.78	9,975	3.31	—	—	—	—	—	4.28	(dd) 13.80 / (ee) 1.39 / (gg) 4.81 / (hh) 1.00 / (jj) 1.21 / (kk) 3.34 / (nn) 8.22 / (pp) 1.01
34	BICC	26.4.78	74,303	2.66	1.42	1.45	—	1.18	1.35	6.15	—
35	Allied Breweries	31.3.78	131,559	—	1.24	—	—	—	—	13.19	—
36	Thorn Electrical Industries	30.3.78	34,282	3.59	—	—	—	1.60	1.20	7.56	(ww) 3.24 / (hh) 1.53
38	Bass Charrington	23.3.78	69,450	4.37	—	1.65	—	—	—	5.11	(h) 1.26
39	Sears Holdings	23.3.78	112,134	2.68	—	—	—	1.35	—	10.63	—
40	Cadbury Schweppes	24.4.78	91,697	1.51	1.26	—	—	1.09	—	6.36	—
41	S. & W. Berisford	31.3.78	19,759	5.04	—	—	—	2.30	1.19	7.98	(qq) 1.01 / (gg) 1.60 / (rr) 2.81 / (pp) 1.01 / (t) 1.05 / (ss) 1.27
42	Unigate	29.3.78	49,620	2.05	—	—	—	1.37	—	8.71	—
45	Boots Co.	31.3.78	89,042	2.9	—	—	—	1.4	—	2.7	—
47	Tube Investments	31.12.77	58,259	1.53	1.31	2.19	—	2.04	1.01	11.34	(tt) 3.02
48	Metal Box	15.3.78	59,604	1.92	1.06	—	—	—	1.46	6.60	(pp) 1.43 / (h) 1.28 / (hh) 1.08
49	Distillers Co.	31.3.78	181,585	2.84	—	1.38	—	—	—	4.64	—
50	Consolidated Gold Fields	31.3.78	36,641	2.57	—	—	—	—	—	8.13	(uu) 2.71

NOTES: *Based on holdings of 1% or more. **This column is the sum of nominee holdings of 1% or more. It is possible that by aggregating the true beneficial interests of nominee holders of less than 1%, undisclosed holdings of 1% or more may exist.
(a) Her Majesty's Government. (b) Bank of England. (c) The Distillers Co. Ltd. (d) Imperial Investments Ltd. (e) Trustees of The Leverhulme Trust. (g) National Enterprise Board. (h) Royal Insurance Co. Ltd. (j) National Coal Board Staff Superannuation Scheme. (k) National Coal Board Mineworkers Pensions Scheme. (n) Church Commissioners for England. (p) Maybank Enterprises Ltd. (q) Patino N.V. (r) J. D. Bannerman. (s) Norddeutsche Affinerie. (t) Scottish Amicable Life Assurance Society. (u) The British Petroleum Pension Trust. (v) Mrs V. M. Eveson. (w) Williams & Glyn's Bank Ltd. (x) Eagle Star Insurance Co. Ltd. (y) National Coal Board Pensions Fund. (z) The Official Custodian for Charities. (aa) Glenapp Estate Co. Ltd. (bb) Inchcape Family Investments Ltd. (cc) John W. M. M. Richard and others. (dd) Barclays Bank International Ltd. (ee) Cushion Trust Ltd. (gg) The ITC Pension Trust Ltd. and another (The ITC Pension Investments Ltd.) (hh) The Royal London Mutual Insurance Society Ltd. (jj) Sun Alliance & London Assurance Co. Ltd. (kk) Westments Ltd. (nn) General Cable Corporation. (pp) Merchant Navy Officers Pension Fund Trustees Ltd. (qq) Alliance Assurance Co. Ltd. (rr) E. S. Margulies. Esq. (ss) Sun Life and London Assurance Co. Ltd. (tt) British Steel Corporation (UK) Ltd. (uu) Société Interprofessionelle pour la compensation des Valuers Mobilières. (vv) Airways Pension Fund Trustees Ltd. (ww) Sir Jules Thorn and others.

For all of you who've wanted to see what an invisible export looks like.

Inside this building are some of the country's most successful exporters.

And a product that's always been one of Britain's most valuable assets.

The building is the home of Guardian Royal Exchange Assurance – and the product is international insurance.

Every year GRE underwrite business in over 120 countries, and every pound, dollar and mark earned that comes back to the UK helps to improve our balance of payments.

Altogether the Insurance and Banking expertise of this country contributed more than £1,000 million to last year's trade figures.

And GRE, as one of Britain's largest insurance companies, are proud to have played their part.

For over 200 years we've been helping to establish the British Insurance Industry as one of the most respected institutions in the world. A period that included the Great Fire of Hamburg

in 1842, the 1906 San Francisco Earthquake and the Darwin Disaster in 1974. All occasions on which GRE and other British Insurers were heavily involved.

Today, even though we have millions of policyholders here in Britain, over 60% of GRE's premium income is drawn from overseas sources who depend on our integrity and experience.

So next time you hear the television pundits say how much invisible exports have helped to close the trade gap, you'll know one company that they're talking about.

And then just think to yourself what would happen to Britain's export record without us.

Head Office: Royal Exchange, London EC3V 3LS.

 Guardian
Royal Exchange
Assurance

A good name to insure with.

BOC International ahead of 「THE TIMES」

This year 'The Times' will have us around the sixties in the turnover ratings. And so we were, until recently.

But times have changed since they did their sums, and when they do them again you will have to look much higher up the list to find BOC International—much higher, we suspect, than you would have imagined.

The integration of Airco Inc in May 1978 has made BOC International one of the largest industrial gases groups in the world: 55,000 employees in more than 100 companies in 50 countries. Last year the sales of the two groups together amounted to £1,185 million.

In a fluctuating world economy, competitive muscle is important, but our aim is more than mutual protection. Airco joins the other companies in the Group to share management strengths, gain understanding of each other's markets, combine technological knowhow and together produce more wealth for the world than we could ever do separately.

BOC International Ltd
Hammersmith House London W6 9DX
Telephone:01-748 2020 Telex: 934664

The Stripe Symbol and letters BOC are BOC Group Trade Marks

4: Nationalised inds., State holding cos.

| Rank | Name—Chairman | Turnover £000 | *Capital employed £000 | NET PROFIT BEFORE INTEREST & TAX | | | INTEREST PAID | | Employees |
				Latest year £000	†% To capital employed Latest year	Previous year £000	Latest year £000	Previous year £000	
1	Electricity Council & Boards *Sir Francis Tombs*	4,779,200	6,510,600	**747,400**	12·0	654,200	**454,700**	447,700	158,723
2	Post Office *Sir William Barlow*	4,183,200	6,881,100	**1,110,700**	18·0	947,200[1]	**390,400**	389,900	401,292
3	National Enterprise Board *Sir Leslie Murphy*	3,501,100	1,370,200	**115,400**	10·2	115,900[2]	**86,800**	66,400	252,805
4	British Steel Corporation *Sir Charles Villiers*	3,153,900	3,951,900	**Loss236,100**	—	77,500	**197,400**	167,700	201,800
5	National Coal Board *Sir Derek Ezra*	2,733,100	1,494,200	**99,000**	8·6	107,900	**91,700**	82,300	303,000
6	British Gas Corporation *Sir Denis Rooke*	2,556,800	2,102,200	**473,400**	21·8	321,000	**147,300**	187,200	99,601
7	British Railways Board *P. Parker*	1,677,800	1,216,900	**68,400**	5·8	13,700	**43,000**	36,800	240,073
8	British Airways *Sir Frank McFadzean*	1,355,300	829,500	**62,000**	9·0	92,000	**23,000**	18,800	57,277
9	British Aerospace *Lord Beswick*	859,645	290,383	**72,839**	25·1[3]	—	**10,111**	—	68,800
10	S. of Scotland Electricity Board *R. Berridge*	407,676	722,569	**89,911**	12·3	85,294	**67,392**	63,008	13,632
11	National Bus Company *F. A. S. Wood*	391,742	179,465	**20,255**	12·3	16,447	**12,044**	10,899	65,118
12	National Freight Corporation *Sir Daniel Pettit*	373,000	137,800	**9,360**	7·0	Loss 1,059	**16,506**	14,376	41,453
13	London Transport Executive *K. Robinson*	292,312	864,650	**Loss 2,777[4]**	—	176[4]	**N/A**	N/A	59,676
14	British Broadcasting Corporation *Sir Michael Swann*	247,995	107,918	**5,768**	5·8	14,563	**822**	440	25,719
15	N. of Scotland Hydro-Electric Bd. *Sir Douglas Haddow*	146,285	494,983	**46,839**	10·5	40,444	**41,501**	34,556	3,910
16	British Airports Authority *N. J. Payne*	125,132	328,947	**32,280**	10·2	25,112	**4,029**	4,097	5,506
17	British Transport Docks Board *Sir Humphrey Browne*	108,813	169,281	**29,047**	18·0	25,819	**6,852**	6,770	11,592
18	Scottish Transport Group *A. M. Donnet*	93,955	65,344	**1,648**	2·8	1,646	**975**	1,095	14,545
19	British National Oil Corporation *Lord Kearton*	25,498	586,661	**6,125**	1·7	8,306	**8,006**	9,393	568
20	Independent Broadcasting Authority *Lady Plowden*	19,685	41,020	**2,814**	7·1	2,611	**184**	167	1,200

NOTES: *Total tangible assets less current liabilities (other than bank loans and overdrafts). † As percentage of capital employed at beginning of year. [1]After deducting £101m provision for elimination of Telecommunications profit above price code reference level. [2]Incorporating results of sub. cos. and associates only from 15.2.76 or later date. [3]As percentage of capital employed at end of year. [4]After interest. N/A Not available.

5: Clearing banks

| Rank | Name—Chairman | GROSS DEPOSITS | | TOTAL ASSETS | | NET PROFIT AFTER TAX | |
		Latest year £000	Previous year £000	Latest year £000	Previous year £000	Latest year £000	Previous year £000
1	Barclays Bank* *A. F. Tuke*	**19,348,000**	17,254,206	**22,077,000**	19,320,053	**118,200**	81,107
2	National Westminster Bank** *R. Leigh-Pemberton*	**17,602,637**	15,383,598	**19,187,765**	17,070,044	**108,830**	87,500
3	Lloyds Bank[1] *Sir Jeremy Morse*	**12,393,716**	10,745,537	**13,529,780**	11,788,019	**83,511**	78,591
4	Midland Bank *Lord Armstrong of Sanderstead*	**11,754,188**	10,441,104	**13,382,640**	11,843,390	**90,078**	77,198
5	National & Commercial Banking Group *Sir Michael Young-Herries*	**3,292,686**	3,160,691	**3,882,571**	3,677,529	**30,507**	28,735
6	Bank of Scotland *Lord Clydesmuir (Governor)*	**1,618,910**	1,351,820	**1,979,710**	1,674,594	**12,593**	12,320
7	Co-operative Bank *Sir Arthur Sugden*	**365,007**	322,467	**415,896**	366,403	**1,760**	1,281

NOTES: *Including Barclays Bank International Ltd., see Table 9. **Including International Westminster Bank Ltd., see Table 9. [1]Including Lloyds Bank International Ltd. and the National Bank of New Zealand Ltd., see Table 9.

6: Finance houses

Rank	Name—*Chairman*	OUTSTANDING BALANCES		CAPITAL EMPLOYED		NET PROFIT BEFORE INTEREST AND TAX	
		Latest year £000	Previous year £000	Latest year £000	Previous year £000	Latest year £000	Previous year £000
1	Lombard North Central *Earl of Crawford and Balcarres*	883,339	828,484	912,917	846,842	110,263	98,727
2	United Dominions Trust *L. C. Mather*	488,100	550,400	906,200	1,077,600	112,100	106,700
3	Lloyds and Scottish *G. Duncan*	292,870	215,833	431,022	346,802	51,619	40,149
4	Mercantile Credit Co. *A. Victor Adey*	291,482	197,308	621,080	410,304	69,673	44,475
5	Forward Trust *J. A. Cave*	268,979	206,336	321,063	239,680	37,033	26,905
6	Hodge Finance *Sir Julian Hodge*	228,364	189,048	173,207	157,870	23,925	21,116
7	Bowmaker *P. Bowring*	147,747	114,852	212,459	173,020	23,772	21,097
8	Provident Financial Group *Lord Chelmer*	135,298	119,177	83,778	76,556	15,834	14,401
9	First National Securities* —	124,281	117,118	126,059	122,156	20,223	19,273
10	North West Securities *Lord Balfour of Burleigh*	119,168	94,483	201,851	164,687	20,806	17,786
11	Commercial Credit Services *R. J. Harrison*	56,403	39,776	62,851	57,671	5,480 p.a.	4,130
12	Wagon Finance Corpn *S. M. de Bartolome*	37,363	30,303	27,141	22,178	4,698	4,113
13	F. C. Finance *Sir Arthur Sugden*	35,925	27,002	74,516	63,131	5,704	5,931
14	British Credit Trust *G. N. S. Horsley*	32,942	25,480	26,557	21,920	3,752	2,835
15	Yorkshire Bank Finance *J. P. R. Glyn*	25,530	19,517	20,991	16,552	2,586	1,896
16	Wessex Finance Corpn *P. N. Grice*	24,050	23,427	25,352	21,689	Loss 1,124	1,643
17	HFC Trust *I. Martindale*	23,176	16,029	18,045	11,174	1,924	75
18	Raleigh Industries (Gradual Payments) *T. E. Barnsley*	22,421	17,243	16,025	13,911	2,365	2,077
19	Security Pacific Finance *H. G. Simms*	14,322	4,151	12,371	3,453	479	150
20	AVCO Financial Services —	12,767	9,189	11,500	8,933	1,681	933
21	Bank of Ireland Finance (UK) *M. J. Dargan*	11,845	6,492	11,549	6,955	784	384
22	Boston Trust & Savings *P. N. Vonckx, Jr*	9,893	8,868	7,640	6,817	748	703
23	Medens Trust *J. A. K. Collins*	8,661	8,162	5,601	5,550	948	846
24	London Scottish Finance Corpn *R. H. Landman*	7,914	6,161	3,996	3,465	938	850
25	Industrial Funding Trust *J. K. Dick*	5,905	3,744	4,985	3,581	448	327
26	Shawlands Securities *N. R. Frizzell*	4,170	4,004	6,229	6,355	717	765
27	Cattle's Holdings Finance *R. Waudby*	1,656	1,118	1,630	1,119	171	159
28	Milford Mutual Facilities *J. Handford*	1,263	1,287	1,002	1,017	123	101
29	Service Finance Corpn *K. Wright*	816	821	655	661	82	77

NOTE: * Figures extracted from combined accounts of First National Securities Ltd. and other related companies (not prepared for statutory purposes).

Bowring scores for Britain

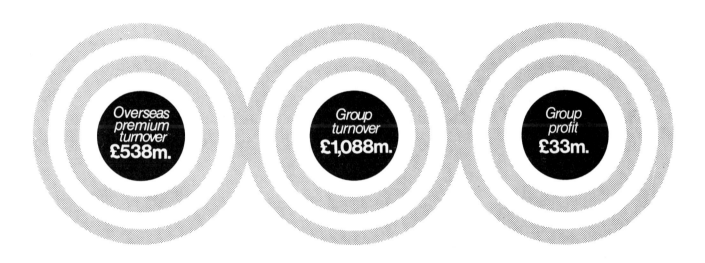

Overseas premium turnover £538m.

Group turnover £1,088m.

Group profit £33m.

The continuing contribution by Bowring to the British economy reached new peaks in 1977.

Already one of the largest single contributors to this country's vital invisible earnings, Bowring this year surpassed its own export record in premium turnover in overseas currencies.

Add to this the other 1977 records in Group turnover and Group profit and a clear-cut picture is presented of the kind of positive productivity that most organisations aim for but few achieve.

Bowring success comes from world-wide activities which include insurance and reinsurance broking, insurance underwriting, credit finance and leasing, merchant banking, shipping, trading and engineering.

These results are evidence of Bowring's continued endeavours towards the well-being of Britain.

C. T. Bowring & Co. Limited
The Bowring Building, Tower Place, London EC3P 3BE
Telephone: 01-283 3100   Telex: 882191

1977
Awarded to C. T. Bowring
(Insurance) Holdings Ltd.

7: Accepting houses

Rank	Name—*Chairman*	*TOTAL ASSETS		ACCEPTANCES		NET PROFIT AFTER TAX	
		Latest year £000	Previous year £000	Latest year £000	Previous year £000	Latest year £000	Previous year £000
1	Kleinwort, Benson, Lonsdale *R. A. Henderson*	1,234,052	1,091,863	196,138	182,586	7,479	6,542
2	Hill Samuel Group *Sir Kenneth Keith*	1,094,638	976,182	209,066	174,902	6,852	6,712
3	Schroders *The Earl of Airlie*	1,066,060	895,230	110,731	109,854	3,504	2,213
4	Hambros *J. O. Hambro*	1,049,598	968,973	257,960	225,952	4,851	5,488
5	Samuel Montague & Co. (inc. Drayton) *P. Shelbourne*	898,539	925,788	57,139	54,154	1,650	1,560
6	Morgan Grenfell Holdings *J. E. H. Collins*	752,583	624,979	110,370	73,773	5,165	2,496
7	S. G. Warburg & Co. *Lord Roll of Ipsden*	651,472	524,314	100,955	94,406	9,704	9,887
8	Lazard Brothers & Co. *D. Meinertzhagen*	517,870	483,079	51,161	40,740	3,807	2,629
9	N. M. Rothschild & Sons *Evelyn de Rothschild*	416,855	362,392	37,439	32,760	500	403
10	Baring Brothers & Co. *J. F. H. Baring*	284,118	251,524	42,145	34,164	650	525
11	Guiness Mahon & Co. *D. Robson*	198,475	191,041	30,540	26,550	1,200	950
12	Brown, Shipley Holdings *Lord Farnham*	196,288	169,561	25,557	22,909	1,693	1,482
13	Anthony Gibbs Holdings *Sir Philip de Zulueta*	176,228	150,954	45,634	36,968	455	521
14	Singer & Friedlander *A. N. Solomons*	175,577	137,421	31,803	22,044	1,187	1,310
15	Arbuthnot Latham Holdings *A. R. C. Arbuthnot*	170,354	153,625	17,304	15,929	1,088	1,008
16	Charterhouse Japhet *M. H. W. Wells*	88,091	71,709	26,268	17,537	815	402
17	Rea Brothers *W. H. Salomon*	77,372	58,669	11,655	11,159	501	471

NOTES: This table comprises all members of the Accepting Houses Committee.
*Excluding acceptances.

8: Discount houses

Rank	Name—*Chairman*	GROSS DEPOSITS		TOTAL ASSETS		NET PROFIT AFTER TAX	
		Latest year £000	Previous year £000	Latest year £000	Previous year £000	Latest year £000	Previous year £000
1	Gerrard & National Discount Co. *R. G. Gibbs*	1,010,877	784,571	1,034,588	801,948	5,708	3,410
2	Union Discount Co. of London *A. J. O. Ritchie*	948,506	613,718	968,439	629,066	6,114	1,869
3	Alexanders Discount Co. *J. P. R. Glyn*	496,461	358,353	509,099	368,023	2,139	264
4	Cater Ryder & Co. *E. D. D. Ryder*	422,759	393,305	433,800	403,337	1,732	1,330
5	Clive Discount Holdings *N. H. Chamberlen*	395,278	228,075	403,425	234,848	2,119	1,324
6	Smith St. Aubyn & Co. (Holdings) *J. F. E. Smith*	326,786	297,973	334,532	304,304	1,948	1,375
7	Jessel Toynbee & Co. *M. R. Toynbee*	259,005	271,752	265,504	277,356	1,299	1,011
8	King & Shaxson *T. S. Hohler*	256,743	228,279	263,844	234,477	1,217	972
9	Allen Harvey & Ross *M. E. R. Allsopp*	249,801	189,812	255,989	194,117	1,201	697
10	Gillett Brothers Discount Co. *R. D. Whitby*	237,151	168,467	243,029	172,962	1,014	469
11	Seccombe Marshall & Campion *D. G. Campion*	74,301	101,880	77,526	104,973	304	473

NOTE: This table comprises all members of the London Discount Market Association.

9: British banks trading mainly overseas

Rank	Name—*Chairman*	GROSS DEPOSITS		TOTAL ASSETS		NET PROFIT AFTER TAX	
		Latest year £000	Previous year £000	Latest year £000	Previous year £000	Latest year £000	Previous year £000
1	Barclays Bank International* *A. F. Tuke*	10,355,000	8,863,762	12,173,000	10,129,099	49,300	31,185
2	Standard Chartered Bank *Lord Barber*	7,110,114	6,583,989	8,493,657	7,653,025	54,510	48,301
3	Hong Kong and Shanghai Banking Corpn[1] *M. G. R. Sandberg*	6,801,046	6,037,598	7,772,298	6,919,865	59,391	49,504
4	Lloyds Bank International[2] *Sir Reginald Verdon-Smith*	4,841,871	3,777,397	5,463,457	4,328,903	19,035	16,577
5	International Westminster Bank[3] *Viscount Sandon*	4,296,818	3,901,818	5,298,133	4,652,328	16,801	11,591
6	Grindlays Holdings *N. J. Robson*	2,640,719	2,368,429	2,760 456	2,487,631	10,558	6,554
7	National Bank of New Zealand [2,4] *Sir John Marshall*	482,183	477,799	508,489	496,892	1,848	1,795
8	Bank of Tokyo and Detroit (International) *Y. Kashiwagi*	139,376	124,322	155,722	158,933	1,016	758

NOTES : *Subsidiary of Barclays Bank Ltd.
[1] Incorporated in Hong Kong, a British Colony.
[2] Subsidiary of Lloyds Bank Ltd.
[3] Subsidiary of National Westminster Bank Ltd. (Previous year figures extracted from statement for Stock Exchange purposes.)
[4] Residence transferred to New Zealand as from 1.1.1978.

WHERE IN THE WORLD WILL YOU FIND STANDARD CHARTERED?

HERE, BUT NOT JUST HERE

Clements Lane is the nerve centre of the Standard Chartered world, but to our customers it's only one of 1500 Group addresses in 60 countries around the world.

This exceptional network could save you time and money for your business; if your bank can't offer you the same, come and see us at Clements Lane or ring Keith Skinner on 01-623 7500.

Standard Chartered
Bank Limited
helps you throughout the world

10: Largest unit trusts

Rank	Name	Managers	*Value of fund £000	Number of unit holders	Rank	Name	Managers	*Value of fund £000	Number of unit holders
1	Investment Trust Units	S. & P.	178,386	92,064	40	M. & G. Second General Trust Fund	M. & G.	25,940	8,438
2	M. & G. Dividend Fund	M. & G.	93,320	35,383	41	Target Preference	T.T.M.	24,798	22,786
3	M. & G. General Trust Fund	M. & G.	85,276	23,723	42	Tyndall Income	T.M.	24,547	6,239
4	Scotbits	S.S.	64,324	67,828	43	Hill Samuel Income	H.S.	24,538	5,087
5	Financial Securities	S. & P.	64,306	49,266	44	National High Income	B.T.M.	24,209	18,671
6	TSB General	T.S.B.	63,949	42,408	45	Hill Samuel British	H.S.	22,851	14,086
7	Unicorn Capital	B.U.	62,762	39,701	46	Hill Samuel International	H.S.	22,717	12,436
8	Charifund	M. & G.	62,521	3,670	47	Target Equity	T.T.M.	22,331	6,344
9	Guardhill	G.R.E.	58,565	1,583	48	M. & G. Recovery Fund	M. & G.	22,238	10,585
10	Unicorn Income	B.U.	57,310	19,634	49	Schroder Special Exempt Fund	H.S.W.	22,174	116
11	Unicorn '500'	B.U.	53,018	27,290	50	Prudential	P.	21,970	1,565
12	Scotyields	S.S.	51,607	38,491	51	Unicorn Growth Accumulator	B.U.	21,564	21,843
13	M. & G. American & General Fund	M. & G.	49,049	13,709	52	Growth	B.T.M.	21,314	22,559
14	UK Equity	S. & P.	48,667	41,755	53	Lloyds Bank Second	L.B.	20,730	31,799
15	Hill Samuel Dollar	H.S.	47,262	8,596	54	Allied First Trust	A.H.G.	20,463	14,465
16	High Yield	S. & P.	44,989	35,595	55	High Income	H.	19,189	8,957
17	Abbey General	A.M.	44,573	3,551	56	Electrical & Industrial Development Trust	A.H.G.	19,121	9,881
18	Income	S. & P.	44,134	44,295	57	Barclaytrust Investment Fund (Income)	B.U.	18,798	1,016
19	Unicorn Extra Income	B.U.	42,629	22,337	58	Metals Minerals & Commodities Trust	A.H.G.	18,331	17,038
20	Growth	N.W.	42,567	40,957	59	Equity & Law	E. & L.	18,000	346
21	Unicorn General	B.U.	40,360	67,723	60	Shield	B.T.M.	17,586	23,008
22	Capital	S. & P.	38,656	37,600	61	Norwich Union Group Trust Fund	N.G.T.	17,516	137
23	Universal Growth	S. & P.	36,573	25,940	62	Allied Growth & Income Trust	A.H.G.	17,014	2,919
24	Tyndall Capital	T.M.	36,100	8,745	63	Scotshares	S.S.	16,810	29,453
25	United States Growth	S. & P.	36,027	12,702	64	The Hambro Fund	A.H.G.	16,560	425
26	Commodity Share	S. & P.	33,914	25,648	65	Allied Capital Trust	A.H.G.	16,559	5,375
27	Allied High Income	A.H.G.	33,256	19,245	66	Hambro Smaller Companies Fund	A.H.G.	16,447	3,180
28	Practical	P.I.	33,186	3,632	67	M. & G. Compound Growth Fund	M. & G.	15,973	13,959
29	M. & G. Extra Yield Fund	M. & G.	31,640	11,352	68	Japan Growth	S. & P.	15,479	6,370
30	Hambro Accumulator Fund	A.H.G.	31,181	33	69	M. & G. Pension Exempt Fund	M. & G.	15,121	196
31	High Return	S. & P.	30,919	11,915	70	Gartmore High Income	G.F.M.	15,100	5,600
32	Unicorn Financial	B.U.	29,675	16,004	71	Domestic	B.T.M.	14,685	32,433
33	Lloyds Bank First	L.B.	29,506	28,030	72	Scottish	T.S.B.	14,600	836
34	Lloyds Bank Third	L.B.	28,317	10,492	73	North American	H.	14,599	3,901
35	M. & G. High Income Fund	M. & G.	27,650	12,556	74	Grantchester Fund	G.M.	14,219	3,629
36	Hill Samuel Capital	H.S.	27,600	4,124	75	Financial Securities	B.T.M.	14,162	21,837
37	Allied Equity Income	A.H.G.	27,584	11,093					
38	Target Financial	T.T.M.	27,463	15,350					
39	Select International	S. & P.	26,121	5,090					

NOTE: *At 31 May 1978.

MANAGERS

A.H.G.	Allied Hambro Group	L.B.	Lloyds Bank Unit Trust Managers Ltd.
A.M.	Abbey Unit Trust Managers Ltd.	M. & G.	M. & G. Group Ltd.
B.T.M.	Britannia Trust Management Ltd.	N.G.T.	Norwich General Trust Ltd.
B.U.	Barclays Unicorn Ltd.	N.W.	National Westminster Unit Trust Managers Ltd.
E. & L.	Equity & Law Unit Trust Managers	P.	Prudential Unit Trust Managers Ltd.
G.F.M.	Gartmore Fund Managers Ltd.	P.I.	Practical Investment Co. Ltd.
G.M.	Grieveson Management Co. Ltd.	S. & P.	Save & Prosper Securities Ltd.
G.R.E.	Guardian Royal Exchange Unit Managers Ltd.	S.S.	Scotbits Securities Ltd.
H.	Henderson Unit Trust Management Ltd.	T.M.	Tyndall Managers Ltd.
H.S.	Hill Samuel Unit Trust Managers Ltd.	T.S.B.	T.S.B. Unit Trust Managers Ltd.
H.S.W.	J. Henry Schroder Wagg & Co. Ltd.	T.T.M.	Target Trust Managers Ltd.

The M&G Pension Fund Investment Service.

For some years now M&G have been providing an investment management service for the pension funds of companies and public corporations, as well as charitable foundations.

We are now extending this facility and taking on new clients for our Pension Fund Investment Service. Our independent status, wide contacts with stockbrokers and the very substantial volume of investments under M&G management place us in an ideal position to provide an investment service of this type.

For a copy of our new booklet "The M&G Pension Fund Investment Service," or to arrange an appointment to discuss the investment management of your Company's pension fund, please write to:

David Morgan,
M&G Investment Management Ltd.,
Three Quays, Tower Hill,
London, EC3R 6BQ. Tel: 01-626 4588

M&G

THE M&G GROUP

11a: Insurance companies - Life

Rank	Name—*Chairman*	LIFE ETC. FUNDS Latest year £000	Previous year £000	INSURANCES IN FORCE Latest year £000	Previous year £000	NEW BUSINESS Latest year £000	Previous year £000
1	Prudential Assurance Co. *R. H. Owen*	4,259,187	3,813,559	25,155,200	22,023,200	8,736,300	8,109,500
2	Legal & General Assurance Society *Viscount Caldecote*	2,612,600	2,160,500	—	—	2,628,610	2,068,457
3	Commercial Union Assurance Co. *Sir Francis Sandilands*	1,972,700	1,872,800	—	—	1,975,200	2,002,900
4	Standard Life Assurance Co. *A. M. Hodge*	1,808,064	1,616,656	—	—	1,453,878	1,388,477
5	Guardian Royal Exchange Assurance *J. E. H. Collins*	1,477,300	1,239,200	—	—	2,568,900	3,472,600
6	Norwich Union Insurance Group *D. E. Longe*	1,282,893	1,114,679	—	—	—	—
7	Scottish Widows' Fund & Life Ass. Society *A. I. Mackenzie*	932,919	716,908	—	—	705,046	726,879
8	Eagle Star Insurance Co. *Sir Denis Mountain*	932,100	777,200	—	—	1,605,300	1,324,600
9	Pearl Assurance Co. *F. L. Garner*	919,013	850,210	3,320,100	3,080,000	544,917	609,428
10	Royal Insurance Co. *D. Meinertzhagen*	765,871	662,858	—	—	939,500	893,400
11	Sun Life Assurance Society *P. G. Walker*	754,986	606,155	—	—	767,000	906,500
12	Co-operative Insurance Society *H. A. Toogood*	719,045	660,871	—	—	729,106	674,528
13	Equity & Law Life Assurance Society *P. D. J. H. Cox*	631,189	453,966	4,102,872	3,728,056	796,331	914,239
14	Friends' Provident Life Office *E. W. Phillips*	594,853	506,143	—	—	695,000	758,000
15	Hambro Life Assurance *J. M. Clay*	508,448	353,734	1,900,000	1,300,000	730,000	512,000
16	Scottish Amicable Life Assurance Company *Sir Robert Fairbairn*	495,055	382,773	2,527,445	2,036,291	763,796	498,798
17	General Accident Fire & Life Ass. Corpn. *I. H. S. Black*	483,558	442,780	—	—	1,144,300	1,151,400
18	Abbey Life Assurance Co. *R. F. Richardson*	414,736	323,723	—	—	—	—
19	Liverpool Victoria Friendly Society *E. Robertson*	410,396	385,828	—	—	157,078	144,206
20	Sun Alliance & London Insurance *Lord Aldington*	394,400	344,943	—	—	637,075	661,804
21	Clerical Medical & General Life Ass. Society *Sir Robert Black*	367,068	303,575	2,174,800	1,912,300	513,100	525,800
22	Royal London Mutual Insurance Society *T. Cowman*	362,617	294,440	1,108,312	1,020,861	196,353	175,838
23	Phoenix Assurance Co. *J. Hambro*	351,500	299,400	—	—	1,123,900	1,207,100
24	Britannic Assurance Co. *J. F. Jefferson*	347,676	318,729	1,100,452	982,510	232,152	204,968
25	Refuge Assurance Co. *P. W. D. Smith*	327,704	311,376	—	—	175,413	154,902

Depend on us...

Royal Insurance covers the world, handling over £950 million of overseas premiums; writing business in 85 different countries and 16 languages.

Fair dealing, unrivalled service and stability are the hallmarks of Royal Insurance worldwide.

New U.K. head office: New Hall Place, Old Hall Street, Liverpool L69 3EN.

Royal Insurance
looks after you. Fast

11b: Insurance companies - Non-life

Rank	Name—*Chairman*	PREMIUM INCOME Latest year £000	Previous year £000	GROSS INVESTMENT INCOME Latest year £000	Previous year £000	UNDERWRITING PROFIT Latest year £000	Previous year £000
1	Royal Insurance Co. *D. Meinertzhagen*	**1,235,476**	1,091,832	**113,694**	93,959	**15,155**	Loss 17,829
2	Commercial Union Assurance Co. *Sir Francis Sandilands*	**1,072,500**	1,148,900	**127,700**	123,900	**Loss 20,900**	Loss 59,800
3	General Accident Fire and Life Assurance Corpn *I. H. S. Black*	**674,582**	620,331	**75,316**	59,988	**Loss 6,304**	Loss 17,649
4	Guardian Royal Exchange Assurance *J. E. H. Collins*	**591,500**	560,700	**65,300**	58,500	**Loss 6,600**	3,800
5	Sun Alliance & London Insurance *Lord Aldington*	**465,500**	426,126	**53,400**	46,815	**1,100**	Loss 11,019
6	Prudential Assurance Co. *R. H. Owen*	**358,400**	321,915	**37,257**	34,459	**Loss 12,431**	Loss 12,997
7	Phoenix Assurance Co. *J. Hambro*	**323,000**	323,400	**41,600**	36,300	**Loss 1,000**	Loss 9,400
8	Eagle Star Insurance Co. *Sir Denis Mountain*	**315,000**	258,200	**39,600**	34,400	**Loss 4,300**	Loss 7,200
9	Norwich Union Insurance Group *D. E. Longe*	**125,869**	139,384	**20,150**	18,220	**5,468**	4,961
10	Legal & General Assurance Society *Viscount Caldecote*	**123,200**	109,000	**16,700**	14,500	**Loss 3,900**	Loss 3,700
11	Co-operative Insurance Society *H. A. Toogood*	**90,625**	79,054	**10,631**	8,384	**2,821**	576
12	National Employers' Mutual General Insurance Association *M. H. R. King*	**78,292**	71,532	**8,863**	6,638	**Loss 1,747**	Loss 296
13	Cornhill Insurance Co. *D. W. G. Sawyer*	**76,441**	65,583	**7,247**	5,647	**381**	218
14	Provincial Insurance Co. *C. F. E. Shakerley*	**63,647**	55,733	**5,768**	4,662	**Loss 1,243**	Loss 1,048
15	Excess Insurance Group *W. L. Samengo-Turner*	**63,127**	54,610	**12,044**	9,467	**Loss 3,811**	Loss 4,649
16	National Farmers' Union Mutual Insurance Society *R. Cary*	**53,745**	47,130	**6,779**	5,232	**2,115**	844
17	Municipal Mutual Insurance Co. *Sir Francis Hill*	**52,955**	41,765	**8,074**	5,215	**Loss 1,844**	Loss 1,324
18	Iron Trades Employers Insurance Association *D. Rebbeck*	**52,471**	42,517	**6,539**	5,610	**Loss 1,440**	Loss 1,376
19	Minster Insurance Co. *D. S. A. Pearce*	**43,020**	41,768	**7,033**	5,831	**Loss 1,666**	262
20	Pearl Assurance Co. *F. L. Garner*	**36,390**	31,287	**5,340**	4,697	**Loss 3,466**	Loss 3,013
21	Orion Insurance Co. *Sir Antony Part*	**26,479**	24,936	**4,886**	4,569	**Loss 256**	4
22	Dominion Insurance Co. *D. A. H. Johnson*	**22,460**	20,406	**3,334**	3,013	**Loss 2,223**	Loss 2,309
23	Norwich Winterthur Reinsurance Corpn *D. E. Longe*	**19,798**	12,507	**3,378**	2,179	**1,365**	Loss 869
24	National Insurance & Guarantee Corpn *E. Carter*	**19,644**	17,640	**2,166**	1,509	**Loss 755**	47
25	United Friendly Insurance Co. *R. C. Balding*	**15,036**	13,375	**719**	452	**907**	875

Bain Dawes

12: Other financial institutions

Rank	Name	Chairman	NET PROFIT AFTER TAX Latest year £000	Previous year £000	*Equity mkt. cap. £m
1	Mercantile Credit Co.	A. Victor Adey	8,244	2,707	—
2	Yorkshire Bank	J. P. R. Glyn	6,449	5,797	—
3	Lombard North Central	Earl of Crawford and Balcarres	6,218	4,029	—
4	United Dominions Trust	L. C. Mather	3,900	Loss 5,300	43.8
5	Agricultural Mortgage Corpn.	J. P. R. Glyn	2,536	1,801	—
6	John James Group of Companies	John James	2,269	1,229	12.5
7	Cattle's (Holdings)	R. Waudby	615	462	6.8
8	Cedar Holdings	S. Coorsh	580	455	—
9	London Scottish Finance Corpn.	R. H. Landman	242	157	2.1
10	HFC Trust	I. Martindale	193	Loss 445	—
11	Ionian Securities	Sir Robin Brook	27	Loss 699	—
12	Goode Durrant & Murray Group	L. E. Robinson	Loss 3,289	Loss 138	5.3
13	Britannia Arrow Holdings	G. Rippon	Loss 3,742	Loss 4,794	12.0
14	First National Finance Corpn.	J. P. R. Glyn	Loss 4,109	Loss 31,476	3.0

NOTE: *At 14 July 1978.

13: Mining finance

Rank	Name—Chairman	Headquarters	*CAPITAL EMPLOYED Latest year £000	Previous year £000	NET PROFIT BEFORE INTEREST AND TAX Latest year £000	Previous year £000	**Equity market cap. £m
1	Anglo American Corpn of South Africa[1] H. F. Oppenheimer	Johannesburg	2,129,840	898,234	148,235 p.a.	75,721	703.9
2	Federale Mynbou Beperk W. B. Coetzer	Johannesburg	674,276	620,038	88,657	89,320	—
3	Consolidated Gold Fields Lord Erroll of Hale	London	526,500	608,329	73,800	64,291	264.4
4	Anglo American Gold Investment Co. J. Ogilvie Thompson	Johannesburg	463,530	391,225	26,770	28,301	367.7
5	Charter Consolidated M. B. Hofmeyer	London	383,099	361,125	48,815	44,508	148.9
6	Gold Fields of South Africa A. Louw	Johannesburg	262,018	300,577	15,436	19,249	212.0
7	Johannesburg Consolidated Investment Co. Sir Albert Robinson	Johannesburg	252,694	305,797	35,233	32,676	92.4
8	Selection Trust J. P. du Cane	London	240,934	254,596	26,959 p.a.	24,362	133.1

NOTES: *Total tangible assets less current liabilities (excluding bank loans and overdrafts) but including investments at market value.
**At 14 July 1978.
[1] Merger of Anglo American Corpn of South Africa and Rand Selection Corpn. (Figures for previous year are those of Anglo American Corpn of South Africa.) Converted at R1.61735 to £1.

Facts and figures don't always speak for themselves.

Your company's results – and future prospects – have to be communicated and interpreted to a wide audience.

To the City, shareholders, employees, financial press, the public at large.

As a leading financial advertising and PR agency, we know a thing or two about getting company results read – and remembered.

How your Chairman's Statement can be made to come across with clarity and conviction.

What a healthy injection of creative design will do for your Report and Accounts.

The kind of lively communication needed to put your employees in the picture.

Or the ways in which corporate campaigns can help small names grow big, and big names bigger.

And that's only half the story. Our Public Relations department also has a vital part to play in keeping the press up to date with what you're doing – and why.

It all adds up to a complete service called Streets Financial.

Now, what about seeing how we'd make your facts and figures speak up loud and clear?

Ring Jem Miller or Mike Lomax on 01-247 8752.

Streets Financial Limited

62 Wilson Street, Finsbury Square, London EC2A 2BU. Telephone 01-247 8752. Telex 888369.

14: Property companies

Rank	Name—*Chairman*	*CAPITAL EMPLOYED		GROSS RENTS		NET PROFIT BEFORE INTEREST AND TAX		**Equity mkt. cap. £m
		Latest year £000	Previous year £000	Latest year £000	Previous year £000	Latest year £000	Previous year £000	
1	Land Securities Investment Trust *Lord Samuel*	870,998	871,117	56,258	52,559	48,337	44,926	413.3
2	English Property Corporation *Sir Denis Mountain*	723,840	892,574	75,952	88,212	61,517	72,628	39.4
3	MEPC *Sir Gerald Thorley*	530,799	717,086	55,386	55,737	42,223	40,386	133.9
4	Town & City Properties *J. M. Sterling*	365,180	431,065	34,033	33,093	13,583	14,753	31.9
5	Hammerson Property & Investment Trust *S. Mason*	209,941	223,037	33,909	33,353	21,818	24,249	91.6
6	Slough Estates *G. N. Mobbs*	192,798	193,537	15,205	12,863	13,912	11,195	108.1
7	British Land Co. *J. Ritblat*	165,281	283,642	15,725	14,941	14,279	14,223	22.4
8	St. Martins Property Corporation *F. M. Al-Sabah*	157,798	216,042	13,744	10,709	10,868	7,193	—
9	Stock Conversion & Investment Trust *R. Clark*	130,627	112,034	7,681	6,734	6,273	5,758	71.9
10	Bernard Sunley Investment Trust *D. C. G. Jessel*	118,860	116,264	5,505	4,814	8,891	5,183	35.2
11	Haslemere Estates *F. E. Cleary*	109,797	105,084	8,643	7,363	6,899	5,698	53.7
12	Capital & Counties Property Co. *K. H. Wallis*	102,646	127,310	10,052	9,971	8,127	4,821	38.4
13	Brixton Estate *M. J. Verey*	96,875	82,161	6,180	5,086	2,631	1,220	35.6
14	Great Portland Estates *B. Samuel*	83,928	76,932	7,191	6,500	4,958	4,780	83.2
15	Daejan Holdings *L. L. Tobin*	80,244	81,526	7,561	7,185	7,966	6,410	14.7
16	Centrovincial Estates *J. Gold*	67,966	77,663	8,776	7,739	4,116	3,655	10.8
17	Berkeley Hambro Property Co. *J. O. Hambro*	65,887	123,605	6,265	10,033	5,803	10,174	19.4
18	Samuel Properties *Viscount Bearstead*	59,246	62,534	5,219	4,013	3,566	2,725	23.1
19	Land Investors *J. J. Rose*	50,477	49,874	3,408	3,010	2,837	2,562	37.0
20	Peachey Property Corporation *Lord Mais*	48,220	41,435	4,089	3,809	1,783	2,749	17.1

NOTES: *Total tangible assets less current liabilities (other than bank loans and overdrafts and future tax).
**At 14 July 1978.

Invest in Experience.

If you are about to be involved in a Commercial or Industrial property situation, dealing with acquisition, disposal, leasing, financing or project management, invest a little time with us now. In return you will gain a great deal in experience.

Hampton & Sons

6 Arlington Street, London SW1A 1RB
Tel: 01-493 8222 Telex: 25341

9 Dowgate Hill, London EC4R 2TD
Tel: 01-236 7831

Also in Paris, Channel Islands and Branches

15: Investment trusts

Rank	Name—Chairman	Investments at market value £000	NET REVENUE BEFORE INTEREST AND TAX		*Equity market cap. £m.
			Latest year £000	Previous year £000	
1	Globe Investment Trust[1]—A. F. Roger (Governor)	268,455	17,428	7,374	171.6
2	Industrial & General Trust—Sir Anthony Touche	169,242	8,506	7,504	110.8
3	Foreign & Colonial Investment Trust Co.—H. C. Baring	159,978	6,475	5,137	111.5
4	Alliance Trust Co.—D. F. McCurrach	142,613	6,619	6,229	113.7
5	Witan Investment Co.—J. R. Henderson	125,145	5,163	4,432	77.2
6	Philip Hill Investment Trust—Sir Kenneth Keith	123,093	7,077	6,418	87.3
7	British Investment Trust—F. B. Harrison	114,880	5,322	5,070	103.6
8	Scottish Investment Trust Co.[2]—A. Grossart	112,495	4,194	1,280	89.0
9	Scottish Mortgage & Trust Co.—T. R. MacGregor	112,030	5,103	5,153	83.0
10	British Assets Trust—Sir Alastair Blair	107,916	5,121	4,399	71.6
11	Atlas Electric & General Trust—Sir Anthony Touche	93,662	4,547	3,964	63.7
12	Mercantile Investment Trust—G. J. A. Jamieson	92,423	5,422	4,748	53.7
13	Scottish United Investors—R. C. Smith	92,028	3,627	3,219	71.8
14	Investment Trust Corpn—D. M. C. Donald	90,427	3,862	3,503	—
15	Edinburgh Investment Trust—I. R. Guild	84,086	3,970	3,473	63.1
16	Scottish Eastern Investment Trust—A. L. McClure	83,859	4,245	3,751	76.6
17	Border & Southern Stockholders Trust—C. A. McLintock	82,083	2,886	2,530	58.9
18	Investors Capital Trust—C. F. Sleigh	78,720	3,089	2,460	51.3
19	United States Debenture Corpn[3]—W. M. Cunningham	77,549	4,389	2,500	66.2
20	Drayton Premier Investment Trust—P. Shelbourne	76,246	4,228	3,998	54.1
21	Anglo-American Securities Corpn—G. J. A. Jamieson	75,943	3,712	3,238	58.1
22	London Trust—E. D. G. Davies	74,202	3,936	3,645	44.0
23	Scottish American Investment Co.—P. J. Oliphant	73,465	3,399	2,903	50.9
24	Scottish National Trust—A. Rintoul	71,478	2,695	2,326	47.4
25	United British Securities Trust—Sir Geoffrey Kitchen	69,634	2,979	2,596	58.0
26	Drayton Consolidated Trust—P. Shelbourne	67,242	3,542	3,194	44.0
27	Scottish Western Investment Co.—J. A. Lumsden	66,480	2,604	2,387	52.7
28	Great Northern Investment Trust—Viscount Weir	65,113	3,225	2,864	50.9
29	Clydesdale Investment Co.—J. A. Lumsden	64,256	2,315	2,031	49.4
30	Guardian Investment Trust—M. B. Baring	59,351	2,845	2,506	40.3
31	Monks Investment Trust—M. Hamilton	58,796	2,734	2,510	41.1
32	Stockholders Investment Trust—C. A. McLintock	58,619	1,845	1,673	37.8
33	Trustees Corpn—Sir Anthony Touche	57,826	2,727	2,475	40.7
34	Rothschild Investment Trust—Jacob Rothschild	56,461	6,211	6,429	36.2
35	Lake View Investment Trust—C. A. McLintock	56,355	2,134	2,029	41.7
36	Scottish Northern Investment Trust—R. J. C. Fleming	52,380	2,465 p.a.	2,339	36.6
37	Continental & Industrial Trust—A. L. Hood	52,188	2,336	2,111	33.1
38	American Trust Co.—A. L. McClure	51,945	2,621	2,984	37.1
39	Securities Trust of Scotland—J. G. Wallace	51,559	2,559	2,379	38.0
40	Northern American Trust Co.—I. R. Guild	49,787	2,157	1,970	31.7
41	Sphere Investment Trust—C. M. Hughes	49,722	2,136	1,778	33.6
42	Merchants Trust—M. W. Jacomb	48,767	2,383	2,052	38.8
43	Second Alliance Trust Co.—D. F. McCurrach	47,538	2,055	1,813	37.4
44	Raeburn Investment Trust—D. Meinertzhagen	45,938	2,306	2,080	34.0
45	Drayton Commercial Investment Co.—P. Shelbourne	45,546	2,505	2,330	29.9
46	Whitbread Investment Co.—F. O. A. G. Bennett	45,334	3,037	2,727	37.9
47	London & Provincial Trust—Lord Wyfold	45,231	1,833	1,711	35.2
48	Aberdeen Trust—J. S. R. Cruickshank	45,054	2,048	1,856	30.9
49	Caledonian Trust—J. A. Lumsden	42,879	1,525	1,344	30.6
50	English & New York Trust Co.—I. M. L. D. Forde	42,536	1,901	1,628	30.2

NOTES: *At 14 July 1978.
[1] Merger of Globe Investment Trust and Cable Trust. (Revenue for previous year relates to Globe Investment Trust.)
[2] Merger of Scottish Investment Trust Co. and Second Scottish Investment Trust. (Revenue for previous year relates to Scottish Investment Trust Co.)
[3] Merger of United States Debenture Corpn and London Scottish American Trust. (Revenue for previous year relates to United States Debenture Corpn.)

95

16: Largest building societies

Rank	Name	TOTAL ASSETS		LIQUID ASSETS		RESERVES	
		Latest year £000	Previous year £000	Latest year £000	Previous year £000	Latest year £000	Previous year £000
1	Halifax	6,508,587	5,411,078	1,282,957	962,456	184,366	142,352
2	Abbey National	5,413,528	4,346,320	1,126,609	718,323	200,325	144,608
3	Nationwide	2,804,016	2,278,111	558,899	414,767	107,296	76,492
4	Leeds Permanent	1,891,831	1,622,377	365,633	305,738	57,556	46,162
5	Woolwich Equitable	1,772,871	1,486,497	327,424	246,247	58,368	48,084
6	Alliance	1,277,854	1,019,870	306,181	219,202	41,169	33,754
7	Leicester	1,120,879	901,867	243,779	151,717	38,493	31,005
8	Provincial	1,085,548	861,621	264,498	171,121	43,829	36,374
9	Britannia	965,230	781,249	267,869	196,027	38,730	31,312
10	Bradford & Bingley	874,911	692,499	200,278	112,790	37,446	26,044
11	Anglia	710,954	587,711	146,100	105,416	22,719	19,695
12	Burnley	595,610	498,123	131,275	94,236	25,374	18,666
13	Bristol & West	569,186	437,559	178,419	113,730	19,787	11,676
14	Hastings & Thanet	554,052	454,360	127,963	88,634	22,365	16,248
15	Gateway	538,297	441,138	108,265	70,398	20,218	16,375
16	Cheltenham & Gloucester	504,961	399,278	125,692	66,438	19,763	15,463
17	Huddersfield & Bradford	497,554	414,554	114,327	78,832	20,925	15,311
18	Northern Rock	435,066	351,782	96,769	56,447	15,388	11,433
19	Town & Country	235,872	202,480[2]	58,545	46,573[2]	14,140	11,119[2]
20	South of England	213,911	175,386	45,407	30,044	9,594	7,943
21	Coventry Economic	210,883	181,309	38,890	30,178	8,636	6,664
22	Guardian	207,734	177,607	57,849	45,711	11,035	8,940
23	Derbyshire	192,191	159,167	42,277	31,389	7,037	5,735
24	Chelsea	189,687	155,728	44,298	29,578	7,561	5,342
25	West Bromwich	181,484	147,019	51,133	37,648	7,964	6,148
26	Leeds & Holbeck	168,712	139,977	36,701	25,071	5,962	4,919
27	Portman	159,773	131,585	33,839	25,455	8,251	7,039
28	Skipton	150,813	128,650	36,751	25,535	6,404	5,484
29	Principality	124,070	103,468	26,513	20,336	5,934	4,083
30	Wolverhampton & Mercia	123,614	103,630	27,703	19,004	7,614	6,110
31	Bridgwater	117,571	96,342	32,928	22,518	4,610	3,806
32	Staffordshire	111,774	91,849	31,415	23,078	4,251	3,570
33	Heart of England	109,069	91,962	22,439	15,172	4,592	3,725
34	Birmingham	101,719[1]	57,092	22,666[1]	10,004	5,785[1]	3,343
35	London Goldhawk	98,989	83,128	28,227	14,451	4,377	3,699
36	Liverpool	90,947	73,445	21,880	10,499	4,080	3,181
37	Nottingham	90,578	72,320	22,212	18,526	5,338	4,021
38	Sunderland & Shields	81,839	69,973	16,022	12,467	3,881	3,045
39	Hearts of Oak & Enfield	81,151	69,744	19,510	13,316	3,292	2,899
40	National Counties	81,070	73,085	15,352	14,219	7,442	6,076
41	Lambeth	80,984	66,514	17,323	13,990	4,208	3,543
42	Cheshire	79,802	64,445	18,117	12,073	3,884	2,805
43	Property Owners	79,534	60,426	23,530	9,201	3,074	2,387
44	Sussex County	75,004	57,451	19,934	9,485	2,710	2,107
45	Midshires	74,040	62,637	16,173	11,577	2,874	2,138
46	Norwich	68,370	57,223	15,796	10,266	3,037	2,532
47	Sussex Mutual	65,366	52,780	17,592	12,003	2,991	2,461
48	Eastbourne Mutual	65,042	48,222	19,420	11,082	2,180	1,865
49	Cumberland	63,122	53,305	13,322	13,043	3,117	2,579
50	Newcastle Upon Tyne Permanent	61,814	51,362	14,617	8,227	2,662	2,156

NOTES: [1] Combined figures of Birmingham Incorporated B.S. and Birmingham Citizens B.S. Previous year figures are those of Birmingham Incorporated B.S.
[2] Combined figures of Town & Country B.S. and Magnet & Planet B.S.

17: The 500 leading European companies

The following letters are used to indicate countries: A - Austria; B - Belgium; D - Denmark; F - France; Fin - Finland; G - Germany; I - Italy; L - Luxembourg; N - Netherlands; No - Norway; S - Sweden; Sp - Spain; Sw - Switzerland.

Rank	Name	Country	Main activity	Turnover 1977 £M	Turnover 1976 £M	Reported profits 1977 £M
1	Royal Dutch Petroleum Co.	N	Oil and petroleum	13,640·0	11,992·9	2,203·8
2	Philips' Lamps Holding	N	Electrical products	7,172·5	7,004·6	272·9
3	ENI	I	Holding co. (petroleum, chemicals, engineering, textiles, etc.)	7,027	6,006	(61)
4	Veba AG	G	Holding co.	6,821·7	6,781·8	198·1
5	Daimler-Benz AG	G	Motor vehicle and engine manufacturers	6,441·8	5,853·8	555·5
6	Siemens AG	G	Electrical and general engineering, electronics	6,275·9	5,149·7	357·8
7	Volkswagenwerk AG	G	Motor vehicle manufacturers	6,015·4	5,335·6	466·6
8	Cie. Française des Petroles	F	Holding co. (oil and petroleum)	5,957·6	5,282·4	29·0
9	Hoechst AG	G	Chemicals, dyes, plastics, etc.	5,802·7	5,849·3	270·4
10	BASF AG	G	Chemical products, plastics	5,773·6	5,767·6	276·2
11	Renault (Régie Nationale des Usines)	F	Automobile production	5,488·3	4,976·5	1·3
12	Bayer AG	G	Chemical products	5,327·9	5,200·6	273·2
13	Nestlé Alimentana S.A.	Sw	Holding co. (chocolate, milk and food products)	5,239·9	4,970·8	357·5
14	Unilever N.V.	N	Food products, detergents, animal feedstuffs, toilet preparations	5,206·7	4,770·5	223·5
15	Thyssen AG	G	Iron and steel	4,910·0	5,077·7	120·7
16	Peugeot-Citroën (P.S.A.)	F	Automobiles, engines	4,669·5	3,909·2	0.3
17	SNEA	F	Petrol, oil, natural gas, sulphur	4,125·0	4,010·0	138·0
18	Saint-Gobain-Pont-à-Mousson	F	Construction materials	3,548·4	3,181·6	153·9
19	OIAG-Oesterreichische Industrieverwaltungs AG	A	State industrial holding co.	3,455·9	3,347·6	3·8
20	Petrofina S.A.	B	Oil exploration	3,347·9	3,125·5	223·1
21	Montedison SpA	I	Chemicals, pharmaceuticals	3,286·5	2,891·9	279·3
22	AEG-Telefunken	G	Electrical engineering	3,065·2	2,824·8	26·6
23	Deutsche Shell AG	G	Oil and petroleum	3,048·6	3,115·3	(8·6)
24	Esso AG	G	Oil producers	3,037·4	3,113·8	(2·5)
25	RWE Rheinisch-Westfälisches Elektrizitätswerk AG	G	Generation and distribution of electricity	3,017·4	2,899·4	276·8
26	Nederlandse Gasunie (N.V.)	N	Purchase and sale of natural gas	2,938·3	2,596·1	27·0
27	Mannesmann	G	Pipe mills and steel processing	2,917·6	2,938·5	145·7
28	Pechiney Ugine Kuhlmann	F	Holding co. (chemicals, aluminium, etc.)	2,895·4	2,481·0	15·8
29	Rhône-Poulenc S.A.	F	Holding co. (chemical and pharmaceutical products)	2,632·2	2,408·0	9·4
30	Ciba-Geigy AG	Sw	Chemicals, pharmaceuticals, dyes, etc.	2,592·2	2,474·1	109·5
31	Ford-Werke AG	G	Car manufacturers	2,531·3	2,156·2	309·9
32	Gutehoffnungs-Hütte Aktienverein	G	Holding co. (shipbuilding, iron and steel trades, etc.)	2,452·2	2,249·4	77·9
33	Ruhrkohle AG	G	Coal mining	2,440·3	2,836·9	N/A
34	Deutsche BP AG	G	Petroleum, natural gas	2,415·9	1,876·6	(13·4)
35	Akzo N.V.	N	Holding co. (chemicals, fibres, etc.)	2,401·2	2,474·1	(1·3)
36	Finsider	I	Holding co. (iron and steel)	2,338·1	1,933·9	(3·2)
37	Estel N.V.	N	Steel	2,333·4	2,142·7	(121·8)
38	D.S.M. N.V.	N	Chemical products	2,332·7	2,141·6	12·7
39	Aral AG	G	Petroleum	2,307·7	2,240·3	5·8
40	Fiat	I	Motor vehicles, ships, engines, diesel trains, aeroplanes	2,304·2	2,160·4	70·6
41	Opel (Adam) AG	G	Car manufacturers	2,291·4	2,192·8	84·7
42	Esso S.A.F.	F	Oil producers	2,254·6	1,933·7	27·6
43	Schneider S.A.	F	Holding co. (heavy industry, iron and steel)	2,218·5	2,062·4	4·7
44	Denain Nord-Est Longwy	F	Iron and steel manufacturers	2,193·6	1,954·2	(229·5)
45	KF/Konsum	S	Wholesale and retail distributors	2,162·1	1,875·8	3·3
46	BBC–Brown Boverie & Cie AG	Sw	Electrical engineering	2,135·3	2,198·4	17·3
47	Shell Française	F	Petroleum products	2,106·0	1,968·3	—
48	Bosch (Robert) GmbH	G	Electronic engineers and auto-electrical manufacturers	2,071·9	1,813·4	191·8
49	Salzgitter AG	G	Iron and steel manufacturers	2,067·2	2,216·7	(23·7)
50	Cie. Générale d'Electricité	F	Holding co. (electrical engineers)	2,040·1	1,746·9	46·0

Rank	Name	Country	Main activity	Turnover 1977 £M	Turnover 1976 £M	Reported profits 1977 £M
51	Michelin & Cie.	F	Holding co. (tyres)	1,944·1	1,756·8	168·1
52	Karstadt AG	G	Department stores	1,928·1	1,806·9	57·9
53	SHV Holdings N.V.	N	Shipping, natural gas, oil, transport	1,910·8	1,868·6	26·0
54	Migros-Genossenschafts-Bund	Sw	Department stores, supermarkets	1,885·6	1,741·9	4·1
55	Deutsche SPAR-Zentrale	G	Wholesale distributors, supermarkets	1,878·5	1,815·0	N/A
56	Volvo AB	S	Motor vehicles, marine, industrial and aero engines, etc.	1,812·6	1,764·9	35·5
57	Metallgesellschaft AG	G	Non-ferrous metals	1,742·0	1,550·7	N/A
58	East Asiatic Co. Ltd.	D	Ship owners, global traders, plantation owners, forest developers	1,681·7	1,377·9	30·6
59	Flick (Gruppe Friedrich)	G	Holding co. (iron, steel, mechanical engineering)	1,659·0	1,489·3	71·1
60	Kaufhof AG	G	Department stores	1,618·9	1,581·7	35·7
61	Wintershall AG	G	Potash and mineral oil producers and refiners	1,618·9	1,544·2	8·4
62	IBM Deutschland GmbH	G	Computers	1,589·4	1,484·4	474·0
63	Reemtsma Cigarettenfabriken GmbH	G	Cigarette and drink manufacturers	1,564·7	1,539·8	63·7
64	Voest-Alpine AG	A	Iron and steel	1,517·7	1,548·8	N/A
65	Solvay & Cie.	B	Chemicals, plastics	1,478·8	1,398·8	93·4
66	Stet-Societa Finanziaria Telefonica	I	Electrical machinery, apparatus and supplies	1,448·6	1,171·0	16·1
67	BSN-Gervais Danone	F	Food products	1,436·2	1,310·5	1·6
68	Hoffman-La Roche (F.) & Co. AG	Sw	Chemicals and pharmaceuticals	1,430·6	1,333·9	87·6
69	Alusuisse	Sw	Aluminium	1,418·9	1,260·6	39·7
70	Deutsche Texaco AG	G	Oil refinery	1,412·5	1,444·1	50·7
71	Thomson-Brandt	F	Electrical engineers	1,399·8	1,880·2	52·1
72	Carrefour	F	Hypermarkets	1,389·9	1,075·5	40·8
73	Pirelli-Dunlop Union SpA	I	Rubber products	1,388·3	1,076·1	79·2
74	BMW-Bayerische Motorenwerke AG	G	Motor and motor cycle manufacturers	1,377·5	1,184·6	92·8
75	Italsider SpA	I	Iron and steel	1,349·9	1,323·0	(235·9)
76	Henkel KgaA	G	Detergents, cleaning agents	1,335·7	1,270·7	39·4
77	Esso Italiana	I	Oil, petroleum	1,313·0	998·9	(18·3)
78	GB-Inno-BM SA	B	Supermarkets, department stores	1,259·5	1,061·6	20·8
79	Mobil Oil AG	G	Oil and natural gas	1,251·5	1,222·5	14·0
80	Sandoz AG	Sw	Dyestuffs, pharmaceuticals, chemicals, etc.	1,244·6	1,071·4	55·8
81	Saab-Scania Aktiebolag	S	Vehicles, aircraft, electronics, etc.	1,210·3	1,077·7	33·4
82	ICA-Koncernen	S	Foods, restaurants, consumer goods	1,184·3	N/A	9·5
83	Creusot-Loire SA	F	Iron and steel	1,177·7	959·1	(22·7)
84	BAYWA AG	G	Agricultural products and machinery	1,174·1	1,127·5	7·7
85	Ruhrgas AG	G	Gas supply	1,172·4	998·3	79·7
86	Deutsche Lufthansa AG	G	Airline operator	1,144·0	1,045·1	35·9
87	Degussa	G	Precious metals, chemicals, furnace construction	1,109·6	1,059·3	32·8
88	IBM France	F	Computers	1,099·4	976·6	87·8
89	ASEA	S	Electrical power equipment	1,089·5	941·7	35·3
90	Usinor	F	Steel production	1,081·2	1,082·1	(229·4)
91	Electrolux Aktiebolag	S	Refrigerators, cleaning and office machines	1,035·7	857·1	57·6
92	Klöckner-Werke AG	G	Iron and steel producers, heavy engineering	1,026·6	1,037·7	(16·0)
93	Printemps SA	F	Department stores	995·9	922·2	N/A
94	Ahold NV	N	Supermarkets, food manufacturers	952·3	781·1	15·9
95	Saarbergwerke	G	Coal, electric power	947·9	802·5	N/A
96	Marquand & Bahls GmbH & Co.	G	Holding co. (mineral oils)	946·4	783·3	N/A
97	Sulzer (Gebrüder) AG	Sw	General engineering	913·3	920·3	21·9
98	Chrysler France SA	F	Automobile manufacturers	906·8	625·5	31·0
99	SKF Group (AB Svenska Kullagerfabriken)	S	Roller bearings	897·3	782·6	40·8
100	Sacilor-Acieries et Laminoirs de Lorraine	F	Iron and steel	888·7	888·4	(254·5)

The legend you meet.

The Mercedes-Benz S-class is just one part of a range that begins with the 200D and goes up to the 450SEL 6.9. Each car is built singlemindedly to the principle that a car should combine superb styling with excellent engineering, outstanding performance, concern for safety and luxurious comfort.

If it's impossible, get Bovis to build it.

Rank	Name	Country	Main activity	Turnover 1977 £M	Turnover 1976 £M	Reported profits 1977 £M
101	Klöckner-Humboldt-Deutz AG	G	General engineering	886·1	800·1	36·9
102	Ericsson (Telefonaktiebolaget L.M.)	S	Electrical engineering and telecommunications	878·1	819·7	52·4
103	Vereinigte Industrie-Unternehmungen AG	G	Holding co. (utilities, chemicals, metals)	874·7	886·3	45·2
104	Edeka Zentrale AG	G	Consumer goods	862·7	733·0	4·8
105	Horten AG	G	Department stores	823·4	826·8	15·6
106	Gevaert Photo-Produkten NV	B	Photographic equipment	816·3	769·5	27·0
107	Neste Oy	Fin	Oil and gas	814·4	689·8	29·5
108	Intercom	B	Electricity and gas production and distribution	811·2	766·1	51·4
109	Ogem Holding N.V.	N	Industrial holding co.	806·7	752·8	10·7
110	CEPSA	Sp	Oil refining	741·8	602·7	19·4
111	Deutsche Babcock AG	G	General engineering	800·5	875·8	20·6
112	Beijerinvest AB	S	Holding co.	797·3	713·3	8·9
113	Sté. Lyonnaise des Eaux et de l'Eclairage	F	Public utilities	788·8	617·2	33·1
114	Nouvelles Galeries Réunis	F	Department stores	788·1	725·7	6·5
115	Casino	F	Food manufacturers and distributors	763·6	657·1	20·5
116	Internatio-Muller N.V.	N	Holding co.	758·6	702·9	11·4
117	Krupp (Fried.) Hüttenwerke AG	G	Iron and steel production	754·2	796·8	(2·2)
118	Cockerill	B	Steel manufacturers	752·0	822·2	(115·7)
119	SOK—Suomen Osuuskauppojen Keskuskunta	Fin	Co-operative wholesalers	751·0	726·0	1·7
120	Oerlikon-Bührle Holding AG	Sw	Holding co. (general engineering)	702·6	614·0	53·4
121	Charbonnages de France	F	Coal mining	737·7	726·9	(21·1)
122	Neckermann Versand KGaA	G	Mail order house and department stores	734·7	774·5	(28·3)
123	Skanska Cement-Gjuteriet	S	Builders	733·3	637·7	17·8
124	SCOA	F	International wholesale and retail distribution	731·4	667·7	22·8
125	Wolff AG (Otto)	G	Iron and steel production	725·5	744·1	10·4
126	Oetker-Group	G	Holding co. (food and beverages)	719·6	764·1	N/A
127	Thyssen Bornemisza N.V.	N	Cement, machinery, transport equipment, water transport, general wholesale trade	708·8	590·4	37·6
128	Bertelsmann AG	G	Publishers	708·1	539·5	35·9
129	Lafarge	F	Cement production	704·6	669·8	16·8
130	VEW-Vereinigte Elektrizitäts-Werke Westfalen AG	G	Electricity supply	700·5	680·9	57·8
131	Viniprix	F	Supermarkets	694·0	460·9	6·1
132	Sté. Internationale Pirelli SA	Sw	Holding co. (cables, tyres, rubber articles)	693·6	743·2	8·0
133	Snia Viscosa	I	Textiles, chemicals, engineering	686·9	622·8	(27·7)
134	Grundig AG	G	Electronic equipment	684·9	626·2	N/A
134	Chemische Werke Huls AG	G	Petrochemicals	684·9	670·0	N/A
136	Standard Elektrik Lorenz AG	G	Electrical engineering	681·2	671·5	35·4
137	Chimique, Routière et d'Entreprise Générale	F	Civil engineering	680·0	561·4	8·7
138	Cebeco-Handelsraad	N	Wholesale trade	679·7	534·9	4·8
139	Brinkmann AG (Martin)	G	Tobacco	676·7	666·9	29·0
140	Olivetti & C. SpA (Ing. C.)	I	Business machinery and systems manufacturers	676·6	514·4	N/A
141	Métallurgie Hoboken-Overpelt	B	Non-ferrous metals	673·1	608·6	6·1
142	Systembolaget AB	S	Beer, wine, etc.	663·9	574·2	15·0
143	Radar SA	F	Holding co. (supermarkets)	658·2	526·2	8·6
144	Preussag AG	G	Coal, oil, non-ferrous metals	652·3	666·2	15·5
145	Haniel & Cie. (Franz)	G	Petroleum products	642·0	554·8	22·3
146	Swissair	Sw	Airline	635·3	569·4	13·5
147	Avions Marcel Dassault-Breguet Aviation	F	Aircraft	635·1	660·8	49·8
148	KLM-Royal Dutch Airlines	N	Air transport	632·7	579·3	31·5
149	Cie. Générale des Eaux	F	Water purification and distribution	626·9	518·1	N/A
150	S.A.S.	S	Airline	617·1	538·9	10·2

Our clients say more about us than we ever can.

THE FERRARI BERLINETTA BOXER BB512. 5·0 litre flat 12. The Ultimate Sports Car.

Rank	Name	Country	Main activity	Turnover 1977 £M	Turnover 1976 £M	Reported profits 1977 £M
151	Grånges Aktiebolag	S	Iron and steel, mining	604·1	603·0	53·2
152	Rijn-Schelde-Verolme Machinefabrieken	N	Shipbuilding, mechanical engineering	599·0	618·8	(10·7)
153	Holderbank Financière Glaris SA	Sw	Holding co. (cement)	591·5	556·4	30·7
154	Chargeurs Réunis SA	F	Holding co. (transport)	587·0	494·9	10·2
155	Compania Telefonica Nacional de España	Sp	Telephone and data transmission service	581·1	416·9	137·8
156	Demag AG	G	Mechanical engineering	576·1	530·2	13·2
157	Heineken N.V.	N	Holding co. (brewers, etc.)	568·5	491·8	·0
158	Swedish Match Co.	S	Building and interior products, matches, packaging materials	564·6	518·2	(0·4)
159	Boehringer Ingelheim Gruppe	G	Pharmaceuticals	564·1	547·4	56·5
160	Hollandsche Beton Groep N.V.	N	Holding co. (building and civil engineering)	562·0	470·6	16·2
161	Televerket	S	Telephones, telegraphy, broadcasting	555·0	513·0	14·0
162	Hapag-Lloyd AG	G	Shipping	545·6	474·5	19·7
163	SEAT	Sp	Vehicle manufacturers	538·3	490·6	2·6
164	Spie-Batignolles	F	Constructional engineers	537·5	409·8	4·5
165	ARBED	L	Iron and steel producers	537·1	563·3	65·8
166	L'Oreal	F	Hair products and cosmetics	536·2	470·5	32·7
167	Nedlloyd Groep N.V.	N	Shipping	534·8	549·8	23·1
168	VAW-Vereinigte Aluminium-Werke AG	G	Aluminium production	532·9	523·8	6·0
169	Schering AG	G	Chemicals and pharmaceuticals	531·2	497·1	46·9
170	Hachette (Librairie) S.A.	F	Publishers	527·2	463·1	2·1
171	Norsk Hydro A/S	No	Producers of nitrogen and magnesium products, plastics	526·9	484·3	24·3
172	Union Explosivos Rio Tinto SA	Sp	Chemicals, industrial explosives, etc.	525·9	437·6	17·8
173	Delhaize Frères et Cie.	B	Supermarkets	517·4	442·5	4·5
174	SCA-Svenska Cellulosa A/B	S	Chemical pulp, paper, timber and chemical products	515·5	465·6	21·0
175	Wessanen N.V. (Koninklijke)	N	Food manufacturer	508·6	438·0	6·9
176	Sandvik AB	S	Iron and steel	506·4	438·2	33·2
177	Rütgerswerke AG	G	Raw material processors	499·1	536·0	12·7
178	Holzmann AG (Philipp)	G	Civil engineering and construction co.	498·0	438·6	N/A
179	Vereinigte Edelstahlwerke	A	Steel	497·8	494·4	N/A
180	Entreprise Minière et Chimique	F	Mining and metals	491·8	526·1	14·3
181	Alitalia	I	Airline	491·6	350·4	6·8
182	OK-Okjekonsumenternas Förbund	S	Wholesale and retail of cars, hotels and boarding houses, water transport	490·0	382·1	2·8
183	Office Commercial Pharmaceutique (O.C.P)	F	Pharmaceutical distributors	487·4	444·9	3·2
184	Beghin-Say	F	Paper, sugar refinery	484·7	444·0	(14·1)
185	Zahnradfabrik Friedrichshafen AG	G	Vehicle component producers	474·0	444·8	8·5
186	KBB N.V.-Koninklijke Bijenkorf Beheer	N	Holding co. (shops, department stores)	474·0	418·9	8·1
187	Ferodo (SA Française du)	F	Motor components	472·3	426·2	25·9
188	Alfa-Laval AB	S	General engineering	471·8	421·0	19·3
189	Dragados y Construcciones SA	Sp	Builders and civil engineers	470·7	411·6	9·4
190	United Breweries Ltd.	D	Breweries	467·2	451·0	16·3
191	Atlas Copco AB	S	Compressed air equipment	466·1	425·0	37·8
192	Stora Koppabergs Bergslags AB	S	Mining, steel	465·8	495·8	11·4
193	Otra NV	N	International traders	465·7	430·4	1·8
194	Continental Gummi-Werke AG	G	Manufacturers of tyres and industrial rubber articles	462·8	443·0	13·2
195	IBM Italia	I	Computers	455·6	384·4	47·8
196	Valmet OY	Fin	Machinery, transport, equipment	454·7	452·5	(0·4)
197	Freudenberg & Co.	G	Holding co. (leather, rubber, chemicals)	453·5	426·4	N/A
198	Bayernwerk AG	G	Electricity	453·3	362·8	33·3
199	Mobil Oil Française	F	Oil refinery and distribution	451·9	375·0	N/A
200	Strabag-Bau AG	G	Building and construction	450·6	405·0	20·0

We're very accomplished in obtaining the lowdown on European stocks and shares.

The Extel European Company Card Service gives you all the figures and facts that matter - in English - on some 700 large firms quoted on the Bourses. It's the safe, easy way to keep abreast of all that's going on across the Channel.

Write or ring for complete details. *Toute de suite,* monsieur. You don't know what you might be missing.

Extel Statistical Services Limited
the <u>fact</u> getters

37-45 Paul Street, London EC2A 4PB · Phone 01-253 3400 · Telex 263437

Rank	Name	Country	Main activity	Turnover 1977 £M	Turnover 1976 £M	Reported profits 1977 £M
201	Douwe Egberts BV	N	Coffee, tea, tobacco	447·3	391·0	6·8
202	Stahlwerke Röchling-Burbach	G	Steel	444·8	483·1	N/A
203	Générale d'Entreprises	F	Civil engineering	441·5	351·8	2·5
204	Pernod Ricard SA	F	Holding co. (wines and spirits)	437·0	415·4	28·8
205	Dumez	F	Building and construction	429·2	358·0	21·3
206	Honeywell Bull	F	Business machines, etc.	422·3	350·1	18·1
207	Andrae-Noris Zahn AG	G	Pharmaceuticals	420·5	413·2	4·2
208	Dyckerhoff & Widmann AG	G	Construction and cement production	420·2	402·5	N/A
209	Linde AG	G	Refrigeration equipment, chemical engineering machinery	415·3	387·0	22·6
210	Deutsche Marathon Petroleum GmbH	G	Refining and wholesale of petroleum	415·2	310·3	4·2
211	Hankkija	Fin	Wholesale co-operative	415·2	375·2	1·4
212	VFW-Fokker mbH	G	Aircraft manufacturer, etc.	414·0	423·7	37·0
213	Stevin Groep N.V.	N	Civil engineering	411·0	390·3	10·2
214	Groupe Docks de France	F	Supermarkets	410·8	367·3	6·0
215	E.B.E.S.	B	Electricity production and distribution	409·9	371·7	39·7
216	Axel Springer Verlag AG	G	Printing and publishing	408·5	356·1	4·5
217	Rheinische Braunkohlenwerke AG	G	Coal, electricity	408·1	386·3	41·8
218	Verenigde Machinefabrieken Stock N.V.	N	Engineers	407·4	436·6	(9·3)
219	Hochtief AG	G	Civil engineering and construction	403·4	306·5	24·1
220	Deli Mij N.V.	N	Wholesale trade (timber, tobacco and commodities)	399·1	317·4	8·3
221	Tabacofina S.A.	B	Holding co. (tobacco)	394·5	358·1	7·5
222	Roussel Uclaf S.A.	F	Pharmaceutical and biological products	392·9	364·5	21·4
223	Routière Colas (Société)	F	Civil engineering	392·0	355·9	11·3
224	Nederlandse Spoorwegen N.V.	N	Railways	389·6	359·5	N/A
225	Gotaverken AB	S	Shipbuilding	385·5	235·5	58·2
226	Norddeutsche Affinerie	G	Smelter and refinery of non-ferrous and precious metals	384·3	385·9	16·5
227	Carl-Zeiss-Stiftung	G	Holding co. (glass, optical equipment)	382·6	350·0	10·2
228	Steag AG	G	Electricity, gas and steam supply, construction	382·1	331·3	8·9
229	Dollfus-Mieg et Cie. (S.A.)	F	Holding co. (textiles)	381·7	344·5	(4·0)
230	HEW-Hamburgische Electrizitätswerke AG	G	Electricity and heat distribution	377·8	350·9	56·6
231	Bouygues S.A.	F	Building constructors	377·6	289·2	5·6
232	Snecma	F	Aircraft, engines, etc.	374·5	375·4	10·6
233	Kügelfischer Georg Schäfer & Co.	G	Ball and roller bearings	373·1	350·2	4·2
234	Grands Travaux de Marseille	F	Civil engineering	367·9	367·9	7·8
235	Merck (E.)	G	Chemical and pharmaceutical manufacturers	367·0	355·4	5·6
236	Fischer (Georg) AG	Sw	Machinery and castings	365·1	349·4	11·2
236	Rinascente (La)	I	Department stores	365·1	313·9	(2·5)
238	Hagemayer N.V.	N	Cosmetics, pharmaceutuicals, electrical engineering	365·0	312·6	11·3
239	Steyr-Daimler-Puch AG	A	Motor vehicle and engine manufacturer	364·4	343·8	10·8
240	Cit-Alcatel	F	Telecommunication systems	360·7	313·0	9·3
241	Industrie A. Zanussi SpA	I	Electrical machinery, apparatus and supplies	360·0	254·0	18·0
242	Buhrmann Tetterode N.V.	N	Holding co. (paper manufacturers)	359·6	315·5	16·1
243	Bekaert S.A.	B	Holding co. (wire and wire products)	358·9	338·0	17·4
244	Poliet	F	Holding co. (building materials)	358·4	300·6	9·2
245	Nordwestdeutsche Kraftwerke AG	G	Electricity production and distribution	355·0	329.7	40·1
246	International Sleeping Car and Tourism Co.	B	Transport, hotels, restaurants, tourism	352·8	359·3	3·4
247	Liebherr Holding GmbH	G	Building equipment	352·7	285·9	N/A
248	Rauma-Repola Oy	Fin	General engineering	351·3	298·1	6·3
249	Euromarché	F	Supermarkets, hypermarkets	350·8	283·1	5·2
250	Lauritzen A/S	D	Shipping co.	345·4	308·9	38·8

Rank	Name	Country	Main activity	Turnover 1977 £M	Turnover 1976 £M	Reported profits 1977 £M
251	Fougerolle	F	Public works, road works, civil engineering	344·2	307·9	4·6
252	Radiotechnique	F	Radios, televisions, electrical equipment	342·2	295·2	24·8
253	Energie-Versorgung Schwaben AG	G	Electricity supply and distribution	340·7	332·3	41·2
254	Chevron Oil Belgium N.V.	B	Petroleum products	335·5	324·7	3·4
255	Babcock-Fives (Cie. Industrielle et Financière)	F	Holding co. (mechanical, structural and electrical engineers)	332·3	363·3	10·6
256	Chatillon (Cie. Industrielle)	F	Iron and steel	331·3	343·3	N/A
257	Enso-Gutzeit Osakeyhtio	Fin	Wood, paper	329·4	298·9	1·3
258	Mjolkcentralen Arla	S	Food manufacturers	328·2	300·1	1·9
259	PWA-Papierwerke Waldhof-Aschaffenburg AG	G	Chemicals, pulp and paper manufacturers and converters	326·8	296·9	8·6
260	DCGG Deutsche Continental-Gas Gesellschaft	G	Gas and electricity production and supply	323·8	307·1	13·9
261	Schmalbach-Lubeca GmbH	G	Manufacturer of packaging materials	323·8	310·6	3·4
262	Wacker-Chemie GmbH	G	Industrial chemicals, plastics	323·7	318·4	14·8
263	Carnaud S.A.	F	Iron	322·8	222·8	3·5
264	Usines Cnausson (S.A. des)	F	Motor components	320·1	231·2	N/A
265	Eschweiler Bergwerks-Verein	G	Coal production	316·3	404·5	N/A
266	Olida et Caby Associés S.A.	F	Foods	315·6	289·1	1·1
267	Lesieur Cotelle et Associés	F	Holding co. (fats and oils)	314·1	307·5	9·6
268	Redoute à Roubaix S.A.	F	Mail order	313·9	278·2	10·3
269	Boliden AB	S	Mining, metallurgy and chemicals	313·7	276·6	7·3
270	Smidth (F. L.) & Co.	D	Engineering	312·9	302·6	21·7
271	Badenwerk AG	G	Electricity supply	309·6	304·5	23·5
272	Schindler Holding AG	Sw	Holding co. (general engineering)	307·6	296·8	13·2
273	Langnese-Iglo GmbH	G	Frozen foods	306·4	291·7	N/A
274	Nokia AB (Oy)	Fin	Pulp, paper, power, etc.	305·5	275·8	6·4
275	Sidmar	B	Iron and steel	305·3	271·6	(17·3)
276	Bos-Kalis Westminster Group N.V.	N	Dredging co.	304·9	264·7	13·0
277	Diehl KG	G	Data systems, clocks, defence products	303·9	274·0	N/A
278	Borregaard A/S	No	Holding co. (paper, chemicals)	302·1	271·2	0·1
279	Auxiliaire d'Entreprises	F	Civil engineering	300·2	254·8	18·7
280	Södra Skogsägarna	S	Wood, paper	299·9	279·3	3·6
281	Varta AG	G	Holding co. (batteries and plastics)	298·7	285·8	17·2
282	UNERG	B	Gas, electricity, etc.	298·5	248·2	23·1
283	Cellulose du Pin S.A.	F	Wood pulp, paper	292·1	284·3	21·3
284	Uddeholms Aktiebolag	S	Steel, paper and chemicals	291·5	242·4	(42·6)
285	Svenska Esso AB	S	Petroleum	286·5	290·3	8·6
286	Buderus AG	G	Iron and steelworks	286·4	276·4	1·5
287	Semperit AG	A	Tyres, rubber goods and plastics	284·3	276·2	(5·6)
288	Telefonbau-und Normalzeit	G	Electrical machinery, apparatus and supplies	284·1	254·4	28·3
289	Akergruppen	No	Shipbuilding	284·0	309·6	0·8
290	BPA Byggproduktion AB	S	Civil engineers	279·5	248·4	0·3
291	Meneba	N	Holding co. (flour millers, etc.)	278·3	266·1	(4·1)
292	UTA-Union de Transports Aériens	F	Airline	276·5	234·1	5·3
293	Kymi Kymmene	Fin	Paper, engineering, chemicals	276·2	217·2	1·8
294	D.B.A.	F	Manufacturers of equipment for motor and aircraft industries	274·8	234·5	2·5
294	Süddeutsche Zucker-AG (Südzucker)	G	Sugar refiners	274·8	242·4	12·2
296	Euroc AB	S	Cement production	274·7	251·0	7·9
297	Esselte AB	S	Printing, publishing, packaging	274·2	241·2	12·3
298	Esso Suisse	Sw	Oil and petroleum	274·1	226·5	0·5
299	AGA Aktiebolag	S	Gas, batteries, radiators, electronics	273·8	281·0	19·0
300	UCB S.A.	B	Chemical and pharmaceutical manufacturers	273·6	269·0	(5·9)

Rank	Name	Country	Main activity	Turnover 1977 £M	Turnover 1976 £M	Reported profits 1977 £M
301	Elkem-Spigerverket A/S	No	Ferro-alloys, steel, etc.	271·8	265·1	4·0
302	Dortmunder Union-Schultheiss Brauerei AG	G	Brewers	271·0	279·3	14·1
303	OCE-Van Der Grinten N.V.	N	Equipment and materials	270·7	172·9	15·4
304	Iberduero S.A.	Sp	Electricity	270·4	228·3	89·7
305	Landis & Gyr AG	Sw	Electrical equipment	270·1	236·7	11·0
306	Dansk Shell	D	Petroleum	269·9	246·9	9·9
307	Nixdorf Computer	G	Computers	267·4	213·9	8·5
308	Mielewerk GmbH	G	Machinery, metal products, furniture	267·0	220·7	N/A
309	Lonza AG	Sw	Chemical manufacturers and electricity supply works	266·2	250·6	4·1
310	PRB	B	Polyurethane, chemicals	265·3	237·8	9·1
311	O & K Orenstein & Koppel AG	G	General engineering	265·0	242·7	9·6
312	Chemie Linz	A	Chemicals	264·5	256·5	2·2
313	Dansk Esso A/S	D	Petroleum products	263·0	238·9	(0·3)
314	Ballast-Nedam Groep N.V.	N	Builders, constructors and engineers	262·0	269·6	5·5
315	Bofors AB	S	Arms, tanks, steel products	260·7	215·8	4·4
316	Grunzweig & Hartmann und Glasfaser AG	G	Building materials	260·6	245·9	8·9
317	Superfos A/S	D	Fertilisers	259·9	243·8	5·6
318	Cedis	F	Supermarkets	258·7	225·8	5·8
319	Grands Magasins Jelmoli S.A.	Sw	Department stores and mail-order houses	256·7	244·4	6·7
320	Felten & Guilleaume Carlswerk AG	G	Holding co. (electrical engineering)	256·6	253·6	5·9
321	Van Leer B.V.	N	Fabricated metal products	255·7	255·0	N/A
322	Ford Motor Co. (Belgium) S.A.	B	Motor manufacturers	254·6	236·3	10·4
323	Molkerei-Zentrale Süd GmbH & Co. KG	G	Milk and milk products	254·5	238·6	0·1
324	Usego-Trimerco Holding AG	Sw	Holding co. (food industry)	254·4	224·7	(1·3)
325	Kemanobel AB	S	Chemicals	253·9	200·6	11·5
326	Heraeus GmbH	G	Pottery, glass, electrical machinery, photographic and optical goods	251·9	214·3	14·3
326	Svenska Fläktfabriken AB	S	General engineering	251·9	247·4	7·9
328	Porsche AG	G	Motor vehicles	249·7	150·5	8·0
329	International Harvester Co. mbH	G	Agricultural machinery, etc.	245·9	225·6	27·0
330	Wella AG	G	Hair products	244·8	226·2	4·5
331	Kvaerner Industrier A/S	No	Holding co. (ship building, construction, engineering)	244·5	222·2	3·4
332	Lainière de Roubaix	F	Holding co. (wool textile manufacturers and merchants)	243·8	207·8	3·9
333	Energieversorgung Weser-Ems AG	G	Electricity supply	242·9	214·4	20·2
334	NKL	No	Wholesale co-operative	242·7	282·6	4·3
335	Allgäuer Alpenmilch AG	G	Milk products	242·1	167·1	16·0
336	C.E.M.-Cie. Electro-Mecanique	F	Electrical engineering	237·9	170·1	1·4
337	Maizena GmbH	G	Food and starch manufacturer	237·4	220·8	23·0
338	Jean Lefebvre (Ehtreprise)	F	Civil and public works contractors	237·0	205·9	9·6
339	Fromageries Bel-La Vache Qui Rit	F	Dairy products	236·7	218·1	4·7
340	Radiologie (Cie. Générale de)	F	X-ray equipment	235·5	209·6	2·4
341	A/S Ardal og Sunndal Verk	No	Aluminium	234·7	212·7	3·1
342	Boehringer Mannheim GmbH	G	Pharmaceuticals	233·6	204·3	24·5
343	Sommer-Allibert	F	Holding co. (wall and floor coverings, plastic products, etc)	233·5	187·5	8·5
344	Italcementi Fabriche Riunite Cemento SpA	I	Cement manufacturer	232·9	182·5	3·4
345	Vorwerk & Co. KG	G	Holding co. (electrical appliances, carpets)	232·6	207·5	N/A
346	Pricel	F	Holding co. (textiles)	232·0	189·3	3·7
347	Incentive	S	Metal products, machinery	231·1	216·6	5·5
348	PLM (Aktiebolaget Platmanufaktur)	S	Metal, plastic and glass containers	230·3	210·1	5·8
349	Stadtwerke Köln GmbH	G	Suppliers of gas and electricity, public transport	230·1	202·2	5·7
350	Gist-Brocades N.V.	N	Chemicals, pharmaceuticals	229·8	213·0	7·9

Hamlet Enterprises

Producers of International Commercials

For Show-Reels contact
Harry Brooks or Diana Hayward
at 46 Lowndes Square London SW1
01-235-1811

Rank	Name	Country	Main activity	Turnover 1977 £M	Turnover 1976 £M	Reported profits 1977 £M
351	V.N.U. Verenigde Nederlandse Uitgevers- Bedrijven B.V.	N	Publishing, printing	229·5	210·2	17·4
352	Fichtel & Sachs AG	G	Vehicle components	229·3	205·7	20·3
353	Hunter Douglas N.V.	N	Building products, etc.	228·3	215·3	8·0
354	Campenon-Bernard S.A.	F	Holding co. (civil engineering)	228·2	207·7	1·6
355	Olympia Werke AG	G	Office machinery	228·0	228·1	N/A
356	Kockums Mekaniska Verkstads Aktiebolag	S	Shipbuilding	225·3	223·7	1·4
357	Mo Och Domsjo Aktiebolag	S	Forest products	224·7	202·3	2·6
358	Broström Shipping Co. Ltd.	S	Shipping	224·2	214·8	(7·4)
359	Générale de Fonderie	F	Heating, sanitary and kitchen equipment	223·4	248·1	(4·9)
360	BIC (Société)	F	Pen distributors	217·7	196·6	24·3
361	Pressbyraföretagen AG	S	Wholesale and retail of consumer goods	217·4	255·3	0·7
362	Motor Iberica S.A.	Sp	Motor vehicles	215·9	150·8	8·5
363	Publicis S.A.	F	Holding co. (advertising and public relations consultants)	215·6	181·3	1·2
364	Dragages et Travaux Publics (Entreprises)	F	Builders and civil engineers	213·7	168·8	4·4
365	S.C.A.C.	F	Fuel trading	213·4	189·8	1·4
366	Borsumij Wehry N.V.	N	Consumer goods	211·8	178·9	5·8
367	Hutchinson-Mapa	F	Rubber products	210·6	192·5	3·3
368	Cie. Générale Maritime	F	Shipping	210·1	247·6	N/A
369	Ciments Français (Sté des) S.A.	F	Cement production	209·7	191·6	8·4
370	Cie. Optorg	F	International traders	206·2	177·8	11·2
371	Metallurgique Hainaut-Sambre (Sté)	B	Iron and steel	206·1	241·4	(43·0)
372	Kléber-Colombes	F	Tyres, aircraft and motor components	204·0	183·6	(5·3)
373	Merlin Gerin	F	Electrical engineers	201·1	169·5	7·6
374	Altana Industrie-Aktien und Anlagen AG	G	Holding co. (pharmaceuticals, dietetics, etc.)	200·7	184·0	14·6
375	Engins Matra	F	Aero engineering, motor vehicles	200·1	160·3	9·8
376	Knorr-Bremse	G	Light engineering	199·8	193·5	N/A
377	Papeteries de Belgique S.A.	B	Paper and cardboard manufacturers	199·7	185·3	0·5
377	Magazine zum Globus AG	Sw	Department stores	199·7	193·4	2·1
379	Österreichische Elektrizitätswirtschafts AG 'Verbundgesellschaft'	A	Gas and electricity production and supply	198·6	182·6	(6·7)
380	Gerresheimer Glas AG	G	Glass manufacture	197·9	194·8	(3·1)
381	Ford Motor Company A/S	D	Motor dealers	197·8	174·5	5·7
382	Bremer Vulkan Schiffbau und Maschinenfabrik	G	Shipbuilding and repair	197·7	135·7	12·3
383	Gelder Papier (Van)	N	Paper manufacturers	194·8	202·2	(7·3)
384	Telemécanique Electrique	F	Electrical engineering	194·3	173·9	16·1
385	Borel (Jacques) International	F	Restaurateurs and caterers	193·8	163·1	17·3
386	Didier Werke AG	G	Refractory products	192·5	212·5	2·7
387	Maisons Phénix	F	Building and construction	192·4	155·2	22·4
388	Yhtyneet Paperitehtaat Oy	Fin	Paper manufacturers, forestry	189·2	173·0	1·1
389	Rheinmetall Berlin AG	G	Holding co. (engineering)	189·1	194·1	5·6
390	Züblin AG (Ed.)	G	Civil engineering	189·0	190·3	2·5
391	Moulinex	F	Household appliances	188·6	170·5	13·2
392	N.C.B.	S	Cellulose paper, etc.	187·7	142·9	(0·8)
393	Ruhrchemie AG	G	Chemicals	187·6	190·3	5·6
394	Economats du Centre	F	Food chain	186·1	161·4	3·4
395	Acciaiere e Ferriere Lombarde Falck	I	Iron, steel	185·5	177·1	3·2
396	Eisen und Metall AG	G	Iron and steel	185·2	211·7	(2·4)
397	Elektrizitäts-Aktiengesellschaft Mitteldeutschland	G	Electricity supply	184·5	178·0	11·7
398	Hussel Holding AG	G	Holding co. (wholesale and retail)	183·7	167·5	5·5
399	Thomassen and Drijver-Verblifa N.V.	N	Tin boxes and packaging materials	183·3	172·8	13·0
400	Klein, Schanzlin & Becker AG	G	Pumps, valves and compressors	183·2	189·7	9·0

Rank	Name	Country	Main activity	Turnover 1977 £M	Turnover 1976 £M	Reported profits 1977 £M
401	Flachglas AG	G	Glass manufacturers	182·9	158·4	19·1
402	Rochette Cenpa S.A.	F	Paper and woodpulp	182·2	176·4	(6·7)
403	Luossavaara-Kiirunavaara AB	S	Metal production	182·0	230·9	(15·3)
404	Pripps Bryggerier (AB)	S	Brewers	181·9	169·6	4·6
405	Outokumpu Oy	Fin	Metal production	181·6	153·3	2·3
406	Wienerwald GmbH	G	Restaurant chain	180·6	150·2	N/A
407	IBM	S	Computers	179·8	154·6	10·1
407	SEB S.A.	F	Holding co.	179·8	162·9	3·4
407	Siab Byggen AB	S	Building and construction	179·8	141·5	0·4
410	Dunlop AG	G	Tyres	177·2	130·5	2·6
411	Schuitema N.V. (Gebr. D.)	N	Retail sale of food, etc.	177·0	151·0	1·7
412	Cie Française des Ferailles F	F	Railways	175·4	174·6	(0·6)
413	Bilspedition (AB Godstrafik &)	S	Transport and haulage	174·9	146·7	1·1
414	Burmeister & Wain AS	D	Shipbuilders	174·1	197·6	7·5
414	Tampella (Oy) AB	Fin	Forest products, pulp and paper	174·1	136·2	0·7
416	Kemira Oy	Fin	Chemicals	173·3	181·9	1·0
417	Norcem AS	No	Plastics, glass and cement production	173·2	138·5	6·2
418	Dyckerhoff Zementwerke AG	G	Cement producers	172·4	162·6	5·5
419	Triumph-Adler Group	G	Computers, office machinery	171·9	164·4	7·9
420	Kone Oy	Fin	Textiles, metals machinery	171·3	148·1	3·8
421	KNSM Group N.V.	N	Shipping	171·2	175·4	(0·2)
422	Poclain	F	Manufacturers of excavators	171·1	146·3	(6·8)
423	Moët-Hennessy S.A.	F	Champagne, cognac and perfume	170·6	146·4	N/A
424	Salamander AG	G	Footwear manufacturer	168·5	149·6	7·8
425	Fabrique Nationale Herstal S.A.	B	Small arms, ammunition and machinery	166·7	131·1	5·7
426	Voith-Beteiligungen GmbH	G	Engineering	165·9	156·9	6·5
427	KNP-Koninklijke Nederlandse Papierfabrieken N.V.	N	Paper production	165·8	155·0	(0·4)
428	Fecsa-Fuerzas Electricas de Cataluna S.A.	Sp	Electricity production and distribution	164·9	135·4	29·9
429	Goldschmidt (T.H.) AG	G	Organic metals, chemicals	164·6	165·0	4·0
430	Galerias Preciados	Sp	Department stores	164·4	129·4	2·4
431	Billeruds AB	S	Manufacturers of pulp, paper and timber	163·0	156·2	5·4
432	Rousselot S.A.	F	Chemicals, polymers, adhesives	161·2	118·7	9·3
433	Holmens Bruk AB	S	Paper and wood production	160·6	139·3	3·7
434	International Service System A/S	D	Security Maintenance	160·5	164·4	6·8
435	SSIH–Sté Suisse pour L'Industrie Horlogère S.A.	Sw	Holding co. (horological products)	159·1	163·3	N/A
436	Nordostschweizerische Kraftwerke AG	Sw	Electricity production and distribution	158·8	139·5	7·9
437	Danske Sukkerfabrikker A/S	D	Sugar producers	158·5	160·0	14·5
437	Eridania Zuccherifici Nazionali SpA	I	Sugar production	158·5	153·2	3·8
439	Blohm & Voss	G	Ship building and repair	157·6	248·6	10·7
440	CM Industries	F	Holding co. (pharmaceuticals, surgical instruments, food stuffs)	156·8	134·2	4·7
441	Lyon Alemand Louyot (Comptoir)	F	Electrical appliances, electronics, telephones, metals	156·5	131·3	3·0
442	Korf Stahl AG	G	Holding co. (steel and iron)	156·2	156·1	(9·0)
443	Fagersta AB	S	Iron and steel	155·7	140·6	7·5
444	Bazaar de L'Hôtel de Ville	F	Department stores	155·1	137·1	0·3
445	Oelmühle Hamburg AG	G	Edible oils, etc.	155·0	116·9	2·4
446	Stadtwerke Hannover AG	G	Gas and electricity supply, public transport	154·4	149·8	11·0
447	Neunkirchener Eisenwerk AG	G	Iron, steel, fertilisers	153·7	187·3	13·9
447	Petrochim S.A.	B	Petroleum and coal products	153·7	195·1	1·5
449	Iggesund Bruk AB	S	Forestry, timber	153·4	142·5	3·5
450	Kodak AG	G	Films and cameras	153·2	157·2	2·1

Rank	Name	Country	Main activity	Turnover 1977 £M	Turnover 1976 £M	Reported profits 1977 £M
451	Magneti Marelli SpA	I	Electro mechanical equipment	151·5	120·7	0·4
452	S.A.T. (S.A. de Télécommunications)	F	Telecommunications	150·9	131·7	12·1
453	Club Méditerrannée S.A.	F	Hotel and holiday village operators	150·7	118·5	7·6
454	Eternit AG	G	Cement, concrete, asbestos	147·7	146·0	1·5
455	Grands Moulins de Paris S.A.	F	Flour milling, animal feedstuff	147·1	126·9	1·3
456	Comptoirs Modernes	F	Supermarkets and food retailers	146·9	129·2	1·5
456	Husqvarna	S	Sewing machines and domestic products	146·9	141·2	0·5
458	ESAB	S	Engineering	145·9	132·8	3·4
459	Portland-Zementwerke Heidelberg AG	G	Cement, concrete, cement products	144·9	141·2	16·3
460	OBAG-Energieversorgung Ostbayern AG	G	Electricity production and distribution	144·6	180·6	13·1
461	Goulet-Turpin S.A.	F	Holding co. (hypermarkets, supermarkets)	144·1	138·5	0·4
462	Bols (Erven Lucas)	N	Liqueurs and spirits	143·7	115·4	8·8
463	Braun AG	G	Consumer goods	143·6	136·0	6·9
464	Dunlop S.A.	F	Tyres	142·5	131·2	—
465	Locabail-Cie. pour la Location d'Equipements Professionels	F	Leasing of commercial and industrial equipment	142·1	120·7	3·9
466	Industrie-Werke Karlsruhe Augsburg AG	G	Industrial machinery	141·7	135·5	1·9
467	Carbochimique S.A. (Sté)	B	Fertilisers, nitrogen products, organic chemicals	137·0	N/A	0·4
468	Elsevier	N	Publishers and printers	136·5	116·0	7·6
469	Claas (Gebr.)	G	Agricultural machinery	136·0	153·5	5·1
469	Serlachius Oy (G.A.)	Fin	Pulp and paper products	136·0	133·5	1·3
469	Verenigde HVA Mij. N.V.	N	Industrial holding co.	136·0	140·1	0·4
472	Vieille-Montagne S.A.	B	Non-ferrous metals	133·5	147·1	(6·8)
473	Lech-Elektrizitätswerke AG	G	Generation and distribution of electricity	131·5	113·1	16·1
474	Monberg & Thorsen A/S	D	Chemicals, building and construction	129·1	132·6	2·8
475	Pfalzwerke AG	G	Electricity (transmission and distribution)	128·7	123·9	10·9
475	Phoenix Gummiwerke AG	G	Tyres, industrial rubber goods, rubber footwear	128·7	133·7	2·2
477	Losinger AG	Sw	Civil engineering	127·8	130·4	N/A
478	Stahlwerke Bochum AG	G	Steel production	127·1	135·7	1·3
479	SASM Alsacienne de Supermarchés	F	Supermarkets	127·0	115·9	1·8
480	D.L.W. AG	G	Floor coverings	125·7	118·4	12·3
481	Alivar SpA	I	Food production	125·6	129·1	0·4
482	Standard Telefon og Kabelfabrik A/S	No	Machinery, electrical apparatus and supply	125·5	117·6	9·2
483	WMF Wurttembergische Metallwarenfabrik	G	Cutlery and tableware manufacturers	124·7	116·8	4·6
484	Centrale Suiker Mij	N	Sugar production	122·6	94·1	5·8
485	Von Roll AG	Sw	General engineering	121·9	130·8	0·6
486	Locafrance S.A.	F	Leasing	121·5	106·7	3·0
487	Lepetit SpA (Gruppo)	I	Chemical, pharmaceutical and cosmetic products	121·3	122·5	10·3
488	Nutricia N.V.	N	Food products	121·2	108·3	3·1
489	Forbo S.A.	Sw	Holding co. (floor and wall coverings)	120·5	120·3	4·2
489	Holec N.V.	N	Holding co. (electrical engineering)	120·5	120·6	2·8
491	Dietrich et Cie. S.A.	F	Holding co. (mechanical construction, smelting, metal shaping)	120·2	121·9	7·9
492	Kluwer N.V.	N	Holding co. (publishing)	119·4	99·0	7·1
493	C.E.C. Carbonisation Entreprise et Ceramique	F	China, sanitary ware, tiles	118·5	110·8	(2·1)
494	Luchaire S.A.	F	General engineering	117·7	104·5	4·6
495	Galeries Lafayette	F	Department stores	117·5	108·8	1·1
496	Securitas International AB	S	Industrial security	117·4	95·0	(0·9)
496	Pfaff (G.M.) AG	G	Sewing machines	117·4	115·6	9·3
498	Gamma Holding N.V.	N	Textiles	116·9	105·3	1·1
499	Holland America Lijn Holding N.V.	N	Holding co. (shipping, tourism, transport)	116·7	107·9	(4·9)
500	Wuppertaler Stadtwerke AG	G	Energy supply and distribution, public transport	116·4	111·8	0·7

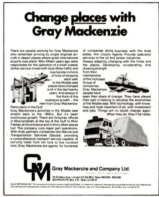
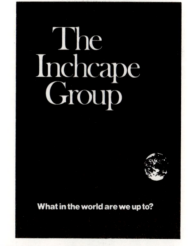

Bank of Boston House, 5 Cheapside, E.C.2.

If banking is a service business, then it should be on service that you judge a bank.

We've spent 56 years in the City, building an organisation to cater for the toughest judge of all: the financial professional.

That's why The Bank of Boston's account officers prefer long instead of short-term relationships. Why they stay with their accounts longer than their counterparts at other banks.

Why we have an exchange specialist based on the dealing floor devoted exclusively to keeping corporate customers abreast of developments.

Why our two hundred people in London aim at the highest standards (if you give the best service, you've got the best bank).

And it works.

Our dealers have put us among the top banks in making markets in all major trading currencies.

And six out of the top ten companies in the prestigious 'The Times One Thousand' are our customers.

Do you put a premium on service too?

We look forward to meeting you.

Boston. The bank for financial professionals.

BANK OF BOSTON 1784

THE FIRST NATIONAL BANK OF BOSTON

Bank of Boston House, 5 Cheapside, London EC2P 2DE (Tel: 01-236 2388). Also at: 31 Lowndes Street, Belgravia, London SW1X 9HX (Tel: 01-235 9541).

118

ARGENTINA; AUSTRALIA; BAHAMAS; BOLIVIA; BRAZIL; CHANNEL ISLANDS; DOMINICAN REPUBLIC; FRANCE; GERMANY; HAITI; HONG KONG; IRAN; JAPAN; LEBANON; LUXEMBOURG; MEXICO; PANAMA; SINGAPORE; SPAIN; U.K.; U.S.A.; URUGUAY; VENEZUELA.

18: The 100 leading American companies

Rank (sales)	Name	Sales £000	*CAPITAL EMPLOYED £000	Rank	NET INCOME Latest year £000	Previous year £000
1	Exxon Corporation	30,938,004	14,918,032	1	1,303,019	1,420,255
2	General Motors Corporation	29,557,031	9,858,241	2	1,794,837	1,561,065
3	Ford Motor Co.	20,350,363	5,957,677	6	899,597	528,691
4	Mobil Corpn.	18,187,188	7,009,211	5	540,290	506,869
5	Texaco	15,015,057	7,567,157	3	500,559	467,723
6	Standard Oil Co. of California	11,698,007	5,473,179	7	546,577	473,314
7	Gulf Oil Corpn.	10,537,779	5,374,025	8	404,410	438,828
8	International Business Machines Corpn.	9,751,645	7,405,135	4	1,462,444	1,289,644
9	General Electric Co.	9,421,135	4,452,702	13	585,211	500,457
10	Sears, Roebuck & Co.	9,262,723	4,883,505	11	450,649	373,496
11	Chrysler Corpn.	8,985,372	2,462,113	23	67,115	176,499
12	Standard Oil Co. (Indiana)	7,562,555	5,310,574	9	544,004	477,645
13	International Telephone & Telegraph Corpn.	7,069,462	4,671,365	12	302,390	262,826
14	Atlantic Richfield Co.	6,137,908	4,982,370	10	377,260	309,319
15	Safeway Stores	6,049,690	916,123	66	55,017	56,770
16	Shell Oil Co.	5,897,574	3,899,400	15	395,318	379,585
17	K. Mart Corpn.	5,346,275	1,155,378	52	162,903	143,358
18	United States Steel Corpn.	5,168,002	4,410,809	14	74,160	220,651
19	E. I. Du Pont de Nemours & Co.	5,073,837	3,414,735	17	293,143	247,002
20	J. C. Penney Co.	5,038,451	1,448,239	45	158,645	122,667
21	Continental Oil Co.	4,807,914	2,714,148	20	204,693	245,333
22	Western Electric Co.	4,374,619	N/A	N/A	263,553	116,904
23	RCA Corpn.	4,238,182	1,587,255	41	132,831	95,402
24	Tenneco	4,001,237	3,283,087	18	229,578	206,238
25	Great Atlantic & Pacific Tea Co.	3,919,643	355,191	92	1,716	7,411
26	Procter & Gamble Co.	3,917,319	1,824,311	30	248,165	215,702
27	Union Carbide Corpn.	3,783,867	3,229,632	19	207,099	237,268
28	Kroger Co.	3,628,692	446,799	89	32,615	25,991
29	Goodyear Tire & Rubber Co.	3,564,301	1,807,928	33	110,655	65,591
30	Sun Co.	3,451,528	2,178,683	24	194,644	191,547
31	R. J. Reynolds Industries	3,421,941	1,789,513	36	227,749	190,316
32	Beatrice Foods Co.	3,395,476	920,844	65	119,138	98,180
33	Philips Petroleum Co.	3,379,503	2,481,552	22	277,979	221,380
34	Dow Chemical Co.	3,352,651	N/A	N/A	298,845	329,533
35	Westinghouse Electric Corpn.	3,300,705	1,553,691	43	134,864	120,041
36	Union Oil of California	3,245,001	2,091,754	26	179,747	144,563
37	Occidental Petroleum Corpn.	3,236,094	1,804,062	34	117,188	98,801
38	International Harvester Co.	3,213,262	1,562,531	42	109,565	93,621
39	Eastman Kodak Co.	3,208,920	2,503,675	21	346,033	349,889
40	Rockwell International Corpn.	3,150,686	998,494	62	77,494	66,362
41	Caterpillar Tractor Co.	3,145,415	1,822,963	31	239,365	206,077
42	United Technologies Corpn.	2,985,034	996,369	63	105,390	84,648
43	F. W. Woolworth Co.	2,976,338	888,518	67	49,422	58,188
44	Bethlehem Steel Corpn.	2,887,873	2,108,309	25	Loss 241,033	90,347
45	Esmark	2,823,256	691,821	81	36,015	44,394
46	Kraft	2,817,320	808,519	73	82,880	72,950
47	Philip Morris	2,797,514	1,624,304	40	180,116	142,874
48	Xerox Corpn.	2,730,250	2,010,025	27	218,675	193,012
49	Ashland Oil	2,716,802	1,029,096	61	88,338	73,129
50	Federated Department Stores	2,647,700	955,757	64	105,709	90,414

NOTES: *Total tangible assets less current liabilities (other than bank loans and overdrafts).
N/A Not available.
Converted at US$1.8595 to £1.

Rank (sales)	Name	Sales £000	*CAPITAL EMPLOYED £000	Rank	NET INCOME Latest year £000	Previous year £000
51	General Foods Corpn.	2,640,353	788,238	74	95,369	80,897
52	LTV Corpn.	2,529,334	814,241	71	Loss 31,933	16,511
53	Marathon Oil Co.	2,492,332	1,371,765	47	105,920	105,301
54	American Brands	2,482,597	1,062,949	60	84,851	65,605
55	Monsanto Co.	2,470,825	1,954,827	28	148,212	196,988
56	Amerada Hess	2,469,079	1,108,472	57	96,198	82,085
57	Firestone Tire & Rubber Co.	2,380,694	1,314,708	48	59,263	51,628
58	Cities Service Co.	2,359,882	1,709,277	37	113,041	116,698
59	Boeing Co.	2,161,226	760,366	76	96,962	55,337
60	Winn-Dixie Stores	2,149,341	216,431	96	37,860	33,894
61	Minnesota Mining & Manufacturing Co.	2,140,536	1,534,943	44	222,074	182,049
62	W. R. Grace & Co.	2,138,334	1,138,742	54	75,545	70,923
63	Lucky Stores	2,104,906	231,158	95	32,957	24,794
64	Greyhound Corpn.	2,065,857	551,215	86	44,380	41,453
65	Colgate-Palmolive Co.	2,063,568	784,244	75	86,325	80,264
66	Ralston Purina Co.	2,020,059	711,482	79	76,741	67,706
67	Georgia-Pacific Corpn.	1,976,338	1,371,874	46	140,898	115,784
68	International Paper Co.	1,973,057	1,796,020	35	125,679	136,381
69	Continental Group	1,968,755	1,110,567	56	77,333	63,619
70	Gulf & Western Industries	1,959,128	1,683,607	39	80,843	107,647
71	Deere & Co.	1,938,181	1,143,996	53	137,478	129,912
72	Coca-Cola Co.	1,914,428	825,343	70	175,434	153,245
73	Armco Steel Corpn.	1,908,706	1,234,165	50	64,443	66,537
74	McDonnell Douglas Corpn.	1,906,318	608,985	83	66,124	58,540
75	Standard Oil Co. (Ohio)	1,894,715	3,646,576	16	97,366	73,599
76	Borden	1,872,158	703,056	80	68,228	60,665
77	Getty Oil Co.	1,870,268	1,821,287	32	166,236	139,002
78	American Stores Co.	1,863,219	204,324	97	13,885	17,190
79	Litton Industries	1,851,532	752,884	77	30,065	6,355
80	American Can Co.	1,850,874	838,129	69	61,307	54,262
81	Aluminum Co. of America	1,837,322	1,700,457	38	104,974	77,333
82	Lockheed Aircraft Corpn.	1,813,821	423,985	91	29,793	20,812
83	Bendix Corpn.	1,765,636	575,262	85	63,512	56,305
84	Weyerhaeuser Co.	1,765,404	1,904,339	29	163,426	164,543
85	Jewel Companies	1,762,701	343,520	94	14,493	19,449
86	Sperry Rand	1,758,542	1,071,421	59	84,338	78,136
87	TRW	1,755,280	671,436	82	82,935	71,558
88	National Steel Corpn.	1,688,013	1,214,187	51	32,334	46,108
89	Champion International Corpn.	1,681,431	1,128,363	55	74,544	55,458
90	Pepsico	1,665,451	722,004	78	100,747	73,156
91	Signal Companies	1,594,213	812,892	72	54,588	34,846
92	Allied Chemical Corpn.	1,571,794	1,255,491	49	72,736	63,008
93	Johnson & Johnson	1,567,131	879,965	68	133,002	110,447
94	General Mills	1,564,616	480,086	88	62,938	54,067
95	Republic Steel Corpn.	1,564,606	1,071,826	58	22,066	35,423
96	General Dynamics	1,560,196	550,817	87	55,593	53,551
97	Consolidated Foods Corpn.	1,555,244	424,702	90	47,362	48,106
98	CPC International	1,543,318	586,717	84	71,471	65,609
99	Raytheon Co.	1,515,603	352,031	93	60,898	45,841
100	Textron	1,506,984	N/A	N/A	73,604	65,101

NOTES: *Total tangible assets less current liabilities (other than bank loans and overdrafts).
N/A Not available.
Converted at US$1.8595 to £1.

FOR FAST FINANCIAL INFORMATION ON ANY COMPANY...

...ANYWHERE IN THE WORLD

Jordans can offer you the most flexible service in the business.

Whether you need facts from the Registries in London, Cardiff or Edinburgh or in-depth information on overseas companies, our experts are on the spot.

And that means a fast, accurate service which helps you make the right decisions — quickly.

Jordan & Sons Ltd
Jordan House
Brunswick Place
London N1 6EE
Telephone 01-253 3030
Telex 261010

44 Whitchurch Road
Cardiff CF4 3UQ
Telephone 0222-371901
Telex 49167

Jordans

19: The 50 leading Japanese companies

Rank (sales)	Company	Head office	SALES £000 12 MONTHS		NET PROFIT £000 12 MONTHS	
			Latest	Previous	Latest	Previous
1	Nippon Steel	Tokyo	6,137,203	6,612,137	41,815	75,918
2	Toyota Motor	Toyota	6,036,939	5,266,491	308,119	262,689
3	Nissan Motor	Tokyo	5,926,121	5,343,008	212,876	225,045
4	Nippon Oil	Tokyo	4,704,485	4,654,354	38,675	24,161
5	Tokyo Electric Power	Tokyo	4,667,546	4,079,156	198,211	124,660
6	Matsushita Electric Industrial	Osaka	3,786,280	3,459,103	128,248	109,042
7	Hitachi	Tokyo	3,664,908	3,416,887	82,950	80,100
8	Mitsubishi Heavy Industries	Tokyo	3,638,522	3,213,720	39,665	47,404
9	Nippon Kokan	Tokyo	3,171,504	3,263,852	13,739	28,792
10	Kansai Electric Power	Osaka	2,870,712	2,548,813	139,008	94,641
11	Tokyo Shibaura Electric	Kawasaki	2,799,472	2,543,536	36,718	36,417
12	Maruzen Oil	Osaka	2,577,836	2,612,137	828	13,491
13	Sumitomo Metal Industries	Osaka	2,572,559	2,794,195	14,198	11,636
14	Kawasaki Steel	Kobe	2,467,018	2,593,668	17,966	20,451
15	Dai'ei	Osaka	2,311,346	2,079,156	15,789	13,024
16	Chubu Electric Power	Nagoya	2,306,069	2,013,193	115,032	69,963
17	Honda Motor	Tokyo	2,242,744	1,765,172	46,198	41,016
18	Kobe Steel	Kobe	2,197,889	2,366,755	18,549	29,823
19	Mitsubishi Electric	Tokyo	2,089,710	1,836,412	25,752	22,573
20	Ishikawajima-Harima Heavy Industries	Tokyo	2,013,193	1,836,412	15,124	30,934
21	Mitsubishi Oil	Tokyo	1,978,892	2,018,470	43,454	33,979
22	Kirin Brewery	Tokyo	1,765,172	1,580,475	43,631	35,860
23	Toyo Kogyo	Hiroshima	1,656,992	1,551,451	2,995	2,784
24	Toa Nenryo Kogyo	Tokyo	1,630,607	1,620,053	52,077	39,847
25	Daikyo Oil	Tokyo	1,622,691	1,432,718	8,501	4,504
26	Kawasaki Heavy Industries	Kobe	1,493,404	1,424,802	25,549	34,311
27	Nippon Express	Tokyo	1,482,850	1,385,224	11,723	11,913
28	Taisei	Tokyo	1,461,741	1,443,272	20,079	28,259
29	Showa Oil	Tokyo	1,459,103	1,356,201	9,201	5,425
30	Mitsubishi Chemical Industries	Tokyo	1,440,633	1,580,475	13,361	13,401
31	Nippon Electric	Tokyo	1,422,164	1,282,322	18,549	19,892
32	Kyushu Electric Power	Fukuoka	1,408,971	1,205,805	61,934	35,380
33	Nippon Mining	Tokyo	1,408,971	1,532,982	8,203	10,662
34	Sanyo Electric	Osaka	1,403,694	1,234,828	28,836	24,430
35	Tohoku Electric Power	Sendai	1,395,778	1,245,383	63,398	45,230
36	Shimizu Construction	Tokyo	1,390,501	1,253,298	24,063	27,562
37	Kajima	Tokyo	1,387,863	1,480,211	34,723	40,551
38	Taiyo Fishery	Tokyo	1,369,393	1,269,129	2,773	2,789
39	Ohbayashi-Gumi	Osaka	1,358,839	1,126,649	12,834	16,441
40	Isuzu Motors	Tokyo	1,237,467	1,121,372	16,311	19,517
41	Kubota	Osaka	1,126,359	1,081,794	57,201	55,103
42	Mitsukoshi	Tokyo	1,189,974	1,134,565	27,187	24,179
43	Sumitomo Chemical	Osaka	1,179,420	1,467,018	3,525	9,277
44	Seiyu Stores	Tokyo	1,171,504	1,034,301	7,369	6,591
45	Asahi Chemical Industry	Osaka	1,163,588	1,248,021	12,900	11,873
46	Japan Air Lines	Tokyo	1,147,757	1,042,216	21,478	29,090
47	Kanebo	Osaka	1,139,842	1,097,625	Loss 2,393	Loss 7,488
48	Chugoku Electric Power	Hiroshima	1,108,179	992,084	56,960	30,855
49	Tokyo Gas	Tokyo	1,108,179	1,013,193	37,902	26,177
50	Nippon Yusen	Tokyo	1,076,517	1,139,842	7,821	7,887

NOTES: (1) One-year accounting period ending before March 1978. (2) Excluding commerce and financial companies. (3) Parent company figures only. (4) Conversion rate used: 460 yen to £1.

The Gates Learjet Longhorn

At 51,000 feet you may meet Concorde but that's all *(except another Longhorn)*

Because no other commercial traffic flies that high. The advantages of travelling nearly ten miles up are plain: it is above even the highest weather build-ups, it is out of the most penalizing headwind patterns and totally removed from other commercial traffic except the supersonic Concorde. It means you get there quicker, more economically, more comfortably and on schedule.

The wing design (with its distinctive 'winglets') gives the Gates Learjet Longhorn greater lift, and serving as a sail, stretches fuel further by reducing drag and enhancing forward thrust. On approach and landing, the winglets assist in stabilizing the aircraft at slower speeds, providing even greater margins of safety and increased short field operating flexibility.

CSE Aviation Limited
Oxford Airport Kidlington Oxford OX5 1RA
telephone Kidlington (086-75) 4321 Telex 83204

20: The 30 leading Canadian companies

Rank	Name	Sales £000	*Capital employed £000	NET INCOME Latest year £000	NET INCOME Previous year £000
1	General Motors of Canada	2,925,695	N/A	86,420	76,450
2	Ford Motor Company of Canada	2,738,907	471,475	17,558	60,376
3	Imperial Oil	2,377,706	1,333,333	138,261	126,301
4	Canadian Pacific	2,322,925	2,851,926	114,753	91,101
5	Geo. Weston	2,195,953	378,752	13,145	Loss 3,988
6	Gulf Oil Canada	2,026,169	923,717	88,506	79,368
7	Alcan Aluminium	1,546,766	1,464,866	108,366	23,666
8	Chrysler Canada	1,492,196	N/A	4,607	20,344
9	Massey-Ferguson	1,342,070	845,983	15,654	56,411
10	Seagram Co.	1,174,651	956,740	46,826	43,304
11	Shell Canada	1,123,930	759,179	73,956	64,982
12	INCO	934,495	1,601,720	47,774	94,131
13	Canada Packers	898,652	N/A	8,665	9,636
14	Transcanada Pipelines	885,848	667,395	41,231	36,732
15	Macmillan Bloedel	816,773	510,652	29,000	10,928
16	Steel Co. of Canada	690,854	884,376	43,155	43,346
17	Noranda Mines	663,325	843,521	32,138	22,359
18	Moore Corporation	636,671	367,111	41,853	33,145
19	Northern Telecom	606,935	272,808	39,150	35,372
20	Air Canada	568,188	464,429	9,571	Loss 5,002
21	Canadian General Electric Co.	516,554	195,131	14,608	15,644
22	Texaco Canada	513,247	419,961	17,540	13,865
23	Imasco	502,055	159,378	20,609	16,707
24	Abitibi Paper Co.	500,181	370,513	18,136	6,231
25	Genstar	497,226	410,384	30,824	26,648
26	Domtar	482,960	309,337	12,841	5,053
27	Molson Companies	455,409	161,623	14,804	12,454
28	John Labatt	441,188	156,956	13,427	12,856
29	Dominion Foundries and Steel	439,678	587,255	32,780	31,910
30	Burns Foods	491,382	52,746	1,466	2,723

NOTES: *Total tangible assets less current liabilities (excluding bank loans and overdrafts).
N/A Not available.
Converted at CAN$2.09025 to £1 and US$1.8595 to £1.

21: The 20 leading Australian companies

Rank	Name	Turnover £000	*Capital employed £000	NET PROFIT AFTER TAX Latest year £000	NET PROFIT AFTER TAX Previous year £000
1	Broken Hill Proprietary Co.	1,323,952	1,727,792	39,477	39,357
2	Woolworths	921,931	128,717	17,733	14,078
3	C. J. Coles & Co.	827,194	138,648	19,415	14,252
4	Elder Smith Goldsbrough Mort	744,860	163,809	5,370	4,664
5	Conzinc Riotinto of Australia	668,755	906,456	48,049	46,396
6	Myer Emporium	626,855	249,611	28,117	26,567
7	Amatil	545,057	218,912	13,884	9,403
8	CSR	540,236	558,706	24,612	24,425
9	ICI Australia	467,554	323,807	20,348	13,183
10	Australian Consolidated Industries	374,077	266,435	10,607	4,743
11	Dunlop Australia	335,021	150,871	10,437	9,219
12	Carlton and United Breweries	280,641	143,022	10,576	9,445
13	Thomas Nationwide Transport	276,434	115,629	8,902	8,043
14	Ansett Transport Industries	271,791	105,747	10,589	8,860
15	Burns, Philip & Co.	260,813	159,237	3,651	4,759
16	John Lysaght Australia	238,094	311,497	6,116	751
17	Grace Bros Holdings	227,210	78,485	6,710	5,223
18	David Jones	**226,297	118,433	4,719	3,947
19	Ampol Petroleum	209,919	158,634	6,135	6,012
20	Philips Industries Holdings	208,768	100,411	1,500	2,528

NOTES: *Total tangible assets less current liabilities (excluding bank loans and overdrafts).
**Australian Group sales.
Converted at A$1.62185 to £1.

124

Are you profiting from Udisco's professionalism?

When you deal in the Money Market with Udisco on your side, the advantages are considerable.

Your own professionalism is reinforced by ours. You benefit from absolutely up-to-the-minute information on the Market. And you receive a service based on efficiency and personal attention.

Our own professionalism covers every major aspect of the Market–Local authorities, commercial and Inter Bank Markets. We are also brokers in Treasury Bills, Local Authority Bonds and Certificates of Deposit. (Transactions involving £50,000 or more are especially likely to benefit from our service).

If you have not yet profited from Udisco's all-round professionalism, Mike Clark will be pleased to tell you more about it. A conversation with him could be the start of a very rewarding relationship. The number to ring is:

01-626 3292

UDISCO BROKERS LIMITED

The money-broking arm of the Union Discount Company of London Limited.
78-80 Cornhill, London EC3V 3NH.

22: The 20 leading South African companies

Rank	Name	*Capital employed £000	Turnover £000	NET PROFIT AFTER TAX Latest year £000	Previous year £000
1	Barlow Rand	518,543	725,370	51,317	45,700
2	Federale Mynbou Beperk	494,472	540,790	16,397	17,171
3	Rembrandt Group	463,189	N/A	43,117	39,449
4	South African Breweries	436,735	882,913	35,433	32,215
5	AECI	376,666	364,918	36,232	23,124
6	Anglo American Industrial Corpn	212,676	223,976	25,098	26,555
7	Hulletts Corpn	178,664	185,614	8,690	9,381
8	Anglo-Transvaal Consolidated Investment Co.	165,826	287,972	8,095	7,991
9	South African Marine Corpn	146,281	118,172	15,643	10,942
10	Tiger Oats & National Milling Co.	144,603	340,735	14,643	11,723
11	Premier Milling Co.	128,954	421,625	13,423	12,946
12	Anglo-Alpha Cement	128,862	81,681	4,975	7,716
13	C. G. Smith Investments	114,817	100,529	8,933	8,866
14	Federale Volksbeleggings Beperk	114,079	111,587	4,730	5,377
15	Sentrachem	110,132	102,073	12,273	10,646
16	C. G. Smith Sugar	105,218	115,021	11,071	8,620
17	Triomf Fertilizer Investments	102,905	123,691	Loss 5,010	2,030
18	Tongaat Group	102,288	89,799	6,424	5,337
19	Dorman Long Vanderbijl Corpn	92,822	220,161	8,717	7,020
20	Highveld Steel and Vanadium Corpn	89,533	89,313	12,809	9.801

NOTES: *Total tangible assets less current liabilities (excluding bank loans and overdrafts).
N/A Not available.
Converted at R1.61735 to £1.

23: The 20 leading companies in the Republic of Ireland

Rank	Name	Turnover £000	*Capital employed £000	NET PROFIT BEFORE TAX AND INTEREST Latest year £000	Previous year £000
1	Jefferson Smurfit Group	175,686	69,076	17,847	13,257
2	Irish Shell	**161,475	37,683	6,936	1,151
3	Esso Teoranta	†151,820	20,456	5,791	777
4	Cement–Roadstone Holdings	134,368	142,201	16,208	13,618
5	P. J. Carroll & Co.	108,636	21,635	5,402	6,130 p.a.
6	Waterford Glass	100,470	57,218	10,346	7,989
7	Irish Sugar	98,537	38,483	4,819	4,076 p.a.
8	R. & H. Hall	82,480	19,150	2,013	2,567
9	Brooks Watson Group	72,159	14,440	2,303	2,279
10	Youghal Carpets (Holdings)	64,177	23,690	251	3,704
11	Irish Distillers Group	58,478	43,963	6,771	3,577
12	Fitzwilton	40,406	12,715	970	1,136
13	Ranks (Ireland)	36,359	12,441	2,364	2,343
14	Clondalkin Mills Group	34,308	10,655	3,080	659
15	Arnott & Co. Dublin	28,249	13,855	2,537	2,026
16	W. & R. Jacob & Co.	25,420	9,809	212	557
17	Irish Leathers	25,391	7,972	921	1,086
18	H. Williams & Co.	25,308	2,587	547	Loss 90
19	McInerney Properties	25,305	4,754	1,155	1,461
20	Concrete Products of Ireland	23,093	12,896	2,451	2,301

NOTES: *Total tangible assets less current liabilities (excluding bank loans and overdrafts and future tax).
**Including sales taxes and excise duties.
†Including customs and excise duties and VAT.

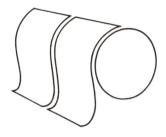

"A SIGN OF THE TIMES"

More and more *top companies
and organisations are turning
to Selwyn Press for their
stationery requirements.
Printed by a unique process
called Thermography
over 1,000,000 fine embossed
letterheads are printed
every week – truly a sign
of the times! . . . .

Send for details of our top
Design Service together with
samples and prices to:

THE SELWYN PRESS
Printers of Fine Embossed Stationery
Northern Way, Bury St. Edmunds
Suffolk IP32 6NR
Tel. (STD 0284) 62201 · Telex 817128

COMPANY INFORMATION-FAST!

Same day searches from the Companies Registries in London, Cardiff and Edinburgh.

Phone Derek Stevenson on 01·251 4941

or Telex 23678

 **Company Information Services**

ICC House, 81 City Road, London EC1Y 1BD

A member of the ICC Group of Companies Publishers of over 200 Business Ratio Reports and Financial Surveys on UK Industry and Commerce

24: Foreign banks in Britain*

American Banks

Allied Bank International
American Express International Banking Corporation
American National Bank and Trust Co. of Chicago
Amex Bank Ltd.
Amex International Ltd.
Bank of America International Ltd.
Bank of America (Jersey) Ltd.
Bank of America National Trust and Savings Association
Bank of California N.A.
Bank of New York
Bank of Tokyo Trust Company
Bankers Trust Co.
Bankers Trust International Ltd.
Chase Bank (C.I.) Ltd.
Chase Manhattan Bank N.A.
Chemical Bank International
Citibank N.A.
Citibank (C.I.) Ltd.
Citicorp International Bank Ltd.
City National Bank of Detroit
Continental Illinois Ltd.
Continental Illinois National Bank and Trust Co. of Chicago
Crocker National Bank
The Detroit Bank and Trust Company
The Fidelity Bank
First Chicago Ltd.
First City National Bank of Houston
First International Bancshares Ltd.
First National Bank in Dallas
First National Bank of Boston
First National Bank of Boston (Guernsey) Ltd.
First National Bank of Chicago
First National Bank of Chicago (C.I.) Ltd.
First Pennsylvania Bank N.A.
First Wisconsin National Bank of Milwaukee
Girard Bank
Harris Trust and Savings Bank
Irving Trust Co.
Manufacturers Hanover Ltd.
Manufacturers Hanover Bank (Guernsey) Ltd.
Manufacturers Hanover Trust Co.
Marine Midland Bank
Mellon Bank N.A.
Merrill Lynch International Bank
Morgan Guaranty Trust Co. of New York
National Bank of Detroit
North Carolina National Bank
The Northern Trust Co.
Rainier National Bank
Republic National Bank of Dallas
Seattle First National Bank
Security Pacific National Bank
Texas Commerce Bank N.A.
Texas Commerce International Bank Ltd.
United California Bank
Wells Fargo Bank N.A.
Western Trust & Savings Ltd.

Japanese Banks

Bank of Tokyo Ltd.
Bank of Yokohama Ltd.
Dai-Ichi Kangyo Bank Ltd.
Daiwa Bank Ltd.
Fuji Bank Ltd.
Hokkaido Takushaku Bank Ltd.
Industrial Bank of Japan Ltd.
Kyowa Bank Ltd.
Long-Term Credit Bank of Japan Ltd.
Mitsubishi Bank Ltd.
Mitsubishi Trust and Banking Corporation
Mitsui Bank Ltd.
Mitsui Trust and Banking Corporation
Nippon Fudosan Bank
Saitama Bank Ltd.
Sanwa Bank Ltd.
Sumitomo Bank Ltd.
Sumitomo Trust and Banking Co. Ltd.
Taiyo Kobe Bank Ltd.
Tokai Bank Ltd.
Yasuda Trust and Banking Co. Ltd.

Other Overseas Banks

Afghan National Bank Ltd.
African Continental Bank Ltd.
Algemene Bank Nederland N.V.
Algemene Bank Nederland (Jersey) Ltd.
Allied Arab Bank
Amsterdam-Rotterdam Bank N.V.
Arab Bank Ltd.
Australia and New Zealand Banking Group Ltd.
Australia and New Zealand Banking Group (C.I.) Ltd.
Banca Commerciale Italiana
Banca Nazionale del Lavoro
Banco Central S.A.
Banco de Bilbao
Banco de la Nacion Argentina
Banco Mercantil de São Paulo S.A.
Banco de Santander
Banco de Vizcaya
Banco di Roma
Banco do Brasil S.A.
Banco do Estado de São Paulo S.A.
Banco Espanol en Londres S.A.
Banco Real S.A.
Banco Totta & Acores
Bangkok Bank Ltd.
Bank Julius Baer International Ltd.
Bank Brussels Lambert (U.K.)
Bank Bumiputra Malaysia Berhab
Bank für Gemeinwirtschaft
Bank Hapoalim B.M.
Bank Leumi (U.K.) Ltd.
Bank Melli Iran

* At 30 June 1978.

Finding the answers takes time.

Handling information is a complex business. Our time could save yours; we have the information and the skills. These have been built up during the last twelve years inside and outside The Thomson Organisation Ltd.

The needs and requirements of our clients from publishing, advertising, manufacturing and finance are very different. We cater specifically for their needs; from simple population statistics to an involved economic forecast, from quick queries over the 'phone to more detailed reports and analysis.

What are your needs and how can we be of service to you?

Contact Christine Hull, Manager, The Times Information and Marketing Intelligence Unit, New Printing House Square, London WC1X 8EZ. Tel: 01-837 1234. Ext. 501.

The Times Information and Marketing Intelligence Unit.

Bank of Adelaide
Bank of Baroda
Bank of Ceylon
Bank of China
Bank of Credit and Commerce-International S.A.
Bank of Cyprus (London) Ltd.
Bank of India
Bank of Montreal
Bank of New South Wales
Bank of New Zealand
Bank of Nova Scotia
Bank of Nova Scotia (C.I.) Ltd.
Bank of Tehran
Bank Saderat Iran
Bank Sanaye Iran
Bank Sepah-Iran
Banque Belge Ltd.
Banque Belgo-Zairoise S.A.
Banque de l'Indochine et de Suez
Banque de Paris et des Pays-Bas
Banque Nationale de Paris Ltd.
Banque pour le Commerce Continental
British Bank of the Middle East Ltd.
Canadian Imperial Bank of Commerce
Central Bank of India
Chase & Bank of Ireland (International) Ltd.
Commercial Bank of Australia Ltd.
Commercial Bank of the Near East Ltd.
Commercial Banking Co. of Sydney Ltd.
Commerzbank A.G.
Commonwealth Trading Bank of Australia
Credit Industriel et Commercial
Credit Lyonnais
Credit Suisse
Credit Suisse White Weld Ltd.
Credito Italiano
Deutsche Bank A.G.
Discount Bank (Overseas) Ltd.
Dow Banking Corporation
Dresdner Bank A.G.
French Bank of Southern Africa Ltd.
Ghana Commercial Bank

Habib Bank Ltd.
Havana International Bank Ltd.
Hong Kong & Shanghai Banking Corporation
Hong Kong & Shanghai Banking Corporation (C.I.) Ltd.
Hungarian International Bank Ltd.
Investitions-und-Handels-Bank A.G.
Korea Exchange Bank
London and Continental Bankers Ltd.
Malayan Banking Berhad
Mercantile Bank Ltd.
Moscow Narodny Bank Ltd.
Muslim Commercial Bank Ltd.
National Bank of Abu Dhabi
National Bank of Australasia Ltd.
National Bank of Greece
National Bank of Nigeria Ltd.
National Bank of Pakistan
Nedbank Ltd.
Oversea-Chinese Banking Corporation Ltd.
Overseas Union Bank Ltd.
Philippine National Bank
Punjab National Bank
Qatar National Bank S.A.Q.
Rafidain Bank
Royal Bank of Canada
Royal Bank of Canada (Channel Islands) Ltd.
Schlesinger Ltd.
Société Générale
Sonali Bank
State Bank of India
Swiss Bank Corporation
Thai Farmers Bank Ltd.
Toronto-Dominion Bank Ltd.
Trade Development Bank
Union Bank of Switzerland
United Bank Ltd.
United Commercial Bank
United Overseas Bank Ltd.
Westdeutsche Landesbank Girozentrale
Western Bank Ltd. (incorporated in South Africa)
Zambia National Commercial Bank
Živnostenská Banka National Corporation

* At 30 June 1978.

Alphabetical Index to Listed Companies

A

B

For Unit Trusts appearing without addresses, see address of the parent companies indicated on page 84

135

138

142

Printed in Great Britain by
WATERLOW (DUNSTABLE) LIMITED

Insuring projects like The Queen's Award

These are only a selection from a long list of insurance and reinsurance projects handled by the C. E. Heath Group around the world.
A high proportion of the premiums involved have been channelled through the London insurance market.
This has helped the Group's overseas currency earnings to be doubled over a three-year period, and has resulted in our gaining The Queen's Award for Export Achievement.

Jack-up drilling rig "Interocean 11" on the Barge "Genmark 105" under tow on a 15,000-mile voyage from Japan to Mexico, which was completed in 77 days.

C. E. Heath has placed in London and world-wide markets the liability and property insurance cover of the Port Authority of New York and New Jersey including the World Trade Centre complex.